To Tahlia,
All the Best
in DC
Clayton Martorella
07/27/20

628 Avenue V

Clayton Martorello

Table of Contents

Prologue

Often Clayton thought about his position in life. He continuously wondered if he was living the good life, being in the moment and taking in all the lessons of the world around him, however small that world might seem to others. He worried that he was closed off to the world beyond his own, that everything around him was passing him by, leaving him out of touch, immobile, and vulnerable. He was ten years old, lying in his bed at the back room of his two-family brick house on Avenue V. The morning sun shone through his window. He could smell fresh green basil growing in the backyard. He knew he was young, and had many more years ahead of him before he grew old. But he believed he would never grow old. "Oh, what a wonderful, restful feeling," he said to himself. It was 1951. So much was happening in the world beyond.

After Clayton finished his paper route, he put on his sneakers and headed over to the lot around the corner on Neck Road. There was a ball game about to take place—the guys from Neck Road against the East 7th Streeters. They had an ongoing neighborhood rivalry. The guys from Neck Road were a diverse cast of characters: Fat Stevee, whose family came from southern Italy; big Jerry Landsmann from Hungary; Bobby Gelfat from a broken marriage, whose father appeared to be of French-Jewish origin; Joey LaRosa; Edward Kwasnewski, known as "the mad Polack";

and Clayton, along with a few other daily stragglers who wandered into the lot looking for a game. East 7th Street had its own cast of characters, mostly Italian: the Iocono brothers, Johnny "Mule Kick" Brunetti and his younger brother Babe, Tommy DiSpigno, and a few other late arrivals from southern Italy. Three out of four times, the 7th Streeters would topple the gang from Neck Road. The winners were the Yanks and the losers were the Dodgers. The 7th Streeters might have been a little hungrier that the Neck Roaders. At the end of the day it was always fun—a lot of shouting, boasting, and name-calling, but in the end everyone wound up across the street on Neck Road in Bill's candy store, gulping down chocolate egg creams and munching on cream-filled Devil Dogs. It was a moment in time when life stood still and allowed the simplest ecstasy to prevail.

For Clayton, being alive was then—and continues to be now—a balance between living the good life and reconciling with the rapidity of a changing world that could transport him beyond his willful parameters. Fear not for Clayton: he has always taken his time when venturing into unfamiliar territory. In his old age he listens to the wondrous music of Johann Sebastian Bach over WQXR at six in the morning. He ponders how he made it this far on this magnificent place called Earth. He occasionally thinks about whether or not he ever existed before, and in some measure, whether he will ever return in the future. But, for now, he is here.

Part One

A family history of life in Brooklyn at the end of the 19th and the beginning of the 20th century

Chapter One

Clayton's story begins in Brooklyn on March 14, 1941, at three o'clock in the afternoon. Rudy, one of his older brothers, was sitting on the front steps of their house on East 5th Street. He was chatting with a boyhood friend, explaining to him how babies are born. Lilly (Liberata in Italian), was inside the house lying in bed, assisted by Mary, her midwife, in the act of giving birth to Clayton. Other than Rudy's not-so-clear explanation of how Frank Sr., Clayton's father, and Lilly, his mother, came together to have him, the boys were left to wonder to what divine inspiration Clayton's arrival on this planet took place. Was it foretold, as in the stories of the Old Testament, or by happenstance, that Clayton arrived when he did to begin a new chapter in the book of life?

There he was swaddled in a warm blanket, nestled in his mother's loving arms. Rumor was that he weighed in at fourteen pounds. Of course in the old days it is likely that the local midwife, perhaps a family relative skilled in delivering babies, while holding him in her arms and waving him up and down as if he were a sack of potatoes, simply guessed that Clayton clocked in at fourteen pounds. His chubby-looking face was likely all the proof necessary to confirm it as fact. He learned at a much later date that Sal, his oldest brother, was born weighing even more than him.

Lilly was 40 years old when Clayton arrived. The prevailing wisdom at the time was that after a nervous breakdown it was good therapy to become pregnant and have another child, as if six children weren't enough. Clayton was the last of seven, with eight years separating him from his sister Barbara, the youngest of the other six siblings.

At the dawn of the twentieth century the common perception among Europeans was that there was gold in them there streets of the good old USA. And many people among the poor and the working classes did find a path to prosperity across the ocean in America. Lilly was only thirteen years old in 1913 when she and the entire Vallefuoco family came to the shores of New York harbor. The ship's manifest listed Augustino and Christina, the parents, along with six girls and three boys. The name Vallefuoco, translated into English, means "valley of fire." Clayton's maternal ancestors lived at the foot of Mount Vesuvius, near the lost city of Pompeii, in Naples, Italy.

Lilly was considered the prettiest child, and therefore the most suitable for a prime male candidate when she would come of age. The Vallefuocos traveled directly from Ellis Island to Stryker Street, between Avenue W and Avenue X, one block east of McDonald Avenue in Brooklyn. This area of Gravesend was home to many Italian American families during the late 19th and early-to-mid-20th century. It was also the place where the Martorellas, Salvatore, Luigi, and Giovanni, took up farming, having arrived from Naples, Italy, in the late 1800s. Salvatore remained in Brooklyn and continued farming while his brothers moved on to other parts of the country. Salvatore and Carmela Martorella's eldest son, Frank, was born in 1898. Of the Martorellas' six boys and five girls, Frank was the brightest and most ambitious member of the family. He was who Christina Vallefuoco had her eyes on for her daughter Lilly to marry.

At the dawn of the twentieth century Italy was not a land of opportunity. Work was not plentiful, especially in southern Italy, where life was a difficult day-to-day existence. A steady stream of boats left the Italian shores and sailed directly to the golden cities of opportunity in the new world, to New York, Boston, Montreal, Philadelphia, Chicago, and San Francisco, in the Old West, the last frontier. New, eager entries rolled up their sleeves and went to work. Among the ranks of Italians who settled in Brooklyn were butchers, carpenters, printers, tool and die makers, brick layers, and grocers. The Martorellas were farmers first, and later on many became sanitation men, in the employ of the City of New York. They also found gainful employment in the carnival world of Coney Island.

Clayton spent all of his youthful years living at 628 Avenue V. The Martorella family owned a semi-attached two-family red brick dwelling connected to the corner house on East 7th Street. The other half of the house was owned by a young Syrian-Jewish family. A second attached two-family house, separated by a party driveway, was shared by the Martorellas and the Tolkins. To the left of the Tolkins were the Weinbergs, and together all four families occupied half of Avenue V, beginning at the southwest corner of East 7th Street. The other half of this avenue was occupied by Dr. Rosenblatt's home, which included a two-car garage and a mansion-style two-story house that extended all the way to Ocean Parkway. For all the years that the Martorellas lived on Avenue V, Dr. Rosenblatt, a balding, formally dressed, heavyset man, was the only doctor Lilly would allow to examine her when she was not feeling well. Across the street was a three-story apartment building which occupied half of Avenue V, and on the remaining half there was another large mansion-style house which extended all the way to

Ocean Parkway. Everyone on the street knew, and helped to look out for, everyone else.

Avenue V was a wide street. It served the youth of the neighborhood in so many ways. Children played stickball, roller hockey, punchball, stoop ball, football, kick the can, and so many other games a kid could think of on the spur of the moment. The Martorella family house had a one-and-a-half-car garage leading to a three-room basement apartment, where Clayton's brother Gus and his wife Louise started a family after World War II ended. The first floor contained seven rooms: a porch, a large living room, a dining room, and an eat-in kitchen in the front part of the house; then a corridor containing three consecutive closets on the left side and one bedroom on the right, which Lilly occupied; then, at the back, with windows facing the backyard, were the remaining two bedrooms. Clayton's two sisters occupied one room, and his father, his unmarried brothers, and Clayton himself slept in the other room. Next to and in front of the boy's bedroom was a single bathroom that everyone competed to be the first in, each and every morning. The second floor apartment had the same number and configuration of rooms and was home to the Lerners, pre–World War II Jewish immigrants from Poland. Like the Martorellas, the Lerners raised a large family. Mr. Lerner was a tailor who traveled to Manhattan daily to earn his living in the fashionable garment district. Throughout their tenure, Frank Sr. never once raised the family's rent.

Augustino Jr. (Augie) was the oldest sibling in the Vallefuoco family, and then came Lilly. The First World War was winding down and daily life in this small part of Brooklyn continued in a seamless manner. Augie and his close friend Anthony worked in an ice-making plant along McDonald Avenue. A large number of homes still received blocks of ice for the preservation of food in the days before affordable refrigerators. One springtime Sunday, Augie invited Anthony to the family's traditional midday dinner. Augie and Anthony could have been two leading men right out of Hollywood. Tall, with jet-black hair, brown almond-shaped eyes, and winning smiles, these two southern Italian American boys, blessed with an abundance of strength and energy, exuded a zestful spirit that filled the air with a joyful essence of life wherever they went, especially among the young ladies.

The six daughters of the Vallefuoco family were dressed in their finest clothes on this Sunday afternoon. Lilly took extra pains to apply just the right amount of lipstick on her lips, applying her makeup perfectly and coaxing the light brown braided and crowned soft hair atop her head into just the right shape and proportion. At five foot four in two-inch heels, wearing a beautifully flowing three-quarter cloud-white dress and weighing a mere one hundred ten pounds, Lilly could have easily modeled for *McCall's*.

When Anthony's and Lilly's eyes met, it was ecstatic love at first sight. After Sunday dinner, with plenty of sunlight left in the day, Augie, Caroline (Lilly's sister and closest friend), Anthony, and Lilly decided to take a walk from Stryker Street toward the Coney Island waterfront. The year was 1919. The war was over and Coney Island was again at its peak of pleasure. After taking in a few rides and some cotton candy, these four lovely birds returned home as nightfall closed in on the Vallefuoco household. Lilly ran into the secure arms of Christina, exclaiming, "Mama, I'm in love with Anthony!"

"Che putz! What is this love? You're too young. Besides, I have someone else in mind for you," replied Christina.

Lilly paused for a moment and then replied, "What do you mean, someone else?"

"Frank Martorella, that's what I mean. He has eyes for you and he's very good looking," Christina said.

"I don't love him—I don't even like him! He's just a dirty farmer who lives in the vegetable garden and rolls around with the pigs," replied Lilly, whereupon she ran off to her bedroom to sulk alone with her romantic thoughts.

Augie and Anthony worked in the ice plant hauling one- and two-hundred-pound blocks of ice from one end of the facility to the other, loading them onto trucks or wagons for delivery to neighborhood households. Augie's brother Carmine worked as a street cleaner for the Department of Sanitation. He was posted to McDonald Avenue between Avenues U and V, a steady gig that he held on to for the rest of his working life. It was Frank Martorella, then a foreman in the Department of Sanitation who supervised the collection of garbage in the Gravesend and Coney Island districts of Brooklyn, who secured this special post for Carmine. Then there was Beniamino (Ben), the third and youngest boy, and the second-youngest child in the Vallefuoco family. He was a curious child, very interested in how radios worked. By the age of ten, Ben had accumulated old radio platforms, taken them apart on his own, and then reworked them. To his amazement he discovered that he could forward and receive radio signals, messages, and conversations from a wide variety of places both near and far.

The Vallefuoco girls were all blessed with clear white skin, healthy bones, soft features, and lovely smiles. Although the girls were quite beautiful, they tended to have a serious and skeptical demeanor, a character trait they inherited from their mother. Caroline, Lilly's sister and closest friend, was the most cheerful of all the Vallefuoco children. For many years, at Christmas time, after returning from midnight mass, all of the children and grandchildren would gather at Caroline's house for good cheer and delightful Italian pastries consumed with her husband Strungone's homemade wine. And when they came of age, some of the girls, including Lilly, found part-time work bottling Italian olives at a neighborhood plant.

Shortly after Lilly's nineteenth birthday, disaster struck the Vallefuoco family. It was on a Tuesday, in the early morning, when the doorbell rang and a voice from the street called out to Mrs. Vallefuoco, "Vieni! Vieni! Come down." With just a robe wrapped around her, Christina raced down the stairs to the front door, where a young man grabbed her right hand and led her into a small truck that took them to the ice plant. Both Augie and Anthony had been crushed to death by an enormous slab of ice that suddenly fell upon them. They died instantly.

When word got back to Lilly of this tragedy, she was devastated and fell into immediate depression over the loss of both her brother and her short-lived lover. She spent several days alone in her room in prayer and seclusion, spending nearly all of her time and energy mourning her losses and the fate that befell them all. Finally, at the end of her tears, Lilly emerged. She confronted her mother and told her she wanted to join a convent. Christina, in her long black dress ending at the mid-point of her black boot-like shoes, cut an imposing figure at the best of times. Now, with the loss of her eldest son and her eldest daughter distraught and confused before her, her classical dark facial features grew gravely severe. Without any hesitation she said to Lilly, "You will not go to a convent and become a nun. I'll have none of this. No! Instead, you will go out with Frank Martorella and discover what a wonderful man he is—and furthermore, he wants you and no one else."

Christina was extremely protective of her six daughters. Augustino Sr. was easygoing and blended into the background and out of the way when it came to family politics, so the topic of matchmaking for his daughters would prove no exception. The Vallefuoco girls considered the Martorellas rough around the edges and crude in their manner, except for the oldest brother, Frank. Christina first observed Frank's charm when he and his younger brother Dominick, traveling by horse and wagon, made the rounds in the neighborhood twice a week, selling produce.

Whenever the women of Stryker Street gathered around the open wagon to buy fruits and vegetables, Christina noticed how quick-witted and articulate Frank was while selling the family produce from the wagon. Christina saw in Frank a handsome and suitable candidate for her beautiful Lilly.

Even though the Martorellas found work for Augustino Sr. on their farm and eventually landed Carmine a spot in the Sanitation Department, Christina looked down on all the Martorellas besides Frank. In her fantasy, Christina believed that her beautiful daughters could do better for themselves; after all, she came to America in pursuit of the American dream.

Salvatore Martorella Sr. had started farming in the Gravesend–Coney Island area of Brooklyn in 1890. Opportunities for economic prosperity in southern Italy had been limited. One was lucky if one could scratch out a living under the Old World system. The elder Salvatore crossed the Atlantic Ocean looking for the land of opportunity, and he was determined to find it, even if it meant building it with his bare hands from the ground up. He knew how to manage a horse and plow, and cut a large, robust figure after years of toil in Italy. On arrival he immediately seized upon the free government land that was available in this rich and potentially active part of Brooklyn. The family he and his wife Carmela would raise—six boys and five girls—flourished in a compound in Coney Island, on West 18th Street between Mermaid and Surf Avenues, a block or two from the where the boardwalk was later built. There was another three-story brick house/barn-like structure located on East 7th Street between Avenue Y and Avenue Z which housed still more of the Martorella family. Behind that house were located a barn and a shed where a horse was kept and plows were stored.

As with many Italian farms, the principle items grown were tomatoes, basil, parsley, turnips, escarole, grapes, fennel, and zucchini, with various other seasonal herbs, spices, fruits, and vegetables. Every other year toward the end of the summer, the Martorellas would gather family and friends for the feast of making tomato sauce; on the off-year, they'd all gather together to make wine. It was always a major production, incorporating large barrels for crushing either tomatoes or grapes, depending on what was in demand. The family could stock up on tomato sauce for as long as two years, even when they sold jars of it at the produce stand on East 7th Street. The wine, on the other hand, never seemed to last very long!

Chapter Two

Frank was the oldest son in the Martorella family and he was also the most literate. In all matters relating to family business, he was the go-to person. Salvatore Sr. barely knew a word of English. Given that the entire Martorella family worked the farm, including other extended family members, and neighbors were even employed when needed, a good overseer was crucial to keeping things going. Being at the right place at the right moment, Frank developed a sixth sense for managing people.

He also took it upon himself to go to grade school and advanced up to the eighth grade, which, at that time in that area, was roughly equivalent to graduating from high school. He was a whiz with numbers and could plot out acreage, deal with money, and seize upon financial opportunities in an instant. In addition to managing the family farm, Frank worked for the New York City Department of Sanitation. He began his career as a street cleaner in Coney Island and eventually advanced to the rank of borough superintendent, responsible for the entire borough of Brooklyn.

Frank's brothers were Joe, Charlie, Dominick, Louie ("Creepy"), and "Toddo" (Salvatore Jr.). His sisters were Antoinette, Lucy, Philomena, Maggie, and Sophie. They were a hardy bunch, ready, willing, and able to roll up their sleeves to do the hard work of maintaining the farm, managing the produce business, and raising their individual families, many of whom lived on West 18th Street in Coney Island.

After a week of hard farm work, the Martorella boys enjoyed playing baseball. Both Frank and his brother Joe were extremely talented ball players. They played for the Nappy All-Stars, a Triple-A baseball team in the Coney Island League. Frank was a hard-hitting shortstop and Joe was the homerun hitter, commanding center field. There was a good deal of grandstand betting on these games. The players received no money. They simply played for the sheer pleasure of the game. The umpires were paid well to call the games, but it was considered blood money. At times, there were disputes over the umpire calls, and, more often than not, they were the ones who received physical blows from the disgruntled ball players and the betting crowd as well. Yet, at the end of the day, all was forgiven.

To some extent the Vallefuoco family was dependent on the goodwill and largess of the hale and hearty Martorellas. In Lilly's family there were six girls and three boys, ultimately reduced by one due to the tragic death of Augie. The girls were Lilly, Vigence, Caroline, Nicoleta, Anna, and Theresa. The boys were Carmine and Ben. Three out of the six sisters named one of their sons Augustine (Augie) in memory of their deceased brother. Lilly's second-oldest son was named Augustine, and he became a celebrated musician. He began taking piano lessons when he was only six years old. By the time Gus, short for Augustine, reached eighteen, he was playing with one of the leading jazz bands of the day.

Upon Augie and Anthony's horrible death, Lilly became severely depressed. It took a while before Lilly came to terms with the dreadful event and regained her composure; and, with some gentle but undoubtedly persistent coaxing from her mother, she finally considered meeting Frank over a Sunday dinner at the Vallefuoco household on Stryker Street.

Frank fell in love with Lilly the moment he set eyes upon her, as he looked down from his wagon in front of the Vallefuoco compound. He told his father in no uncertain terms that he wished to meet this young woman. His father had no qualms about his eldest son falling in love with the beautiful Lilly Vallefuoco. Frank's other siblings, however, thought otherwise of this romance. They saw Lilly as a threat to their well-being. After all, Frank had become the breadwinner for all the Martorellas. They did not wish to lose their meal ticket. For their part, the Vallefuoco girls wanted nothing to do with the other Martorella boys, and dismissed the lot of them as crude farmers. To put it mildly, they looked down their noses at nearly all the Martorellas—the whole family, that is, except for Frank.

One Sunday Easter afternoon, Frank was invited to be the honored dinner guest. The Martorellas were not regular churchgoers apart from the major holidays, Christmas and Easter. On this particular Easter Sunday, Frank wore his best charcoal-black suit, white shirt, and red tie. He made a generous donation at the offering of Our Lady of Solace Church, the local parish in Coney Island. When he arrived at the house at two o'clock, the Vallefuoco girls were quite surprised—indeed, even in awe at how handsome Frank looked. Here was an Italian American with light blue eyes. They wondered where that came from. Lilly and Caroline returned from church shortly after Frank arrived. They'd attended the last service of the morning. Lilly looked stunning in a three-quarter black Spanish laced dress, with her wavy brown hair partially tucked beneath a grey beret topped with several colorful feathers. She and Caroline quickly walked past their guest into the kitchen, to help with the Sunday dinner.

The aromas coming from the kitchen were heavenly, and

swirled in a combination of basilico (basil), parsley, tomato sauce, and a mélange of other wondrous spices. Everyone soon sat down to a dinner of lasagna, meatballs, and braciole (thinly rolled beef filled with parsley, cheese, ham, and fine breadcrumbs, held together with thin sewing thread and allowed to simmer for several hours in a rich, flavorful tomato sauce). It was a joy to the taste buds. Lilly was seated beside Frank on the wall side of the table. Everyone else filed into the remaining chairs in the dining room, with Christina at one end and Augustino Sr. at the other. The dinner began with perfectly baked Easter bread, followed by a plate of lasagna, and topped off with the tender meatballs and braciole. Afterwards, for desert, there were Italian pastries from Cuccio's Bakery on Avenue X, and the Vallefuocos' home-baked, delightfully sweet Easter pie (pastiera di grano). There was Chianti wine, cream soda for the children, and espresso coffee to top off the Sunday meal.

At one point during the dinner conversation, Frank put his right hand over Lilly's left, under the table. After about a minute she became aware that Frank was holding her hand and she slowly withdrew it modestly. The conversation was light. Frank talked somewhat about the farm, and he was curious about what young Ben was doing with all his radios. Ben was eager to show Frank his communication center lodged inside one of his mother's closets. As evening set in, Frank decided to take leave and made his courteous goodbyes to everyone, thanking the talented ladies for the wonderful Easter dinner. He paused for a moment, directing his eyes toward Lilly as she talked to two of her sisters, and then caught her attention by asking if he might call on her again. Lilly briefly glanced at her mother, who responded in an instant with a deliberate nod of the head. Lilly walked over to Frank as he waited at the door and said yes, he could come by again, and she gently kissed him on the cheek. She walked him to the sidewalk and bade him farewell.

Chapter Three

The Martorella family enterprise covered a large swath of territory, extending from Manhattan Beach into Sheepshead Bay, where they managed the Sheepshead Bay race track, a pleasure spot for the Manhattan rich and famous. The tracts of land where the Martorellas worked began at Ocean Avenue, continuing into Brighton Beach and beyond into Coney Island, and stretched all the way to Sea Gate. The Martorellas continued to manage the family farm's produce business and provided caretaking for some of the Coney Island concessions. In 1920 they added a new enterprise, the Riviera restaurant and catering business on Stillwell Avenue and West 16th Street. Antoinette, the second eldest of the Martorella family, and her husband, Zacarino, were the proud owners of this establishment. It was a perfect place for hosting parties on the weekends. Wedding celebrations among the working-class population in Brooklyn were generally beer, wine, and sandwich affairs. The Riviera was an instant success due to its elevating the neighborhood's wedding celebrations to a more formal dining experience.

Again, in true Martorella fashion, the family rolled up their sleeves and went to work. Antoinette and her two sisters, Maggie and Sophie, took over the food preparation. Her younger brothers, Dominick and Charlie, covered various kitchen activities (cleaning dishes, pots, and pans, and food distribution), while her second-youngest brother, Louie, managed the ovens. Frank continued to improve his farming skills by attending the Farmingdale Agriculture School on Long Island. He also became a sanitation man. Shortly after joining the department, he enrolled in the Delehanty School of Business. Frank had a great deal of confidence in his ability to manage people and develop strategies to improve the farming business. As he advanced in the Sanitation Department, Frank was also able to find jobs for some of his brothers and friends.

It was 1920. The First World War was finally over. The country was poised to grow and have a good time. The Roaring Twenties had arrived. Although World War I was supposed to put an end to the many inequities of the hierarchically structured Western society, little was accomplished to alleviate poverty and inequality. It would take the human devastation of a second world war, ending with the explosion of an atomic bomb 25 years later, before Keynesian economics and the Marshall Plan could bring society to a better place. Under the presidency of Harry S. Truman, in support of the New Deal policy of Franklin D. Roosevelt, the United States would at least make a start at putting people back to work and finding new ways to grow an economy in a land on the mend from a severe depression and two horrific wars within less than three decades.

Long before any relief would come to the nation politically or economically, the Vallefuocos and the Martorellas banded together through the marriage of Frank and Lilly. The start of the union would turn out to be a bit rocky, in ways that would have lasting effects upon the marriage of two very different personalities. Lilly agreed to marry Frank under one condition: they were to set up living quarters apart from both families. She did not want to live under the tyranny of her mother, nor did she want to put up with the rough and tumble lifestyle of the Martorella clan. They discovered a lovely apartment in a two-family house just north of Avenue W, neither too far from nor too close to their respective families, where they intended to begin their new life.

The wedding took place at the local church on a springtime Sunday in 1920, followed by an evening reception at Antoinette's Riviera catering hall. All of the day's activity proceeded as planned; the bride and groom were a picture-book couple, and a fine time was had by all. At day's end, when the newlyweds arrived at their newly furnished apartment and crossed the threshold, they discovered that all of their furniture had been removed. Surprise! During the course of the day, the Martorella clan had transferred all of the contents in the apartment to living quarters inside their compound on West 18th Street. Lilly became hysterical, rushing out of the apartment and back into her mother's arms on Stryker Street. Needless to say, Frank was also surprised at this turn of events, and he returned to his family compound none too pleased.

After several days of negotiations with both families, Frank had all of the furniture returned to their new apartment. The newlyweds would indeed make a new beginning, despite their respective families clearly wishing to hold on to them. Shortly after moving in together, Lilly became pregnant with their first child, Salvatore, to be named after Frank's father. After Salvatore, five more children arrived in two-year intervals. In birth order, they were Salvatore, the eldest; Augustine; Frank Jr.; Rudolph; Anna (Anita); and Carmela (Barbara). Clayton, their last child, arrived eight years after Barbara was born.

The new family's early years were filled with growth, style, and direction which led to a family structure that defined the very unique character of Frank and Lilly. As Frank was becoming the leader of the Martorella family, Lilly's talents were beginning to flourish in the areas of art, music, and design. From her mother, she learned how to sew, cook, and clean, and she took pride in maintaining an orderly household. Coming from a family environment of hard work and an earthy style of living, Frank began to appreciate the finer things that were cultivated around him. Lilly embraced fine linens, expensive flatware, and, above all, a meticulously clean house. Lilly perfected her Neapolitan cooking skills and could produce a wealth of wonderful Italian dishes. Her facility with the culinary arts was a trait all of her sisters shared as well.

The Vallefuocos were the nurturers. All of the girls, and their brothers Ben and Carmine, raised large families, with the exception of Caroline, who gave birth to only one child, Mary. She eventually adopted a young boy from a poor family as well. Lilly led the way with seven children. The older boys, Sal, Gus, and Frank Jr., were given music lessons at an early age. Lilly loved to listen to opera over the radio, and she often flexed her vocal cords upon hearing a familiar aria. Her voice was lovely and could make its way up to a high C when she was in good form.

Living north of Avenue W put Frank and Lilly in the company of several other ethnic groups. It was the Jewish influence that had the greatest impact upon Lilly. She realized instantly that her new friends loved music and education. She sensed that this form of discipline could lead to a better way of life for her boys. Sal developed into an excellent violinist and eventually played in the All-City High School Orchestra, representing Brooklyn's Abraham Lincoln High School. Gus honed his craft on piano. By a very early age he demonstrated a special style and skill that formed his musical personality. At the age of eighteen Gus began touring with one of the major jazz bands. Frank Jr. learned how to play the guitar and had a fine singing voice. He was the crooner among the family's three oldest boys.

What distinguished Frank Jr. from his two older brothers was his preference to be by himself. Each day upon returning home from school he liked to go to his room, turn on the radio, and hit the books, away from the noise and hustle and bustle of a very active household. Despite his natural abilities on the guitar, he did not like taking lessons. One day he simply came out of his room and into the kitchen with his guitar. In front of his mother, he smashed the instrument against the kitchen table, stating that he no longer wanted to take music lessons. Upon seeing the guitar smashed to pieces, Lilly was momentarily devastated, but she recovered soon after and silently and sadly gave in to her son's wishes. Yet Frank Jr.'s self-directed planning and personal determination evidently paid off. On graduation day at P.S. 216, located on Avenue X just off East 1st Street, Frank Sr. discreetly slipped into the school auditorium with his Department of Sanitation chauffeur in time to hear that his son, Frank Jr., was to receive an award as the class valedictorian. The proud father shook hands with the surrounding parents and left the school building as quietly as he'd entered. Frank Jr. would go on to study engineering at Brooklyn Tech—a major milestone for the family.

So much of Lilly's mental and physical efforts were invested in her three older boys that, when the next three came along, they received somewhat less of her attention. Rudy, the fourth child, was caught in the middle. In accordance with family tradition, the older boys were named after their forefathers and deceased brother. Lilly chose to name her fourth son after her matinee idol, Rudolph Valentino. After that, Anita and Barbara came along. While Lilly was doing her darndest to raise all six children in the best way that she could, her health and demeanor were beginning to show signs of weakness.

Frank Sr. continued to make a good living, giving to Lilly as much money as she required to maintain the lifestyle she enjoyed. At day's end, though, he too was exhausted from making the daily rounds, overseeing the entire sanitation operation of Brooklyn. At about five o'clock each evening, he would return home from work and change from his suit, shirt, and tie into his khaki overalls and white T-shirt. He often hitched a ride with a local farmhand and headed over to Avenue Z and East 7th Street in order to oversee the activities of the family farm and lend a helping hand. On such long days, Lilly had very little contact with her husband. Yet together they still managed to achieve the impossible: to raise seven children, support their parents' and siblings' businesses, and keep the whole borough of Brooklyn safe and clean. They were unstoppable.

Chapter Four

After the Migliaro family made the trek from Italy to Ellis Island, their first stop was Hoboken, New Jersey. It didn't take long, though, before word spread through the grapevine that Brooklyn, and specifically the Gravesend and Coney Island area, was where they should settle. Jerry and Mary Migliaro moved as soon as they could into a modest two-family house on East 1st Street between Avenues Y and Z. There they raised three boys and seven girls. In later years, Anthony (Tony) Migliaro, the youngest of the three boys, claimed that the Migliaros and the Martorellas were related a few generations back, with their connection coming from the mothers' sides of these two Italian families.

The Migliaros arrived with very little money, and Jerry's prospects for work were limited. He was a large, strapping man who had worked on a farm in the old country. Frank Sr. recruited him to work on the family farm and eventually found him a spot in the Sanitation Department as well. When Jerry worked he was a workhorse—but he liked his wine. There were times when he was missing in action, only to be found later sleeping in a patch of weeds. Placed on the bed of a horse-drawn wagon, he would be unceremoniously delivered back to his home for resuscitation, and recharged to begin a new day. Mary, his wife, a little bitty thing of a woman who gave birth to nine children, would always accept

Jerry with open arms. After Jerry's passing at 61, Mary lived on for nearly four decades, into her mid-nineties.

Mary was a practical woman and an excellent homemaker with a heart of gold. There was always a coffee pot on the stove. While both the Martorella and the Migliaro kids were growing up, so many fun moments were spent in the basement of the Migliaros' loving household. Of the boys, in addition to Tony, there was Marco and Tommy. The girls, in birth order, were Anna, Josi, Rachael, Tootsie, Gloria, Delores, and Geraldine. As soon as Tootsie was of marrying age, she met her mate and took off to California. For the Migliaros, she was the golden girl of the West. Marco set up a successful car repair business out of the double-car garage at the back of the house on East 1st Street.

At first the Martorellas lived in a two-bedroom apartment, but as the family began to grow they moved into a house on East 12th Street with much larger accommodations. Sal, Gus, and Frank Jr. were very active boys and more than a handful for their mother, especially with another child on the way. Lilly's ability to manage a growing household was beginning to take its toll on her mental health. Frequently, she was compelled to ask her mother for some help. Reluctantly, Anna and Theresa, the youngest of the Valle-fuoco sisters, were dispatched to give Lilly some assistance. Frank Sr. was grateful for their help, and at times showed his appreciation by assisting the Vallefuoco family financially.

For Lilly the move to East 12th Street opened up a new world of possibilities in the areas of art and education. The oldest two boys attended kindergarten and first grade at the local elementary school. Lilly was always aware that her comprehension of the English language and her ability to speak it were limited. She realized that she was a work in progress. But over time, her confidence in joining public life began to grow. At home she would study the schoolwork the boys brought into the house, and gradually she learned to read and write in the English language.

From East 16th Street to Ocean Parkway, Avenue U was a shopping paradise as compared to the old neighborhood on Stryker Street. On this new shopping strip, Lilly met other women who were more Americanized. From them she acquired new habits, and she slightly altered her old ones. She loved listening to the radio, especially commercials and classical music. She also enjoyed dressing well. Many of the clothing windows displayed the latest in women's fashion. Fashion magazines introduced Lilly to many different hairstyles and dyes with which she began to experiment.

On a typical springlike day, while strolling along on the avenue, Lilly noticed at the entrance door of a three-story brick building two metal plaques; one advertised "Emilio Corto, violin teacher," and the other, "Murray Schiff, piano teacher." In that instant, she decided that she would send her two eldest boys, Salvatore (Sal) and Augustino (Gus) for music lessons. At the ages of eight and six, respectively, it was Sal on violin and Gus on piano. Lilly was successful in persuading Frank Sr. to purchase a piano. One day to Lilly's surprise, upon returning home from her daily shopping chores, she entered through the front door into the living room to find a slightly used Hamilton free-standing concert piano. This piano still, to this very day, resides in the living room at Gus and Louise's house in Long Beach, California, albeit in a somewhat out-of-tune condition. Gus recently passed away, but at age 92 Louise is still going strong and may get that piano back in tune yet.

The Vallefuoco family, led by their matriarch, Christina, structured their life somewhere between religiosity and old wives' tales. Christina was not very generous in sending help along to Lilly. Often Lilly had to beg her mother for help in caring for her children. Some of the tensions may have been related to Lilly's embrace of the new and vibrant world of modern women. Her developing ability to speak English fluently, coupled with her flair for fashion when choosing her clothing, seemed to place her at the vanguard of her own family. Some jealous rivalry was certainly evident among her female siblings.

After Lilly's four boys were born, Anita and Barbara came along. At that point, Lilly bore the full responsibility of raising six young children. Frank Jr. was the third child to begin taking music lessons, so he was introduced to the guitar. The Martorella family grew zestfully in so many ways. Frank loved his wife dearly, though perhaps he was overly shy at times in letting her know that he found her strikingly beautiful. All too often Frank was very much overworked, which in turn left Lilly overworked with the kids, and the two could do little to change this exhausting pattern.

Chapter Five

The period between 1920 and 1940 was momentous. There was the glitz of the Roaring Twenties, underscored with prohibition, gambling, and the growth of women's emancipation. Then suddenly the crash of 1929 arrived, followed by a prolonged depression which led the United States right into the Second World War. In the meantime, the Martorella family continued to manage the family farm, and work in the ever-present concessions of Coney Island's amusement parks. By 1920, the racing playground of the rich and the famous around town had disappeared, swallowed up in the winds of changing times. However, all of the family's activities kept Frank Sr. constantly busy, with little time left over for him to participate in his own family affairs. For the most part Lilly had to fend for herself, with little help coming from her siblings, and certainly not enough to aid her in raising six very active children.

The colonial house on East 12th Street was quite large, with an interior area of approximately 3,000 square feet. The first floor had the usual large living room, dining room, and kitchen. There was a front and side entrance and a party driveway. The second floor contained four decent-size bedrooms to more than accommodate this growing family. It was altogether a rather large bird's nest that included a stand-up basement as well.

As the older boys began to spread their wings while the younger three were being born, life for Lilly became more and more difficult. The older boys would run around the house, going up and down the staircase, into and out of the house, and everywhere else one could hide and generate some mischief. With each passing day, cooking and cleaning—while at the same time keeping track of everyone—was becoming still more burdensome for Lilly. At times she would have to send one or two of the boys over to her mother's house for a few days in order to relieve herself of the day-to-day physical and mental stress imposed upon her in managing this growing household. Yet despite the constant strain on her nerves and her patience, Lilly retained her strong will, grace, and style in keeping her large house in order and guiding her children to health and happiness through good old-fashioned hard work.

Chapter Six

The Sheepshead Bay Race Track was begun by the Coney Island Jockey Club in 1879 and completed in 1880. The entrance to the club was located at Ocean Avenue between Avenues X and Y. The club and track were formed by prominent backers lead by August Belmont Jr. The course venues were flat and steeplechase. They featured notable stakes for handicap and derby races, some of which are still included in modern-day venues at various tracks around the country. In addition to the Sheepshead Bay Race Track, the Brighton Beach Race Course was also built nearby in the same year, between Ocean Parkway and Coney Island Avenue, alongside the Brighton Beach Hotel. A third entry, the Gravesend Race Track, opened in 1886. It was formed by the Dwyer Brothers, who were wealthy stable owners. It covered an area which extended from McDonald Avenue (then Gravesend Avenue) to Ocean Parkway, and from Kings Highway to Avenue U.

It's no surprise that the Martorella family would become an active part in the maintenance of these wonderful additions to an otherwise sleepy farming community in southwest Brooklyn. The rich and famous crowds of the Manhattan and downtown Brooklyn communities were not to be denied their worldly pleasures. The Long Island Rail Road was a welcome addition to Brooklyn during the same period; combined with an aboveground train and a trolley system, it provided an easy and accessible means of transportation between Manhattan, Prospect Park in Brooklyn, and Coney Island. If that was not enough, there was still the horse and wagon. Well into the twentieth century, the Coney Island farmer's most common form of transportation when bringing his produce to downtown Brooklyn and Canarsie markets was horse-drawn wagon.

Thoroughbred horse racing provided a short-lived boon to the sleepy Gravesend community, transforming it into a pleasure palace for the fashionable as well as the hoi polloi living in and around New York City. In the spring and summer, the upper crust would flock into the swanky hotels and beach houses of Manhattan Beach and Brighton Beach. Following World War I, this part of the world served as a playground for the Great Gatsby era of ostentation and excess.

Throughout southwest Brooklyn, Salvatore Sr., a bull of a man, led the boys and girls of his family in diligently working the farm and caring for the race track grounds. On occasion, Salvatore Sr. might disappear for an hour or two in the late summer afternoon for a little R&R when asked to deliver a parcel of produce to one of the more adventurous ladies of the fast track set. With a package in hand, Salvatore, the invited guest, slightly unshaven and wearing overalls and an undershirt held together with old suspenders, was a formidably handsome, lovemaking specimen of a man. Just what the doctor ordered on a steamy summer afternoon in Coney Island. By nightfall the conquering hero would return home in plenty of time for the family dinner prepared by his caring, unsuspecting wife Carmela and her helpfully unsuspecting daughters. Alongside Salvatore Sr., the boys had to pull their fair share of the workload that came with managing a family farm and the local race tracks. By nightfall there were lots of tired, hungry folks and raucous laughter at the supper table.

This playground for the rich and famous disappeared rather quickly in the annals of time. From 1894 through 1908, Gravesend Race Track hosted the Preakness Stakes, an American Classic Race. In 1908 Governor Charles Evans Hughes signed into law the Hart–Agnew bill that banned all race track betting in New York State. Shortly thereafter, all of the tracks in that part of Brooklyn were closed, eventually giving way to real-estate developers. To take the place of managing race tracks, a new line of work was in order for the family. Thankfully, the Coney Island amusement venues were beginning to take shape and grow. Salvatore Sr. and his hardworking family were in the right place at the right time. It was an easy transition from the race track to the amusement park.

All along Brooklyn's Coney Island coastline stretching from Manhattan Beach to Sea Gate, the wonderful sunny sand and beach bordering the Atlantic Ocean gave a renewed refuge to the rich and the famous. By 1910, after hosting thoroughbred racing for twenty-odd years, the area saw a resurgence of wealthy visitors, and marvelous hotels were built to accommodate those who wished to keep cool during the summer months.

While race track gambling was banned, the need to gamble was not to be denied Manhattan and Long Island's adventurous, risk-taking crowd. Coney Island would become their next best bet. At the dawn of the twentieth century, the rails and the telegraph wire were already linking people to places within mere hours and not days. For that matter, the area's role as host to racing crowds made it the ideal destination for tourists craving a beach holiday alongside the latest amusements. By the time that Nathan's Famous hot dogs had arrived in 1916, marvelous pleasure palaces—namely,

George C. Tilyou's Steeplechase Park—had already been in place since 1897. Luna Park and Dreamland also arrived in 1903 and 1904, respectively. With all the resources in place, the area's shift from racing to amusements meant lots of gainful employment for the Martorellas for years to come.

By the early 1920s the Coney Island boardwalk was completed, stretching from Coney Island Avenue all the way west to the Sea Gate community. The center of amusement activity began at Surf and Stillwell Avenues and ended around the West 20s. In the late 1930s the area was still drawing crowds, and the boardwalk was extended another third of a mile into Brighton Beach.

Dreamland, the most Disney-like of Coney Island's three amusement parks, had a short life. It was completed in 1904 and destroyed by fire in 1911. However, both Luna Park and Steeplechase Park were to continue for several decades to follow, into the 1940s and 1960s, respectively. The rich and famous, along with the rising middle class for whom the parks were designed, were not to be denied their simple seaside pleasures, regardless of the state of things in the outside world. During the dark days of World War I and Prohibition, followed by the Depression, Coney Island, with its fine beaches and amusement parks, provided for the growing masses of humanity an ongoing refuge from their everyday trials and tribulations, a true dreamland despite the nightmares surrounding them in waking life.

Chapter Seven

E ach year when springtime arrived the Martorella family could count on finding extra income from working in the amusement parks of Coney Island, with an abundance of work that carried into late fall. Apart from that, throughout most of the year, farming kept them gainfully employed. On top of all that, in about 1920 the Riviera catering hall came into its own. Antoinette and her husband Zack began the concept of personalized weekend weddings. The Riviera soon developed a reputation as the best place to have a fine wedding ceremony. To this day it is still considered one of the finest catering halls in all of New York City. From its inception, one could find nearly all of the Martorella family working there, weekdays as well as weekends, engaged in preparing the many delicate foods in advance of the weddings soon to follow. Since growing fruits and vegetables was already a part of everyday life for this farming family, it was a natural fit to bring fresh produce to the catering hall. Right from the start, the Riviera took pride in offering a one-of-a-kind catering experience.

From Avenues U and X by Ocean Parkway, to all the way west in Bensonhurst and south by West End Avenue in Brighton Beach, all sorts of Italian American stores arrived. There was Romano's Pork Store, various butcher shops, pastry shops such as Cuccio's Bakery on Avenue X and Lo Bosso's on Avenue U,

George's Bakery on McDonald Avenue, and Luigi Alba's in Borough Park. Italians have always had a sweet tooth. From the turn of the nineteenth century up to the early 1950s, southwest Brooklyn was a melting pot for all ethnicities. Black and white communities emerged, side by side in a rather natural order, in response to the needs of the nouveau riche of Brooklyn and New York.

From Manhattan Beach to Shore Road and from Kings Highway to Brighton Beach and Coney Island rested one large magic carpet of rich soil, sand, and space. The race tracks, the farms, the beaches, and the amusement parks together attracted a rich and vibrant black community into Sheepshead Bay alongside recent Italian, Irish, and Jewish immigrants. The radio advertisements, the horse-drawn electric wagons, and the newly constructed rails carried the well-to-do from their stately mansions out to the lavish hotels of Manhattan Beach and Brighton Beach in pursuit of sun and fun. The good times kept rolling on, albeit with a few temporary setbacks (like war and depression).

The Martorellas were in the middle of all this vibrant activity. It was a time when one could find work both aboveground and "underground," in shadier activities. The idea at the time was to put food on the table and to seek out the good life where and however one could find it. There was room for carpentry, farming, horse-grooming, baking, catering, shopping, and playing. Gambling was an integral part of life in this vibrant community. Up to 1908, for two decades prior, one was allowed to bet on the horses. After 1908 race track betting was prohibited, but other types of betting no doubt took its place. Eleven years later Prohibition was enacted. While the government was trying to clean up society, the good folks of Sheepshead Bay and Coney Island joined forces with the rich and famous in pursuit of the good life. After all, why destroy a good thing?

By 1920, the Coney Island Velodrome was completed and ready for business. It seated ten thousand people, and initially hosted speed bicycle racing. In later years, it added motorcar races, boxing, and football. The gamblers did not stop gambling, they simply went underground—or, more precisely, below the gaze of authorities. During the Prohibition years, the same was true for those who desired the liquid spirits.

If anything could be said of Brooklynites of this era, it's that they were certainly an enterprising people. They enjoyed good food, music, and dancing. They also demonstrated a strong sense of sport and drama. They truly knew how to roll up their sleeves and dirty their hands when there was hard work to be done and pleasure to be had.

Small mom-and-pop stores sprang up everywhere. Jewish merchants tended to settle along Kings Highway, on Avenue U between East 16th Street and Ocean Parkway, and in Brighton Beach as well. The Italians set up food stores, restaurants, and bakeries along Avenues U and X and along McDonald Avenue from Ocean Parkway to Bensonhurst. The black community brought wonderful Southern cooking and a steady sense of quiet calm and levity to the Sheepshead Bay neighborhood, as well as, later on, to Coney Island.

Fishmongers, along with producers and distributors of home-delivered bread, milk, soda, and bakery goods, were woven through the tapestry of this part of Brooklyn. Along with transportation, food was a unifying factor in bringing together this very unique community of recent immigrants and their American-born children. The America of the 1920s marked the beginning of a cross-cultural renaissance in Brooklyn. Skilled carpenters, electricians, and bricklayers from the old country were constantly in demand as New York City bought itself a new suit of clothes, so to speak, in the race to construct newer and bigger buildings, parks, and bridges. Southwest Brooklyn was flourishing economically and culturally for residents willing and able to put in the hard work.

Chapter Eight

The march of time has its own way of playing tricks, as well as granting luck and fortune without any rhyme or reason. All of the children of Salvatore Sr.'s family were born in the years just prior to World War I, and therefore were too young to be drafted into military service. At the dawn of World War II, they were too old to be drafted. In between the wars, they were busy making a living, providing goods and services to their vibrant community.

The decades between 1920 and 1950 were exciting times. By 1922, Frank and Lilly already had one child, Salvatore. Antoinette had married Zack and started their restaurant business. Frank's brother Joe began delivering coal for a living and worked part-time on the farm. He and his wife Lucy went on to have two beautiful girls and a handsome boy. Charles, another brother, found work in the Sanitation Department and started a family as well. He married a German girl and they had a son and a daughter. Still another brother Dominick ("Fumbo") married Millie, a beautiful blond woman of Tuscan origin and the daughter of a rather wealthy concessioner from Sea Gate. Then there was Frank's second-youngest brother Louie, who remained a bachelor and found lasting work as a chef at the Riviera. Louie honed his cooking skills while he served as head cook in the United States Army, stationed at Fort Benning, Georgia, during the Second World War. After the war, he returned to the Riviera and continued to hone his craft as head chef alongside Antoinette. Salvatore Jr. ("Toddo"), the youngest sibling, joined the Sanitation Department and married Viola, a lovely gal who eventually sold Avon cosmetics. They had two lovely children: a girl name Bunny, who was born on March 15th, one day after Clayton was born; and Ricky, her younger brother.

Among Frank's sister, after Antoinette came Lucy, who married and had two boys, Cha Cha and Frank, both very good baseball players. Maggie married and had one daughter. She worked on the farm and at the Riviera. Philomena married and had two children. She settled in Manhattan, where her husband opened up a vegetable store. Sophie was the youngest of the Martorella girls. She was also the prettiest and the most glamorous in the family. She married twice. Both husbands were venture capitalists. She gave birth to a very handsome and debonair son, as well as two beautiful daughters. She had a fourth child with her second husband, a beautiful daughter as well. Sophie also spent her days working at the Riviera. Both of her husbands died prematurely at an early age.

Frank and his siblings certainly had their hands full, and the family grew and prospered with each passing year, even in the midst of Prohibition, depression, and war. The Martorellas were born in the right place at the right time, and the family stuck together while fortune smiled upon them, strengthening them against a time when fortune, in all its fickleness, might not.

Chapter Nine

In late spring or even early summer, the Martorella family manufactured their famous tomato sauce. It was a family event that took place every two years. The center of activity happened at the farmhouse near 1934 East 7th Street. A three-story red brick house stood on a rather large tract of rich farmland that the Martorellas cultivated. They grew Swiss chard, peppers, scallions, turnips, and basilico by the barrelsful, and, above all, fresh ripe plum tomatoes. A huge steel vat was strategically located directly behind the farmhouse. It was eight or ten feet high and approximately eight feet in diameter. It rested about three feet above the ground atop thick concrete cinder blocks placed at each corner of the vat.

The first floor of this farmhouse consisted of two rooms. The front room was more or less a storage room for some farm tools, with shelves and stands to store spices, groceries, and fresh produce. People from the neighborhood could stop by and purchase vegetables, flowers, and various spices off the shelves. The back room, which was the larger of the two, was the kitchen. It contained three large sink bowls, two large stoves, and a very long table with various cooking utensils everywhere, and from the ceiling hung pots and pans of all sizes. The second and third floors contained three or four small bedrooms on each floor, as well as a bathroom on each level of the house, including the basement. The bedrooms were usually rented to individuals or families who worked on the farm. Quite often this domicile was home to first-time immigrants just off the boat from Italy.

First the men of the Martorella family, along with some hired help, delivered, in wooden baskets, freshly picked plum tomatoes into the kitchen at the back door entrance. Salvatore Sr. assigned the women of the household the task of washing the tomatoes and then placing them into large pots of boiling water. When the skins began to crack, the partially cooked tomatoes were transported to Foley handheld strainers to be crushed. Thirty-two-ounce bottles were collectively boiled and placed on racks; after drying, fresh basil leaves and salt were inserted into each bottle. The bottles were then filled with water and the partially cooked and strained tomatoes. Each one was finally capped and then conveyed to the table, to be individually wrapped in newspaper.

The wrapped bottles were then carted en masse to the giant vat. There were two large ladders which were placed at a slight angle against the outside of the vat from the ground up to the top. On the inside of the vat there were two more corresponding ladders to join with the two on the outside. Four young boys were summoned to climb up the ladders and then down again into the vat. The tedious job of handling each of the bottles of tomato sauce began. In a circular pattern, the bottles would be stacked from the bottom up until the vat was filled. Once the giant vat was filled, the boys could exit from the top down by the outside ladders.

The vat was filled with water so that all the bottles were covered. In order to boil the water, a wood fire was started under the vat. After the bottles of tomato sauce were boiled for several hours, the fire was extinguished. Overnight the hot water cooled off, and the next day, in an assembly-like manner, the bottles of tomato sauce were unloaded from the vat, packed twelve to a box, and reloaded onto a horse and wagon for delivery to households in and around the neighborhood.

As with any grand project that has come to a successful conclusion, a family dinner was in order. Antoinette, along with Maggie and Sophie, her two closest allies, would organize a combined Saturday afternoon and evening dinner at the farmhouse on East 7th Street. There was an open invitation to the family along with all of the neighbors and friends who took part in the making of a two-year supply of tomato sauce. As people gradually arrived at the farmhouse, they could sample some of the tasty hors d'oeuvres, ranging from boiled octopus (polpo) to tiny bell-shaped doughy cheese puffs, to stuffed littleneck clams, along with many more tasty vegetable treats.

Dinner started at six p.m. The first course began with a unique Martorella soup prepared in a mildly spicy flavored broth consisted of tiny cut carrots, tiny alphabet pasta, and finely cut celery and onions. The second course consisted of two delicately prepared manicotti served in a mild tomato sauce. Finally, out came either prepared roasted halves of chicken or delicately rolled meatballs and braciole. There was plenty to drink, from homemade wine to mild soda pop for the children.

Cookie and Vinnie, two of Sophie's young children, seven and five years old, respectively, kept running in and out of the house, and every so often Vinnie would give his aunt Maggie, a rather large, buxom woman, a pinch on the behind. In a loud and menacing voice she would holler "Basta! Basta!" Yet secretly, with a smile on her face, she cherished the little rascal. After dinner Leticia, Maggie's beautiful daughter, rose from the table, removed her white apron, and wandered into the front room to gather all the children for a story. There were at least a dozen beautiful young faces gathered around her, for they knew that she could give them a whopper of a story. Being a youthful elementary school teacher, Leticia did not disappoint them. All eyes and ears were intently focused on her as she weaved for them a tall tale of ghosts and intrigue.

At the conclusion of the story, Leticia asked all of the children to turn toward the beautifully framed portrait of the Madonna, veiled in black, resembling a Greek-Byzantine icon. It was on a wooden worktable leaning against a concrete and red brick wall at the far side of the room. She addressed the children all at once, saying, "Let us pray to Our Lady for the less fortunate people of the world and give thanks for our daily bread." "Amen," the circle of children replied. At this time, the grownups were all finished smoking their cigars and cigarettes along with drinking their after-dinner cordials, and were ready to gather their children. It was a day of joy and festivity for everyone to remember. Even Lilly put in an appearance, and allowed herself a rare smile for the gathered family and friends.

Chapter Ten

Time marches on; and, in an evolving society, change often comes from need.

After the stock market crash of 1929, the sleepy community of Gravesend began a transformation, converting itself from a petite laissez-faire farm community into a more modern locale with traffic lights, rules, and regulations. Ocean Parkway once showcased a pleasant bridle path where the upper class generally traveled in friendly formation from Brighton Beach to Prospect Park. By 1935, Ocean Parkway began to look more like a motor speedway. The Horse Path, as the local kids called it, hung around for a few more decades. It somehow disappeared around 1970 or 1980, giving way to an unnecessary Sitting Path along with a complimentary string of synchronized traffic lights.

Coney Island Avenue lost its trolley system around the mid-1950s, yielding to the needs of the automobile. It changed from being an avenue of small stores, movie theaters, and hobby houses to a cluster of three-story apartment buildings, and then finally to a ragtag strip of auto body parts vendors and chop shops filled with broken cars and gasoline stations. It was popularly coined "Gasoline Alley."

The apparent need for more living space led to the conversion of whatever farmland existed in the area into rows of apartment buildings strung all along Ocean Avenue from Sheepshead Bay on north as far as the eye can see. By the mid-1930s, new homes were sprouting up all over the place as one street after another took form. Merchant stores of the mom-and-pop variety began to fill in the gaps of the various shopping strips that had already begun to sprout up in the 1920s. Kings Highway, Avenue U, and Sheepshead Bay developed into major shopping centers where one could find just about anything.

The Martorellas, the Vallefuocos, and the Migliaros were evolving as well. No longer could they depend on the trusty farm that Salvatore Sr. had nurtured; instead, they had to find other means of earning a living. Several of the Martorella boys made their way into the Department of Sanitation. The Vallefuoco girls, for the most part, married men who turned out to be good breadwinners. The same was true for the Migliaros. Anthony (Tony) Migliaro, one of the more flamboyant siblings, became a well-known beautician and hairdresser. In later years, while in the employ of one of the leading beauty salons in New York City, Tony boasted of having such famous clients as Ava Gardner and Audrey Hepburn.

By 1938 the winds of war in Europe were beginning to show signs of spreading across the Atlantic. Germany and Italy were arming themselves out of their respective depressions. The United States, under the second-term presidency of Franklin Roosevelt, was in the midst of reviving itself through various national initiatives geared toward putting more Americans back to work. Sal and Gus were already growing into adulthood, and they both found work in the Catskills that summer. At ages seventeen and fifteen, they were already skilled musicians. Lilly, for some time, worried for the wellbeing of her children. Anita and Barbara had just begun attending elementary school. Rudy and Frank Jr. were at an age where getting into mischief was more the order of the day.

Lilly needed some measure of relief to allay her fears and anxieties. From time to time, while the children were attending school, usually during mid-morning, she would walk over to her mother's house on Stryker Street for a cup of coffee and some family gossip.

Nicoleta, one of Lilly's younger sisters, was married to Jacomo (Jack). They occupied one of the houses inside the Stryker Street quadrangle. Jack built a bocce court and a small café to serve as a leisurely refuge for the local gentry. Caroline married Strungone, the ice delivery man and neighborhood winemaker. They too occupied one of the houses inside the Vallefuoco compound. Sometimes Lilly left her family compound and strolled over to the nearby church, Our Lady of Grace Church on Avenue W, where she took the opportunity to visit with Father DiPasqualito.

Father Gregorio DiPasqualito was a rather fine and gentle man who could effectively reach out to his congregants. Lilly's first acquaintance with him was during confession. He was a good listener and would often find the cause of some sudden upsurge of her depression. They would pray together, generally to our Lady, before concluding each visit. Sometimes the good Father would visit with Lilly at her house on East 12th Street. In this way, Lilly would find some measure of peace and tranquility away from the endless daily chores.

On occasion, in the evenings when the younger children were in bed, Lilly would ask Gus to play some popular tune on the piano. It took little coaxing for Gus, who was a showman at heart, to honor his mother's request. Lilly would change into her loose-fitting nightgown and add to it a finely laced black shawl carefully placed around her shoulders. She would then descend down the stairs from the second floor and float into the living room in tune to a cheerful bolero at eight or nine o'clock in the evening. Not always, but at times, even Frank Sr. would slip into the living room, dressed in overalls and a white T-shirt after having changed from his daytime suit, shirt, and tie. Once a very busy work day had come to an end, Frank Sr. would settle into his favorite chair at the far corner of the living room with a shot glass of scotch in one hand and a Havana cigar in the other. For a brief space in time, the head of this household was at peace with the world.

Watching his beautiful wife dancing and, at the same time, enjoying a good cigar put a genuinely broad smile on Frank's face. Lilly would keep dancing as if her husband was not there. Gus was amused by this scene and cheerfully kept on playing one tune after another. For some reason it was difficult for Frank to pay compliments to his beloved wife, but within his very being he was exalted in this tranquil moment in time. After a while, when Lilly had had enough dancing, with some fatigue she would head on up to her own bedroom. Gus also grew tired, and he too decided to go to bed. Before leaving, however, Gus would walk over to his father, who was by now fast asleep in his favorite chair, to gently tap him on the shoulder, which had the effect of transporting Frank Sr. from his momentary dreams and back into reality. Gus whispered into the ear of his father, "Pop! It's time to go to bed."

Two blocks from the Martorellas' home on East 12th Street lived the Termini family in a grand one-family detached colonial house. The paterfamilias, Giuseppe Termini, was a first-generation Italian banker who organized the Old Colony State Bank at the former site of the Banca Italia on Mulberry Street in lower Manhattan. The Terminis had three sons: Joseph, John, and Albert. All three were about the same age as the three older Martorella boys. Each school day the Termini boys had to pass by the Martorella house on their way to either their elementary school, P.S. 153, or their junior high school, P.S. 234.

From time to time, while on their way home from school, the

Terminis would fall prey to a rather embarrassing situation. Gus and Sal would wait for them to pass by. All three Terminis were rather chubby, cherubic boys. Gus, hiding on the front porch behind short brick stanchions, and Sal, behind a large maple tree, BB guns cocked, took potshots at the three oversized buttocks of these three targets, producing a hop, skip, and a jump, but no physical harm. Later on in life, Joe Termini would get his revenge. Compliments of the US Navy, during World War II, Joe took up dentistry and held the rank of captain. After the war, Joe set up a private practice and was the family dentist for the Martorellas.

In the old days, teeth were held intact with fillings of gold and silver. During the painful procedure of inserting these fillings, painkillers were generally not administered. As grown men, whenever Gus and Sal needed dental work, they invariably would end up in Joe's dental chair. Needless to say, Joe could hardly help taking pleasure in inflicting a little extra pain from his drill in retribution for those annoying BBs bounced off his butt in his youthful years. Still, Joe Termini knew his stuff, and he didn't hold a grudge against any other Martorellas. In fact, as a child, Clayton developed rickets (a softening of the bones), and in later years it was Joe's masterful dentistry that saved Clayton's second set of teeth.

After marrying his lovely wife Rose, Joe Termini moved into her stately house on Fort Hamilton Parkway. In the house where they lived with her family, Joe set up his dental practice. Rose taught chemistry at the local public high school. John and Al Termini studied engineering at Brooklyn Technical High School and eventually started a contracting business, building homes in the Hamptons, on Long Island. In his youth, Al became close friends with Rudy Martorella. He also had a crush on Anita. But their union was not to be; eventually, Al Termini married Eleanor Maratta, Anita's best friend.

Chapter Eleven

There was a two-car garage in between the Martorella and the McCann house, as well as a party driveway. Molly McCann was a registered nurse at the Coney Island Hospital who, since the death of her husband, lived in the house alone. She had no children. She was a good Catholic, attending mass every Sunday at Saint Edmund Church, close by in the neighborhood. She took a liking to Lilly ever since the Martorellas moved in. When she had a spare moment she would stop by to lend a hand with the children, and she was a regular visitor in the sixteen years she resided as a widow next door to the Martorella family.

Lilly's younger brother Ben was a little older than her older boys, and he was eager to help them build and maintain a pigeon coop on top of the garage. At first Frank Sr. objected to this endeavor, but on second thought he changed his mind and allowed Ben and the boys to construct their coop. Taking care of the pigeons, he figured, would give the boys something to do in their spare time and keep them out of trouble. It was on a weekday morning, before school started, when Frank Jr. and Gus had a quarrel over who should clean the coop. They began pushing each other and somehow managed to dislodge the coop. They rolled off the roof, with the coop falling as well, landing on top of the two boys. Pigeons flew off everywhere. Frank Jr. sustained a deep cut on the right side of his head.

Molly McCann saw all of this unfolding while looking out the back window of her house. Since Frank Jr. was bleeding profusely, Molly called out to Lilly while running out the side door toward the back of the house. As Lilly came running out of the house, Molly proceeded to clean and bandage Frank's wound. Another neighbor drove them to Coney Island Hospital, where Frank received further treatment. He returned home that same evening with a new scar but otherwise not much the worse for wear. On that very same evening, when Frank Sr. returned home from a busy day in the city, he proceeded to destroy the empty pigeon coop, putting an end to that "safe" activity.

After the accident, for the remainder of the day, Lilly closed herself up in her room, speaking to no one, alone, to wrestle with the demons that were running around inside her head. The next day was Saturday. Molly came by in the morning to join Lilly for a cup of tea. They were able to talk calmly. The children were on their best behavior, as one might imagine they'd be in the aftermath of such a trying event. The pigeon coop was history, Sal and Gus were astutely practicing their instruments, and Frank Jr. was playing ball outside with his brother Rudy. Josi Migliaro also came by to console Lilly at teatime. It gave Lilly some measure of relief to be able to confide in these two women, as they helped her let go of the stress and strain that had been building up, and which nearly broke her down the day before. These two good neighbors would continue to be important friends to Lilly in the more difficult years to come.

Jerry Migliaro had just begun working with the Sanitation Department, his first full-time job since coming to America. It marked the first time that Jerry and Mary received a steady income, bringing with it good fortune for their family. Mary

Migliaro always had a full pot of coffee brewing on the kitchen stove, in the basement of their one-family house on East 1st Street. There was always warmth, friendliness, and goodwill whenever one entered her house.

To enter the Migliaro basement, one had to walk through the side driveway to the back of the house, open the outside light-weight screen door, descend three steps, and then pass through a heavier inner wood-framed door, which led directly into the kitchen. The doors were never locked. The kitchen and dining area was really one large room. At the entrance, just to the right, was the stove followed by the kitchen sink, a worktable, and an old fridge. Opposite the cooking and cleaning area was a lengthy family dinner table surrounded by several wooden chairs.

Sal, Gus, and Frank Jr., from their early teenage years onward, hung out with Marco and Tommy Migliaro. They were about the same age. The driveway was generally filled with cars that needed some tender loving care. Marco was an excellent mechanic, and it was here at his parents' house where he conducted his auto repair business. Marco's younger brother Tommy and the Martorella boys often extended a helping hand when extra help was needed. These were fun times for all of the boys.

From time to time Lilly would stop by with Anita and Barbara. Lilly's daughters were nearly the same age as Delores and Geraldine Migliaro. They grew up together into their teenage years and later into their marrying years. Josephine (Josi), who was the second oldest of the Migliaro children, had a flair for fashion and grew close to Lilly, who shared a similar knack. They spent a good deal of time glancing at the leading fashion magazines of the day and bought bolts of cloth for making clothing of their own designs. This led to their creating some very original and beautiful skirts, dresses, and various headpieces that were quite unique for their time.

One day while taking a tea break, Lilly, with some poignant suggestions from Josi and Molly McCann, began the task of redesigning the living room of the Martorellas' grand colonial house on East 12th Street. Lilly wanted to create an Italianate setting. They came up with the idea of designing a Venetian boat scene, which included gondolas, bridges, barber poles, and Florentine buildings set against a cloudy blue sky. It would cost a great deal of money to purchase the wallpaper and then to commission an artist to carry out the painting. But as long as the women were able to find the materials and the artisan to accomplish this rather grandiose task, Frank Sr. was willing to cover the cost, albeit with some reservations.

Lilly struck gold when she walked into Oscar Korngold's general, everything store on Avenue U just east of Coney Island Avenue. Even Oscar himself became quite excited over this one-of-a-kind project. He even took the next step in finding a young artist, a recent art school graduate, to paint the rather large mural Lilly had in mind. The artist, Francesco Toni, successfully recreated a wonderful Venetian scene in Lilly's living room, and in his later years he would further advance his craft to become one of the most famous painters of reproduced classic art.

The next step for Lilly was to find a local photographer to agree to take a family picture of her three sons at the piano keyboard with the Venetian scene as a backdrop. The photographer was also a young man whom Oscar recommended. He brandished the latest photographic equipment, and created a classic composition with Gus sitting at the keyboard, on the piano bench, leaning slightly back with hands on the keys and looking slightly left at his brother Frank, who was standing in a crooner's pose. Beside Gus, Sal stood with his violin correctly placed on his right shoulder. On the right side of the piano mantelpiece was an eight-by-twelve-inch framed portrait of Rudy from his waist up, wearing a white shirt and a thin black tie. On the other side was a similar portrait of Anita wearing a silk white blouse, brandishing beautifully combed light brown hair circling a cherub-like face. The three boys were all dressed in dark blue dressy sport jackets and white slacks with white shirts and bow ties to complete this picture. For Lilly, the moment captured in this photograph marked the very apogee of cultural edification.

Chapter Twelve

The radio, telephone, and automobile were the newly available toys of the 1920s and 1930s. These ever-present American iconic goodies were the pacesetters of faster times to come. The Martorellas, like many of their neighbors, adopted these modern gadgets, though a great deal of the earlier way of life in Brooklyn still remained.

While there were moments of exhilaration for Lilly, they were far and few between. Frank did all he could to provide for the household. Money was no object, but time and physical help were in short supply as more and greater responsibility fell on Frank Sr.'s shoulders, especially once he was promoted to the position of Brooklyn borough superintendent of the Sanitation Department. Lilly still had to prepare meals and tend to the additional daily needs of six growing children. It was a Herculean task for these two very different personalities who began their lives together under very unique and difficult circumstances.

In later years Lilly would begin to have stiffness in her fingers and other joints throughout her body. Frank had to live with diabetes for most of his adult life, learning to inject himself with insulin on a daily basis.

In recognition of Frank's appointment as borough superintendent, the Martorella family would celebrate by hosting a grand party at Antoinette and Zack's Riviera catering hall. Both sides of Frank's family were invited along with many relatives, including the Migliaros and the neighbors who worked the farm and the concessions in Coney Island. Even Lilly came to the hall dressed in her finest handmade floral silk dress and white silk blouse (a one-piece with no buttons). Lilly detested buttons; she claimed that buttons carried unwanted germs. She wore her soft light brown hair in a braided crown. Lilly and Frank Sr. sat at the center of the dais flanked by their children and close relatives.

There was a cocktail hour in the downstairs lounge, new for its time, followed by a sumptuous three-course Italian-style dinner in the upstairs main hall. Antoinette and the rest of the Martorella family wished to honor Frank Sr. for all of his accomplishments. The menu included macaroni, wine, and spumoni interspersed with various meats and vegetables to thrill the discerning palates. What more exhilarating moment could Frank Sr. have had than to be honored with his own son, Gus, performing with a twelve-piece dance band in the upper balcony? Frank received two gold watches, a three-diamond-set gold ring, and a host of other gifts in a rare moment of gratitude from all the people whose lives he touched throughout his brief life up to that point in time.

He would also inherit a full set of finely tailored clothes from the husband of his younger and very beautiful sister Sophie. Her husband had passed away suddenly from a weakened heart. Before passing, he managed a thriving haberdashery business in the garment district of midtown Manhattan. Frank Sr. and Sophie's husband just happened to be the same size and build. As a small tribute to Sophie's husband, Frank Sr. would continue to wear those very well-cut clothes for many years to come.

At the dawn of the twentieth century, Europeans flocked to America in search of opportunity and the good life, with many regarding a good education as the key to a better life. Frank and Lilly were no exception in their beliefs and hopes for their off-spring. Lilly wished for her children to follow in her footsteps by seeking out the finer things in life. She so wanted her boys to succeed in music, and for all her children to cultivate their aesthetic sense. Frank knew the value of attaining a good education after seeing so many Italians land on our shores having little or no educational background; he knew the recent arrivals had to learn new skills to distinguish themselves from their countrymen and really get ahead. This desire to educate their children for success was where Frank and Lilly found common ground, and it constituted an important reason for them to stay together. There were also those occasional tender moments in which they shared, unadorned, their abiding love for each other.

In her rare moments of solitude, Lilly enjoyed listening to the radio. Occasionally, during brief interludes from her daily travails, she would even listen to popular tunes played by her own three sons. Sal, Gus, and Frank Jr. delivered a set routine of popular songs over the air at the local radio station. As a young boy, Frank Jr. loved listening to the radio, from which he developed a fine ear for lyrics and music. It was Frank Jr. who put together an ongoing musical revue that could be listened to by the emerging local radio public. For Lilly, those few moments of listening pleasure made her day.

In the summer of 1938, Sal, Gus, and Frank Jr. had their first gig performing in the Catskills. Murray Schiff, Gus's piano teacher, performed in the Borscht Belt during the summer months, and he introduced the boys to a Manhattan booking agent. This moment of good fortune afforded the boys an opportunity to earn a few dollars by playing music at one of the most popular hotels in the mountains. For the trio it was a golden opportunity to earn extra money beyond their usual allowance for doing household chores which, by comparison, held very little appeal. Frank Sr. thought the gig was a good idea, as it kept the boys occupied and away from mischief-making over the summer, while school was closed. It also gave the Martorella household a bit of psychic relief by having three fewer kids to tend to. Lilly, however, thought differently.

The boys were away for only a month, yet Lilly began to miss them. While tending to three children instead of six was some measure of relief for Frank and Lilly, the sudden difference in activity began to weigh on her mind; they were, after all, still only teenagers and away from home for the first time. She started to worry about their wellbeing. On a Thursday, during the first week in July, Lilly telephoned Josi Migliaro and asked, "Could you come by the house today? I want to ask you for a special favor." Josi felt the urgency of Lilly's request and came over immediately. They quietly shared a tea and fresh Italian cookies, whereupon Lilly asked, "How would you and Pino" (that is, Josi's husband who drove a limousine for a living) "like to spend the weekend in the Catskills?" Josi gave it some thought and realized that it would take some convincing to get Pino to give up his weekend of wedding work to make the trip. Yet somehow Josi was able to convince Pino that it was time for a small vacation in the mountains.

It was a go. Lilly convinced her husband to cover the cost of gasoline and any other accommodation expenses for the trip. Frank Sr. would stay at home, wanting no part in the folly. On Friday morning at eight a.m., Lilly, Josi, and Pino took off for the Catskills in Pino's limo. After making a brief stop for breakfast and refueling, they arrived at about noon. No sooner did they enter the town of Ellenville, while driving along Main Street, than they spotted the three boys coming out of a diner, having just finished a late breakfast. The limo pulled up right in front of them, and Lilly immediately jumped out of the vehicle. The boys were momentarily stunned, as if an apparition had suddenly appeared before them. "What are you doing here?" cried Sal. "Oh my lord," Gus chimed in. Frank Jr. just laughed. He was totally amused. "I want you to come home right now," cried Lilly. Gus responded, "We're on for tonight and tomorrow night. We can't leave now; we're expected to perform this weekend."

Lilly and her two cohorts agreed to stay over for the weekend. On Sunday afternoon the boys were to return with Lilly, and that was final. Lilly, Josi, and Pino attended both the Friday and Saturday night shows and, to their surprise, were extremely proud of the boys' performances. Nonetheless, there was no persuading Lilly to let them finish out the summer; she had decided they were leaving on Sunday. While driving back to Brooklyn, the boys lamented their plight, with Sal saying "Back to cleaning floors and painting the attic. What a drag!"

For Lilly, it had momentarily been bliss to be out in the country, seeing two wonderful shows, and retrieving her boys, all at the same time. There was even the added bonus of getting to dress up and show off her finest outfits. When they arrived back home at two in the morning, after the boys and the rest of the family went to bed, Lilly got up and went to the kitchen. She opened up the utility closet where she had her tiny altar and she knelt down in prayer to her patron saint Ann and the Holy Mother, for allowing her to retrieve her sons. For the moment, she felt at peace with herself, if not quite with the world.

Chapter Thirteen

In Brooklyn, as well as in other parts of New York, at the front of many Italian single and two-family homes, one could find lifelike carved figures of various patron saints guarding over the various households. A drive through the Gravesend neighborhood along Avenues X, Y, and Z, between Coney Island Avenue and McDonald Avenue and beyond, featured many of these detailed statues paying homage to the more popular saints, such as St. Anthony, St. Francis, Mary (the Holy Mother), and the Infant of Prague. These were and still are images that many Italian households have looked to for safety and the goodness of a benevolent God. Lilly maintained her own prayer altar in the kitchen of her own home, and she often turned to it to give thanks, and to seek hope and relief.

It wasn't until the fall of 1938, once nearly all of her children had started to attend school, that Lilly began showing noticeable signs of depression. At that time, tending to such family needs as cooking, cleaning, shopping, and making sure that everyone was ready for school became for Lilly more of a burden with each passing day. With each activity, she began to find ways to finish her tasks more quickly by being less meticulous and ultimately less caring about concluding her tasks. Dirty dishes became more prevalent in the sink. She cooked larger quantities of potatoes and pasta and reheated them as leftovers. She would go to the avenue less frequently, relying more on the boys and Frank Sr. to buy fresh vegetables and groceries. Frank Sr. often brought home large slabs of meat that needed cutting and preparation, but, more often than not, they would go bad because Lilly simply didn't have the energy any longer to prepare complete meals. At times Frank Sr. would end up having to do all of the cooking.

Increasingly, Lilly would retreat to her bed, isolating herself from the rest of the family for lengthy periods of time. It was on a Tuesday mid-morning in September 1938 that Lilly, sitting at the kitchen table shortly after all the children were at school, called for Barbara, who was playing in the living room, to come sit by her. Barbara was just four years old, going on five in October, and still not of school age. Lilly put her arm tenderly around Barbara, who sat on a chair next to her, and said, "Go next door and ring Molly's doorbell and ask her to come over. I'm not feeling well." Although she was frightened, realizing, even at her tender age, that her mother looked ill, Barbara did as she was told and ran to Molly's house.

She was barely tall enough to ring the doorbell, and, though she tried to press it, there was no response. Overwhelmed, little Barbara began to cry. Molly happened to look out the side window from the second floor and saw Barbara crying at the side door. She quickly ran down the stairs. Upon opening the door, she faced the innocent crying child. "Please, please come over! Mama is sick, please, please, she's sick," Barbara pleaded. Molly took the sweet child in her arms and hurried right over to see what was wrong.

When Molly entered the house, she saw Lilly drooped over the kitchen table, lying motionless. The kitchen closet was wide open. When Molly looked inside the closet, she witnessed both the kneeling pad and the makeshift altar completely broken to pieces, including even the picture icon of the Madonna. Molly picked up the cleaver that was on the floor at the base of the broken altar. She cleaned it and put it away. Molly then picked up the telephone and dialed Coney Island Hospital, requesting that a doctor come to the house immediately. Lilly was diagnosed as being frail and exhausted and as having had a nervous breakdown. She needed some form of rehabilitation. Molly contacted Frank Sr., apprising him of what had occurred that morning. That same day, as all of the children drifted home from school, they were totally taken by surprise at the sudden change in the household.

Sal, Gus, and Frank Jr. would remain with Frank Sr., while Rudy would stay with Nicoleta, one of Lilly's sisters, who was also married and occupied one of the houses on Stryker Street. Anita and Barbara would end up with their grandmother Christina on Stryker Street. To be closer to the young children, Frank Sr. closed up the house on East 12th Street and decided to rent an upstairs apartment in a two-family house on East 5th Street, just off Avenue W and only a few blocks away from Stryker Street.

At first, Lilly went to a sanatorium in lower Westchester to help regain her physical strength. Not too long after she recovered from her physical weakness, she was transferred to the Downstate Psychiatric Hospital in New York City for continued treatment and psychiatric evaluation. A full year passed before she was released back to her family. It took continuous effort, but Frank Sr. visited Lilly almost every week, to give her some measure of stability, comfort, and much needed encouragement to return to the outside world. Lilly went through a great deal of psychiatric treatment, which included, at that time, a rudimentary form of electric shock. Through the entire ordeal, Lilly desired nothing more than to be reunited with her children.

In September 1939, nearly one year after her breakdown, Lilly came home. It was on East 5th Street, in the upstairs apartment Frank rented in a two-family dwelling, that Frank and Lilly reclaimed their children. For the moment, Lilly's mental stability was quite normal on returning to her own home with her children. She even condescended to sharing the same bed with her husband.

But needless to say, with a mother, father, and six children in a single apartment, living conditions were rather tight. Frank Sr. knew full well that he needed to find larger living quarters. Lilly's sisters helped when they could. Often Anita and Barbara would still sleep at their grandmother's house on Stryker Street.

On one wintry night, while the two girls were sleeping in the same bed at the front of their grandmother's house, Barbara thought that she saw a ghost outside her bedroom window. She started to weep, saying, "I'm afraid, I'm afraid." Grandma Christina came in to see what was wrong. She cuddled Barbara in her arms and said, "Enough! Enough!" She covered them with a woolen blanket and watched over them until they fell asleep. Again, Barbara awakened and called for Christina, who returned with still another blanket. Once again they fell asleep. But soon both girls reawakened in the middle of the night, and they were terribly frightened and calling for help. Their faces and hair were soaking wet from sweat. This time Christina returned with her daughter Theresa, the youngest of the Vallefuoco girls. "Why did you put all these blankets on top of the girls?" Theresa demanded of her mother. Christina replied, "Fa freddo, hanno freddo" (It's cold, they're cold). Barbara explained to her Aunt Theresa that she was afraid of ghosts, but that she was not cold. Being afraid and being cold were not quite the same thing, but evidently the distinction had been lost in translation. Off went the blankets, the ghosts disappeared, and midnight calm was restored.

Living on East 5th Street right near the Vallefuoco compound was one big festival. Frank Sr. would bring home lots of meat, fruit, and vegetables for all to share. In the summer of 1940, Lilly, already past her fortieth birthday, became pregnant with her seventh child. This condition caught everyone by surprise. Doctors used to recommend that women who were depressed become pregnant as a healthy distraction. In this rather cheerful environment on March 14, 1941, Lilly brought into this world her seventh offspring, Clayton. Shortly thereafter Frank Sr. moved his family to larger accommodations at 628 Avenue V.

When the family moved from East 12th to East 5th Street, many things of value were temporarily put into storage. The first thing that arrived out of storage was Gus's Hamilton baby grand piano. It was set up at the center of the right-hand side of the living room. Some of the furniture from the old house on East 12th Street was delivered to the new house along with the piano. The wallpapered Venetian boat scene remained in the old house, but the photo-portrait of the three boys posing as entertainers in front of the wall painting was prominently hung up above the new couch, opposite the piano, on the left-hand side of the living room. These were permanent fixtures that Lilly would never part with, and they also gave Frank Sr. a great sense of pride in his own family.

On December 7, 1941, the Japanese bombed Pearl Harbor, and shortly thereafter President Roosevelt declared war on the Axis powers of Europe and Japan. Frank Sr. had sensed that war with Germany was inevitable already one year before Japan bombed Pearl Harbor. He began hoarding canned goods and various food items at the home on East 5th Street as well as at the family farmhouse on East 7th Street. When the Martorella family moved to Avenue V, Frank Sr. constructed an extensive system of shelving in the basement of the two-family house for the purpose of accumulating food items in anticipation of the war to come. He thought that once the United States entered into the war, shortages of many home products and food rationing would become a reality.

For the seventh time in her married life, Lilly bore the responsibility of tending to a newborn. Eight and one half years had gone by since she tended to Barbara, the last of her six children, before bringing Clayton into the world. Lilly too was beginning to worry about the war to come. Lilly and Frank Sr. both understood that the older boys might have to go off to war. After Pearl Harbor was bombed, their fears became a reality. Sal and Gus were immediately called into the Army and the Navy, respectively. After basic training, Sal was transferred to the West Coast and deployed as military police in the Army Infantry. Gus did his Navy training in the Great Lakes. By a stroke of luck, the file on Gus indicated that he was an accomplished musician, and the US Navy Band in New York City was in need of a piano player of his caliber. Thus, he was transferred to New York to join the band at Hunter College. Lilly's insistence that Gus learn to play the piano at an early age might actually have kept him out of harm's way; the ship that Gus was to have been assigned to was eventually sunk by a German submarine.

Sal was not as lucky. In 1943, during an occupation of one of the islands in the Pacific, Sal, along with three other soldiers, drove over a mine while crossing a small bridge in a jeep. The mine detonated, overturning the vehicle. Sal's three soldier comrades were killed, while Sal was found at the foot of the blown-up bridge, having sustained a broken neck and other severe burns and bruises. He was transferred from the Philippines to a Veterans Administration hospital for the disabled in Utica, New York. After spending six months in intensive care, Sal was then transferred to

Halloran Hospital on Staten Island, where he continued his rehabilitation. After several months of daily physical therapy, aided by
his teenage brother Rudy, who drove him back and forth to the
hospital, Sal could finally settle back into the family household,
returning to a routine lifestyle and giving some comfort to his
worried mother.

Frank Jr. still had one year to go at Brooklyn Technical High
School before the Army caught up with him. In 1942, upon his
graduation, he was drafted. Because of his technical skills that he
acquired at Tech and his very high grades, having been the valedictorian in his graduating class, he was sent to the Pacific island of
New Guinea to conduct work in intelligence. He wasn't sent home
again until one year after the war had ended. Frank Jr. worked as a
comptroller, guiding and directing planes in and out of New
Guinea. On occasion, when Frank Jr. was on leave, he would
sneak off to nearby islands to sit in on a jazz concert performed by
one of the leading bands on tour.

Grandpa Salvatore died in 1942, a few short years after his wife
Carmela passed away. He lived a farmer's life, a friend to all with
practically no enemies. At Sal Sr.'s wake, which lasted for three
days, fifty cases of wine and whiskey were consumed as he rested
peacefully, fully dressed, in an open coffin. Two adjoining rooms
of his home were filled with flowers to beautifully and respectfully
honor his passing.

Chapter Fourteen

Gus met Louise at Hunter College while he was in the US Navy Band. Louise came from Des Moines, Iowa. At the dawn of the Second World War, she joined the Navy. After her basic training, Louise was transferred to New York City to serve in the Navy WAVES, in an administrative capacity. They met on a blind date and it was, appropriately enough, love at first sight. It was not long after they met that the young couple took their marital vows and moved into a modest apartment in the lower Bronx. They had a small wedding, paid for by Frank Sr. Louise was quite beautiful with almost blondish hair, and at five feet four inches tall she cut a Hollywoodish, glamorous figure. She also possessed a heart of gold, combined with good common sense in dealing with everyday situations. Upon their first encounter, Louise instantly captured the heart of Frank Sr.

One springtime weekend, Gus and Louise took the Brighton train all the way from the Bronx to Brooklyn, so Louise could meet Frank Sr. and Lilly for the first time. While taking a walk to the neighborhood candy store, around the corner on Neck Road, privately Frank Sr. asked Louise if her father drank whiskey or smoked cigars. She replied that he did neither; with a mild smiley look on his face, Frank Sr. responded that he didn't think he would like him. Louise hadn't seen her family for nearly two years.

It was Frank Sr. who insisted that both she and Gus return to Iowa for a family visit before they tied the knot. Frank Sr. paid for the airline tickets and chauffeured them to and from LaGuardia Airport. Louise's family got to meet Gus for the first time at Christmas, 1943.

For Lilly, Gus's marriage was a very different story. She had already begun to feel the pain of having three sons drafted into the armed forces. Lilly's momentary pleasure of moving to more spacious living quarters at 628 Avenue V was offset by the absence of her three oldest sons. At the time, she did not yet realize that she was the reason Gus was still alive, due to her insistence that he learn to play the piano at an early age. Had she known, she probably would have fretted over her children even more.

When Lilly came out of her room to greet the newly wedded couple, at her side was Clayton, a little bowlegged boy, who looked frail and pale after having been raised on a rather poor diet of pasta and potatoes. The rest of the family apparently hadn't noticed that Lilly was hoarding her son, keeping and protecting him from the outside world, which, by now, seemed very hostile to her. The greeting was rather cold, and Lilly looked at Louise with drawn, deep-set eyes, brown and piercing, commenting that she didn't like clothing that brandished buttons. Louise was wearing a pretty white button-down blouse. Later on, when they were heading back to their apartment in the Bronx, Louise told Gus that his little brother did not look well and that he needed medical attention.

In the summer months of 1943, right up until Labor Day, Coney Island was ablaze with fun and laughter, filled with sailors and army personnel on leave before going to battle. Dominick ("Fumbo"), Frank Sr.'s younger brother, was the manager of various concessions and the dance hall inside Luna Park. Dominick's wife Millie, born to a fairly wealthy Tuscan Italian family living in the upscale community of Sea Gate, had been influential in procuring the position of amusement park manager for her husband. Millie's neighbor in Sea Gate was Sam Fuganini, the business manager for Bill Miller Enterprises, primary owner of Luna Park and various other pleasure palaces of Coney Island. The Fuganinis and Millie's family had come from the same town in Italy and knew each other for many years.

On a June evening, Fumbo was making the rounds of the various concessions when he spotted a long line of customers waiting for cars carrying young couples into the Tunnel of Love. As he approached this popular concession, Fumbo noticed that it took quite some time for the cars carrying the passengers to exit the tunnel. He discovered that the person running the concession was turning off the motor for a minute or two, thus stopping the cars and affording the couples inside the Tunnel of Love a few extra moments of intimacy. Rudy was in charge of this concession. Needless to say, Rudy was relieved of his duties. He was transferred to another concession selling popcorn, thus ending Rudy's short-lived entrepreneurial venture.

For Bill Miller and the managerial staff of Luna Park, a greater problem was at hand. The dance hall was not attracting enough patrons and the band, it seemed, was being overpaid, as they played to an empty house. He asked Fumbo if he could think of any way to fix this dire situation. Fumbo said to Bill, "Leave it to me." The very next day, Dominick approached Frank Sr. at his office in downtown Brooklyn and asked if he could find a bunch of musicians among the workers of the Sanitation Department who would like to make some extra money playing in Luna Park. They both knew that the Sanitation Band was the best of the three city combos, which included the Police and Fire Department bands. Frank Sr. said to his brother Dominick, "Leave it to me."

By the end of that same week, 32 first-rate dance band musicians showed up to audition for the newly formed band. They all passed with flying colors. The former band was unceremoniously released. Dominick suggested the new band be called Nick Fiorentino and the Californians, a purely fictitious name. Next, Dominick would meet with Bill Miller to request that the first fifty girls be allowed to enter the dance hall free of charge. Request granted, the following Friday night, as the girls filed into the dance hall, looking as glamorous as ever, the eager sailors and soldiers in almost equal numbers followed them in at double the normal price of entry. The music was worthy of the Glenn Miller Orchestra, and the Luna Park Dance Hall turned into one of Bill Miller's more profitable entities. Once in a while, when Gus could find a suitable replacement to cover for him in the US Navy Band, he would put in a guest appearance at Luna Park, sitting in with the "Californians."

Chapter Fifteen

Life at home for the Martorellas remained routine. Lilly and Frank Sr. still did the cooking and cleaning. Both Anita and Barbara, by then a little older, helped out with the cleaning and even with some elementary cooking, like boiling water. Rudy had to take care of his brother Sal, who still required quite a bit of rehabilitation from his wartime injury. Gus and Louise were married and living in the Bronx. Frank Jr. was still far away from home on some island in the Pacific. Unfortunately, Lilly was once again steadily receding into her own world and taking her youngest, Clayton, along for the ride.

Gus initiated a conversation with his brother Sal about what Louise had observed, noting that both his mother and his baby brother were not looking well. Sal was also beginning to realize that his mother was retreating more and more into her bedroom and into her own little world. For days on end, one could hear Lilly and Clayton singing and playing together inside the hallway bedroom which, by then, she had claimed as her own. Lilly sharing a bedroom with Frank Sr. was no longer in the cards.

Sal decided to have a talk with his father. At first Frank Sr. did not wish to acknowledge that his beloved wife was again not well. Sal convinced his father to meet with Dr. Rosenblatt, who lived on the same street as the Martorellas, at the corner of Avenue V and

Ocean Parkway. Being diabetic, Frank Sr. had recently begun visiting Doctor Rosenblatt for his own occasional checkups. Lilly, for the first time, had permitted the good doctor to examine her once before, just after she had given birth to Clayton.

One weekday morning shortly after breakfast, Dr. Rosenblatt appeared at the front door. Anita and Barbara had the day off from school. It was Columbus Day, and the public schools were closed. Anita greeted the doctor and proceeded to usher him into Lilly's bedroom. After examining Lilly, Dr. Rosenblatt also took a look at Clayton. Frank Sr. and Sal met with Dr. Rosenblatt later in the day at his office. Left alone in the patient waiting room for about fifteen minutes, Sal and Frank Sr. concluded that something had to be done. The one question on Frank Sr.'s mind was how long his wife would take to respond to new treatment. Dr. Rosenblatt said that he didn't think Lilly's condition was as severe as the first time she was admitted, but he recommended that she be admitted to a program at Downstate Hospital. After a moment of silence, Dr. Rosenblatt gave some measure of comfort when he said he thought that Lilly could come home in about three months.

The doctor further noted that Clayton had an advanced case of rickets and needed immediate attention. It would be difficult to break this bad news to Lilly, who was noticeably becoming more volatile and reclusive. It was bad, in the sense that something had to be done, but good, in that the action to be taken would result in positive rehabilitation, and an improvement in the overall family condition.

It was decided that Gus would be the one to talk to Lilly. Of all the children, Augustine was the single member of the family whom Lilly felt most comfortable with in almost any manner of conversation. He was somewhat more empathetic than the other members of the family in dealing with grave situations. It was Gus who was, in some way, able to tap into and touch Lilly's emotional core.

No one was prepared for what happened next. When the ambulance arrived at the Martorella household to collect Lilly, she suddenly fled to her bedroom, taking Clayton by the arm and pulling him along with her. She pushed the bed against the door, barricading herself and Clayton inside the room. Anita and Barbara began to cry and pleaded with their mother to come out of her room. Gus took over for the girls, speaking gently to his mother; he was able to calm her down. Suddenly, with the sound of the bed being moved, there followed a moment of silence. The door opened, and Lilly quietly exited her room with Clayton by her side.

It was protocol for psychiatric patients at that time to be placed in a straitjacket. Lilly protested vehemently, but in the end she gave in to this unwelcome procedure. Frank Sr. and his two sons Sal and Gus were able to restore some calm. Barbara cried and reached out to hug her mother as she was about to leave the house. Before leaving, Lilly paused for a moment, then turned to face everyone, and said, "Let no one harm my little boy, Clayton, while I am away."

Clayton spent the next three months at St. Giles the Cripple Hospital, on President Street in Brooklyn. At first the doctors who examined Clayton thought that he would lose the lower parts of both his legs. Dr. Bogart, a Brit, thought that with heavy doses of vitamin D and lots of sunshine Clayton's condition might improve. As if by some miracle, Clayton made a quick recovery. After three months under the good graces of the hospital staff, Clayton was able to leave the hospital. The staff had taken a liking to this rather cheerful young boy, who knew and could sing many of the popular songs of the day and serenaded many of the young nurses, and they responded by giving him extra attention and care. At the end of Clayton's short stay in the hospital, he returned home on a pair of crutches. To ensure that Clayton's legs would continue to grow in a normal manner, he had to wear leg braces for a while.

Clayton returned home in January 1944, one month before his mother was released from Downstate Hospital. It was five months before June 6, D-Day. By that time, the Second World War was concluding at breakneck speed. Frank Jr. was still far away on some unknown island in the Pacific, and Lilly still lived with the fear that one of her sons might not return home. Rarely did Frank Jr. write a letter to his family letting them know where he was or what he was up to. But Sal turned out to be the only family member injured in the war, and even he, thankfully, recovered.

Gus and Louise moved from the Bronx to Brooklyn, resettling in a three-room basement apartment on Avenue V. Frank Sr. successfully converted the apartment from a food-filled grocery store into a livable dwelling, with a new bathroom and kitchen. The living room and bedroom were quite spacious. There was a coal-burning stove in the back room behind the apartment, and there was even a backyard garden.

The twenty-by-twenty-five-foot rectangular plot of dirt in back of the house lay in between two adjacent plots of equal size occupying equivalent spaces at the rear of the two adjacent houses. This was Frank Sr.'s new garden and a source of pleasure on Avenue V. With full acceptance from his neighbors, Frank continued to grow his tomatoes, basil, and a variety of other vegetables. Naturally, he would share this natural bounty with his neighbors. He grew red and yellow roses along the right-hand side of the house, along the corridor fence separating the Martorellas from the Tolkins. Some of the basil was grown in large barrels and grew nearly up to the first floor back room windows of the house. Throughout his youthful years, Clayton woke up breathing in this magnificent fragrance every day.

At age five, Clayton still required crutches, and he would stare out onto the street through a locked gate door, watching the neighborhood boys running and playing on Avenue V. He couldn't wait to join them. By the same good fortune that had graced the Martorella family from one generation to the next in their richly rewarding lives in Brooklyn, New York, Clayton would not have to wait much longer to join the bustling world that thrived in those city streets he eagerly glimpsed just beyond the door.

Part Two

Life Goes On

Chapter Sixteen

It was a bright sunny Sunday morning. Lilly was standing in the middle of the front porch, bouncing a pink rubber ball off of the left wall of the house. She routinely performed this exercise in order to keep her joints from stiffening. She stopped for a moment to look out the front windows. She spotted a young man, dressed in army fatigues, walking on East 7th Street toward her corner house. As he grew closer she recognized him. He crossed Avenue V, and Lilly flung open the front door. Frank Jr. ran up the front stairs, across the outside porch and into the loving arms of his mother. It was just before Christmas in 1946, a year after the war ended. Lilly's missing son had finally come home.

While Lilly was examining her son at the front door, Anita arrived to fetch her mother for breakfast and suddenly saw her older brother. Lilly was shedding tears of joy, and Anita began to jump up and down, adding screams of jubilation at the sight of her older brother. Hearing this commotion coming from the front porch, the rest of the Martorella family leaped out of their chairs in the sitting area of the kitchen and ran to the front end of the house. It was near pandemonium as Frank Jr. was almost carried into the kitchen and royally seated at the head of the breakfast table. Frank Sr. had just finished shaving in the back bathroom as he came through the hallway toward the kitchen. Wearing a pair of light brown khaki work pants and a white T-shirt, still wiping off his face the last of the white shaving cream, he abruptly realized what all the commotion was about.

Everyone came to a halt. Frank Jr. slowly got up from his chair to formally greet his father. There were subtle, unnoticeable tears of joy in Frank Sr.'s eyes as he crossed the room to embrace his third son and namesake. This was a breakfast to remember. The war was over and all of the Martorellas were once again under one roof at 628 Avenue V. It was indeed a very happy moment that arrived just in time for a family more than ready to spread its wings.

With the war at an end and everyone back home, Frank Sr. realized that he needed some domestic help to manage his family and their day-to-day needs. He sat down with his eldest son, Sal, and his two daughters, Anita and Barbara, to urge them to pitch in and take on some of the more critical family chores. At this moment in time, Lilly had become, more or less, a passive member of the household. Anita, who would be fourteen years old in July, and Barbara, turning twelve in October, were to take over the cooking and the cleaning responsibilities of the household. Led by Sal, the boys offered to assist in the running of the house.

But that was wishful thinking. In the beginning, Frank Sr. would give the girls some cooking instructions. When Lilly was in a more lucid mood, she would also participate in offering the girls some of her excellent traditional family recipes. And once a week, on Saturdays, a cleaning woman would be hired to help out with dusting, mopping, and vacuuming all of the rooms and closets. The girls held up their end of the bargain as best they could, but the boys' assistance disappeared almost immediately as more lively and pressing matters—like work, girls, sports, and mischief—lured them away.

Most of the furnishings that filled the house on Avenue V came from the previous home on East 12th Street, except for the dining room set. For a while, the dining room remained empty. As luck would have it, one day shortly after the Martorellas moved into their new home, Frank Sr. was called upon to inspect a furniture warehouse at the downtown waterfront, next door to the Brooklyn Navy Yard, while he made his sanitation rounds. A decision had to be made on how and where to remove a large collection of World War II waste material that was temporarily being stored in the warehouse.

Mr. Seligman, the owner of an import-export operation dealing in new and used furniture, was using one portion of the warehouse to store some clutter left over from World War II, and another portion to conduct retail business. As Frank Sr. made his way from one section of the warehouse to the other, he spotted an astonishingly beautiful dining room furniture set on display made entirely of cherry mahogany wood. Frank knew that, as borough superintendent for the Department of Sanitation, he would have to come to an agreement with Seligman on how to dispose of the World War II clutter; and he also knew, as head of a large household constantly in need of further goods, to always carry a large wad of money in his pants pockets, just in case. A deal was struck with Seligman on the spot, arranging for both the removal of the clutter and the purchase of the furniture set.

That day, Frank Sr. brought home a four-piece set designed in a classical motif. The first piece was a lowboy with two doors that opened from the middle. Each door had a symmetrical classical arch supported by two "pilasters." The second was a slightly larger and longer lowboy, with three drawers in the middle and a door on each side of the unit. Both pieces were supported by heavy, thick, circular mahogany legs, and both were covered by a half-inch-thick green marbleized stone in the same pattern. The third piece was a seven-foot-high china cabinet designed in the same classical style, make, and pattern. And the fourth piece consisted of a very heavy table, supported by thick legs. Six finely clothed, decorated chairs came with the table. It was a complete set of classical furniture, of the finest quality and in excellent condition, which had just arrived at the warehouse from South America.

Lilly took over the three drawers of the larger lowboy. She filled them with her finest linen, scarves, blouses, dining room tablecloths, and some of her fine jewelry. Clayton loved the distinct smell of camphor balls oozing out of the drawers. The two side cabinets were left for Clayton, initially to put his toys in, and in later years for his elementary school books and classroom projects. Some of Lilly's fine china and flatware went into, of course, the china cabinet. This beautiful set of dining room furniture was admired by all who looked upon it, and it was a wonderful addition to a household that clamored for a cheerful moment.

Chapter Seventeen

The war was finally over and many people, at least in the Western world, were feeling pretty good about themselves and looking forward to producing goods and services rather than guns and bullets. Frank Sr.'s newest farm was the backyard of the family house, along with the two adjacent plots. For the first time in one of his gardens, Frank Sr. would be adding some much-needed horse manure. Every once in a while Mother Earth needs some nutritional fortification. At that time, horse manure was still quite plentiful in Brooklyn. The Ocean Parkway bridle path was still very much in vogue with Sunday riders prancing along from West End Avenue all the way to Prospect Park, their horses leaving behind some prime nutritional nuggets for the garden.

One morning, shortly after Gus and Louise moved into the basement apartment at Avenue V, Louise had just finished washing some laundry. With her laundry basket full of wet clothing, Louise ascended the cellar stairs and out the open doors only to be greeted by the intoxicating smell of freshly laid down horse manure. The aroma was enough to make her dizzy, but she was able to maintain enough balance to return down the steps and shut the door behind her before she or the clothing dropped among the droppings.

Jenny McCracken, a healthy looking black woman with a round, cheerful face, appeared one Saturday morning at the front door of the Martorella house. She and her husband were proud owners of a modest single-family house in the nearby neighborhood of Sheepshead Bay. "Mr. Martorella said that I should come by this morning to help you all with some house cleaning," she told Anita. Anita let her into the house as Frank Sr. entered the house from the side door to greet Jenny. Jenny was a welcome addition to the much appreciative family on Avenue V. Later that same morning, shortly after the manure was spread all over the backyard, Jenny opened up one of the back bedroom windows to let in some fresh air. On catching a whiff of this pungent aroma, she immediately turned around and asked Barbara, "Are you all keeping a horse in the backyard?"

Clayton often looked forward to Saturdays. It was house-cleaning day. Jenny arrived at nine a.m. Clayton usually greeted her warmly, almost wanting to hug her before she even came through the front door. It was her warm smile and twinkly eyes that captured his heart.

Jenny worked two full days a week, dusting and mopping the rooms of several offices at the downtown Brooklyn administrative building which housed the Sanitation Department and civil service records. After making his morning rounds of the various Sanitation Department garages, garbage incinerators, and dumping grounds, Frank Sr. usually spent a few afternoon hours at his downtown office. That is where he discovered Jenny.

Clayton had recently been freed of his leg braces, and he was eager to help out with the Saturday housework. For the first time, Frank Sr. commissioned Anita and Barbara to take over all domestic household functions apart from those Jenny had covered. The girls wholeheartedly embraced this new responsibility. Without any reservation or conditions, Frank Sr. entrusted a liberal budget to their management.

Clayton also fell in love with the new dining room set. For hours, he would play underneath the lowboys and the dining room table and chairs, weaving in and out of the many wooden legs of the furniture, maneuvering the numerous rubber toy soldiers, Indians, cowboys, and horses in pursuit of all sorts of good guy–bad guy plots.

Every Saturday, Clayton's job was to dust and polish all of that dining room furniture. He took personal pride in fulfilling this task. Eventually, his father rewarded him with an allowance of 25 cents per week. The girls were given an expense account at Dominic's Grocery Store, which was located at the northwest corner of East 7th Street and Avenue U, one block north of the house on Avenue V.

After a vigorous three and a half hours of hard work, Anita, Barbara, Jenny, and Clayton would feast at lunchtime over delicious ham and Swiss cheese heroes with all the trimmings of potato salad, Hoffman's cream soda, and some sort of baked dessert or ice cream. After all, everyone needed some healthy nourishment in order to carry on with the rest of the day's work. At times, even Lilly would join the group in a moment of merriment. At such times there was good cheer and laughter in the air. As the laughter filtered through the open windows and into the outside world, even Frank Sr. began to secretly laugh to himself while he was tending to his garden behind the house. His children, he felt, were like his fruits, vegetables, and flowers; they all needed to grow and flourish.

Chapter Eighteen

One Saturday morning, Anita and Barbara were in the kitchen preparing the tomato sauce for the next day's afternoon meal. It was part of the weekend ritual of cooking combined with cleaning at the Martorella household. With World War II having come to an end, consumer goods and services were being produced and sold at prices affordable to middle-class families. Suddenly in the kitchen, there was a new refrigerator, a four-burner gas stove, and a new gadget called a floor-waxing machine. Barbara's curiosity led her to this last, foreign machine, which was barely out of the box but already plugged into the wall outlet just above the cooking table. At the same time, Anita was cooking her delicious meatballs on the front burner of the brand new stove. These tasty treats would eventually wind up in a simmering fresh tomato sauce.

Anita repeatedly kept telling Barbara, "Stop playing with that machine and come over here and help me with the cooking." Barbara replied, "But how does this work?" trying one button after another until she pressed the on switch. Suddenly, the waxing machine took off by itself and sped over to the stove, hitting Anita in the back of her legs. The frying pan flew up in the air, with hot cooking oil and meatballs landing all over the place. In an instant, Anita pulled the plug out of the outlet, thus halting the movement of the machine which had already made the rounds of the kitchen. Anita then screamed at Barbara, "You idiot! Get out of here! You've ruined everything; there'll be no Sunday dinner." Barbara replied in an almost sheepish but calm manner, "We can just throw the meatballs into the sauce; the boys won't know the difference."

Louise quickly ran up the stairs from the basement apartment to see what the commotion was all about. She was actually in the midst of putting her newborn baby, Patricia, to sleep for a mid-morning nap. Lilly came out of her bedroom as well, and all four sat down to collect themselves over a cup of coffee. Louise took this opportunity to let the girls know that "while you are away, I will watch Clayton downstairs until you return from school. As soon as you arrive, and don't be late, Clayton goes back upstairs." The girls stared at each other, suddenly realizing that another burden was put upon them.

Thanksgiving was just around the corner, not too long after the waxing machine fiasco. Two days before Thanksgiving, Frank Sr. came home with a 25-pound freshly killed turkey. Of course, the girls were charged with cooking the big bird, with all the trimmings. Of all the people in the household, it was Sal who volunteered to help the girls with the preparations. He was fully recovered from his wartime injury and eager to carry on with his life. All went as planned. When Thanksgiving Day came, the entire Martorella family, including Lilly, gathered around the dining room table to say grace.

Sal went into the kitchen to retrieve the fully cooked turkey. Everyone enjoyed this wonderful Thanksgiving meal, including Gus and Louise. Even little Patty, who was barely a year old, resting in her mother's arms, partook in the festivities. After this sumptuous meal, Sal commented, "Look what a wonderful job the girls did in preparing their first turkey." He then asked them how they managed to cook the turkey. They replied, "We just filled it with cut pieces of bread and pre-cooked mushrooms, onions, salt, and pepper. After that it went into the oven." Sal asked, "Did you remove the neck and the gizzards and clean the turkey?" The girls replied, "No." For a moment everyone looked at each other in silent stupefaction, and then all at once, as if on cue, everyone burst out in laughter. No one complained, and no one became ill. This family, together at last, had much to be thankful for.

The singular item in the dining room that was generally off-limits was Frank Sr.'s closet. Located by the northeast wall, it extended about eight feet into the dining room and was approximately four feet wide. Its side wall went from the floor to the ceiling, and it had a door at the four-foot-wide entrance. It is where most of his private things were kept. It contained a coatrack, and some shelving along the sides and at the back end; there was a light bulb with a pull cord to turn on the light. On the back shelves were kept some unopened bottles of wine accompanied by various brands of liquor. On the side shelves there were some unopened boxes of Cuban cigars and some open trays of dry seeds for planting in his garden. Additionally, a carton about the size of a filing cabinet drawer was on the same shelf, used for storing his important papers. At the entrance of the closet, on one of the top shelves, he usually had a few bars of chocolate candy (including Hershey's and Nestlé's Crunch bars). These treats were left for Clayton, and eventually his two partners in crime, Patty and Frankie, who were born in the basement apartment downstairs and lived there until they were six and four years of age, respectively.

Although this was Frank Sr.'s private closet, it was never locked; and, it seemed, neither were any of the other household doors.

Except for Clayton, no one else bothered to peek into Frank's closet. He seemed to be able to have his privacy while at the same time maintaining an open-door policy when it came to family affairs. As the five boys and two girls continued to grow into their formative years, Frank Sr. insisted that, when dating, they had to return home at a reasonable nighttime hour. However, as far as the girls were concerned, Frank preferred that they spend free time with their friends inside the four walls of 628 Avenue V.

Having the piano in the living room and a piano player living downstairs, there was always music in the air. Gus and his fellow musicians often rehearsed right in the living room. It was always Gus on piano, Tabby on bass, Charlie Papora on sax, and little Angelo on the drums. When the joint was jumping, even the neighbors were treated to a free jazz concert. Anita and Barbara often yanked their little brother off of the couch whenever they needed a partner to dance the Lindy hop—against his free will, of course, but who could resist that jumping rhythm?

Chapter Nineteen

Once the war was over, the immediate task at hand was for the boys to find gainful employment. Sal, ever since he was a young boy, always wanted to become a cop. As soon as he recovered from his wartime injury, he began studying for the police exam. Within a matter of months, Sal was ready to take the written exam. He passed it with flying colors. The garage room, at the front of the house, was used as a gymnasium, containing weights, a punching bag, a heavy bag, jump ropes, and all sorts of other workout material. Inspired by Sal's ambition, all the boys felt the need to work out and stay in shape.

For Sal, though, getting back in excellent shape was not enough to prevent what he considered unexpected disaster from striking again. When it was time to take his physical exam, Sal was told that he could not become a policeman due to his wartime injury. Just after Sal was confronted with this new setback, he returned home and spent the remainder of the day in his bedroom in total despair. That night, as Frank Sr. entered the bedroom, he found his eldest son in tears. Frank sat next to him and said, "Tomorrow morning I want you to go to the Kings County Supreme Courthouse in Brooklyn and ask if you could enter Judge Martuscello's chambers. He is expecting you to be there at ten o'clock in the morning, so make sure you show up at ten sharp."

The conversation with the judge didn't last long. Sal was offered a job in the courtroom, provided he start law school. Sal went to night school for several years to attain his law degree at St. John's. He gained enough expertise at the courthouse that, after obtaining his degree, he was qualified to take the New York State Bar exam. He passed with flying colors. His fate was sealed in the courtroom, as he spent his long and fulfilling career doing legal research for two prominent judges consecutively. In the end, despite his wartime injury, he was a happy camper.

For Frank Jr., though, it was a different story. Upon his return from the Pacific, he discovered that his scholarship to the Massachusetts Institute of Technology (MIT) was momentarily out of reach. He was looking at a two-year waiting list. Unlike his brother Sal, Frank Jr. had no patience for attending school any longer than was necessary. Frank Sr. hinted to Frank Jr., who took on the nickname "Hank," that he might consider studying for the fireman's exam. For Hank it was a no-brainer; he scored number one. Hank worked out vigorously in the Martorellas' garage gymnasium, so he had no difficulty at all in passing the physical. Shortly after joining the department, Hank proceeded to score number one in two consecutive exams for lieutenant and then again for captain; at the age of 34 he had the distinct honor of being the youngest captain commissioned in the Fire Department of New York City.

Gus was still earning a living with the piano. However, the big band sound was gradually giving way to rock 'n' roll, a new breed of music that seemed alien to traditional jazz musicians. By 1950 it had become too costly to maintain a large band. Besides, with two small children and a third one on the way, Gus needed to be home at nights and not on the road, away from the family. His younger brother Hank convinced him to become a fireman. While

Sal was diligently attending law school at night, Hank and Gus grew closer through their common interest in both firefighting and playing the horses at Belmont Race Track. Looking back from one generation to another, one might speculate that the Martorellas seemed to have had a love affair with horses.

For Anita and Barbara, their older brother Gus and his wife Louise were like a second set of parents. Gus was the first to marry and started a family at an early age. Louise realized that the girls needed some parental guidance and should be made aware of "the birds and the bees." Gus, at first, said to his wife, "Why me?" Louise answered, "Because you are the only one they look to for guidance." So, early one Sunday morning Gus trudged up the stairs to have a quiet talk with the girls before breakfast. All three settled down at the kitchen table, with Gus at the end and the girls on either side of him, sitting across from each other.

Slowly and hesitatingly, Gus began to inform the girls on how to conduct themselves when they started dating boys. He sheepishly attempted to caution them about the pitfalls of a boy–girl relationship. Barbara wanted to blurt out that they already knew all this, but Anita kept on gently kicking her ankles and blankly staring into her eyes, hinting that she should be quiet and say nothing. Barbara finally got the silent message. Toward the end of his dissertation, Gus asked the girls if they had any questions or reservations. After watching and letting their older brother labor in agony while trying to deal with this evidently delicate matter, Anita and Barbara suddenly burst into laughter. Together, they put their arms around their loving brother and assured him that they were already aware of "the birds and the bees" and that he need not worry. Gus smiled and put his arms around both girls, saying simply, "Let's all have some breakfast."

Rudy was the wild card in the family. As the older boys returned from being sequestered in the front lines during World War II and were eager to carry on with their lives in a more normal manner, Rudy's thoughts and feelings were somewhat overlooked by the family during this exhilarating moment. In reality, of all seven children born to Frank and Lilly, Rudy was the most energetic and enterprising of the lot. As noted earlier, at Luna Park Rudy had demonstrated his entrepreneurial skill and initiative in working the Tunnel of Love concession to his advantage. "*Carpe Diem*: Seize the Day."

By the age of seventeen, Rudy had no patience for continuing high school and promptly dropped out in his junior year. He wanted to find a job. Like his older brothers, Rudy wanted to find his place in a world that was changing rapidly from a war- to a peace-time economy. Frank Sr. said to Rudy, "If you're not going to continue with your schooling, then you have to go out and find a job in order to continue living at home." By that age, according to Frank Sr., everyone had to pull his or her own weight. So, for a brief period, Rudy lived at his Aunt Caroline's house on Stryker Street.

That's when Rudy hooked up with Emil Casio. Opportunity often knocks when and where it's least expected. The commonly used gambler's expression, "You have to be in it to win it," certainly fit the mood and vitality of this very young man. At that time, whether Rudy realized it or not, the world was his oyster.

As chance would have it, while Rudy wandered along Avenue U on West 5th Street just west of Ocean Parkway, he entered a corner auto repair shop. There was Emil, a medium-built, partially balding man with a friendly smile on his face, in the midst of repairing an automobile engine. Rudy wondered if he could use some help. Before he could say a word, Emil said, "Can you hand me that wrench over there on the table?" Thus began a partnership that would last for many years thereafter.

Emil was a few years older than Rudy and had just finished serving in the military. He was married, with two young girls. The business gave him just enough money to make ends meet. Emil's brother Guido came in twice a week to pay the bills and to lend a hand with miscellaneous repairs. Joe Composto, a friend of Guido's, was a hardy looking man with a sort of smoky voice who periodically pulled in with a yellow school bus that was in need of some minor repairs—usually an oil change or a tune up. The shop was a small but comradely hangout for the four men.

Once Rudy had a job, he found himself back in the good graces of his father. Anita and Barbara's spirits were lifted, happy to once again have their dear brother and next of kin back home in the nest, safely tucked under the wings of 628 Avenue V. After all, like his sisters, Rudy was part of the second trio of children in the Martorella household. Clayton was born eight years after his sister Barbara, so he wasn't really part of the previous "waves" of kids, but he was always happy to have his older siblings around.

Rudy's bus business came together when Jack O'Neil entered the picture. He was a bus dealer for the Superior Bus Company. Having seen a yellow school bus parked at the shop, Jack stopped in to have a word with Emil. He wanted to make a sale. If there was some interest, some buses could be made available at a reasonable price. None of the four really had any extra money with which to buy buses. But somehow, all four—Emil, Rudy, Guido, and Joe—were able to come up with $1500 each. Rudy borrowed $1500 from his father in order to cover his share of the initial investment. The buses went for $2700 apiece, and the deal required that they purchase at least ten units. This meant hiring six or seven additional drivers and finding additional financing to cover the cost of all ten buses. After frenetic telephone calls to some 26 different banks, with not a single one willing to give these young entrepreneurs any credit, it seemed they would have to give up this venture before it could even be started.

Just as they were about to call it quits, Jack O'Neil telephoned Emil and the others to let them know that it was "Their Lucky Day." International Harvester would finance all the buses. The boys were in business. They would incorporate as the Veterans Bus Corporation. Within a few weeks they managed to secure school bus routes to Abraham Lincoln, Lafayette, James Madison, Midwood, and Samuel J. Tilden High Schools, as well as a route to Brooklyn College. It cost a nickel per ride each way for each student who lived at least one mile away from school. Within its first year of operation, the company was a success.

Chapter Twenty

P.S. 153 and Cunningham Junior High 234 were within just a few blocks of each other; at a quick walking pace, the two schools were maybe ten minutes apart. Barbara was elected to bring Clayton to P.S. 153 in the morning, and pick him up in the afternoon, each school day. Clayton's first day of school began in September 1947, shortly after Labor Day. His kindergarten teachers were Mrs. Bichard and Mrs. Autschuler. Having survived rickets in his early childhood years, Clayton led a rather sheltered life. These two wonderful and caring ladies made his transition into the classroom community a rather easy and fun-filled experience. This pleasant moment in time transformed Clayton from being rather sullen and inward-looking to becoming an outward and engaging young lad. Building buildings, drawing pictures, playing house, and singing children's songs were all part of the daily routine imparted to Clayton and his classmates by these two lovely and loving ladies.

Clayton's kindergarten experience set the tone for the many wonderful years to follow, with one early hiccup. During Clayton's first week at school, Barbara was assigned to meet him at a large oak tree, just beyond the entrance gate at the front of the school building. This routine proved successful for the school year's first three days. Then, on the fourth day, Barbara was detained at her school for some reason. When she arrived at P.S. 153, about an hour late, she found her baby brother standing by the oak tree all by himself. Alone and frightened, Clayton's eyes were filled with tears. From that moment on, Barbara was never again late; in fact, she was granted special permission from her school principal to never be kept late because of her obligation to pick up Clayton after school.

Over the many years that followed this scary moment in Clayton's life, he and Barbara shared a special bond. Whenever they agreed to meet each other at some prescribed location or to share precious moments, they could count on each other to come together in good spirits. This included shopping for the next year's school clothing at a local department store, meeting each other at their favorite Chinese restaurant on Avenue U, or simply taking a lunch break together at home. Playing cards was one of their favorite activities; five-hundred rummy was their game of choice.

By that time, Anita and Barbara did all of the household shopping, including the special grocery list that was handed to them by their mother. It was usually written in red lipstick or red crayon on a brown paper bag. Usually Lilly would ask the girls to come into her bedroom. They were to dress properly and under no condition could they wear any article of clothing that brandished buttons. Hopefully, Lilly would be in a good mood. No matter what, the girls loved their mother dearly and would honor her every request. There was no room for error. If they returned home with a grocery item that was slightly different from what she ordered, or even with the slightest imperfection, it was rejected. Lilly insisted that the product be exchanged for the correct item, no questions asked. After a while, the girls became quite skilled at fulfilling their shopping mission and at managing the domestic affairs of the household.

Over time, Frank Sr. grew confident in his two daughters' ability to take matters into their own hands, though, whenever it was possible, Sr. would give them a helping hand. Nevertheless, there were certain moments when Anita and Barbara had disputes among themselves, and that's when the fur would fly.

For instance, Barbara loved having new shoes. Whenever she had some spare change or when she could put the tap on her father, she'd go shopping for a new pair. Anita, on the other hand, became skilled at taking good care to preserve whatever article of clothing she had, including the one or two pairs of shoes that she possessed. The girls shared the larger of the two back bedrooms of the house on Avenue V, and they each had one walk-in closet and shared a rather large chest of drawers that also doubled as a vanity. While Anita took great pains to manage her clothes and shoes neatly and efficiently, occupying perhaps a third of her own closet and drawer space, Barbara almost never had enough room for her clothing. It was not uncommon for many of Barbara's things to wind up inside her older sister's closet, thus intruding on Anita's space, even though that space was otherwise unfilled. This issue of Anita's involuntarily shared space was a perennial point of tension.

In addition, Barbara tended to admire the neatness and elegance of what Anita would wear. Anita somehow managed to take special care of her clothing, and her things always looked trim and stylish. Taking after Lilly, Anita always dressed in a way that looked fresh and really quite beautiful. Every inch of her wavy brown hair was combed, with not a single strand misplaced. Barbara, while beautiful in her own skin, was blessed with larger bones. She too took care of her things, though she had more of everything. Being the younger of the two siblings by two years, Barbara looked up to her older sister and her belongings, perhaps a little too much.

The straw that usually broke the camel's back was when Barbara succumbed to the temptation to try on one of Anita's blouses, just at a moment when Anita happened to enter the room. This sort of conflict could occur at the most inopportune moments, including the middle of the night. The boys would be asleep in their room next door, when suddenly screams would burst out from the girls' room. Things would be flying across their room and bouncing off of the walls. Some nasty words would be exchanged between them as well. After a while, with no end in sight and the intensity of the dispute growing stronger, their father would have to rise out of bed and somehow make his way into the field of battle. While nestled in bed between his two much older brothers, Clayton would giggle to himself, having found the whole kerfuffle to be quite amusing. Frank Sr., as arbiter, always found a way to separate and make peace between these two warring sisters. Silence and sanity would return to the Martorella household, and at last sleep time would be restored.

Chapter Twenty-One

Sunday morning at the Martorella household was like Grand Central Station in New York City; lots of movement and a generally wonderful feeling of adventure permeated this outsized space and time. The windows were open, the sun was out, and the aroma of basil was in the air. Life was good.

From his bedroom, Clayton could hear Anita and Barbara getting ready to head over to Kornfeld's Bakery on Avenue U. Coming down from his mystical moment, Clayton leaped out of bed, threw on his dungarees, socks, shoes, and the T-shirt he had been wearing for the past three days, and raced to the kitchen to join his sisters before they left the house. Horror of horrors, Clayton smelled like a sewer in a slum, and Anita instantly yelled at him, "Go to the bathroom and shower and then put on some clean clothes!" Barbara took her younger brother by the hand and escorted him into the bathroom, making sure that he took a shower. She then brought him some clean clothes from his bedroom. He dressed himself in record time.

Going to Kornfeld's on Sunday morning was one of Clayton's favorite happenings, and the girls knew that he would not want to be left behind. This wonderful Jewish bakery was located just one block north of the house: a simple walk up East 7th Street to Avenue U, and then a right at the corner and four stores down. The owners were Harry and Mildred, husband and wife, and they had a lovely daughter, Natalie, who was just a year older than Clayton. Clayton was captivated by Natalie's innocent good looks. Apart from his heart-throbbing crush, Clayton was addicted to the sweet smell of freshly baked rolls and cakes that filled the air in the store with intoxicating aromas. Except for some dairy products, which were kept in a glass-enclosed refrigerator, everything else was baked on the premises, in the back room of the store.

The Martorellas' order usually called for no less than a dozen mixed rolls, which included some horn, some twist, and some sandwich rolls, as well as some egg and poppy bagels. The girls on that occasion bought a chocolate layer cake to add to the mix. Clayton also loved Kornfeld's delicious Chinese cookies, which were made from sweetened flour baked to a crunchy yellow crisp. Each cookie was circular, about four inches in diameter and half an inch high, with a thick circular blob of rich milk chocolate at the center. Clayton would finish eating his cookie before he and his two sisters arrived home for breakfast.

After Sunday breakfast, everyone would go their separate ways. It wasn't until the late afternoon meal that everyone came together again. The boys were in a dating mood. With the exception of Gus, who was already hooked by his loving and beautiful wife Louise, the boys fanned out of the house in search of their soul mates. Sal was dating a young woman named Jeanne and Hank was attached to a beautiful Macy's clerk named Ann. Rudy was still footloose and fancy-free. Driving a bus gave him the opportunity to play the field. On his way toward Abraham Lincoln High School, his route was filled with many good-looking high school girls, many of whom happened to be friends of his younger sister Anita. Anita was the prettiest and most popular girl in the school. Barbara would join this mix of friends the following year, upon becoming a sophomore at Lincoln. Barbara was, in her own earthy way, as attractive as Anita, and would soon find boys knocking at her front door as well.

In much of humanity, by nature, people can be divided into two camps: one type leans toward perfection, and the other displays a proclivity toward imperfection. Sometimes people can make a transition from being a perfectionist to having a devil-may-care attitude and letting the chips fall as they may. The reverse may also be true. Such moments of revelatory transition quite often occur as one grows older, gaining wisdom and insight in all that has happened throughout one's life. But such a moment can also happen when someone close is about to knock at death's door.

Chapter Twenty-Two

Every growing family needs to have a doctor. Almost by accident, Dr. Nathan Haas came into the picture for the Martorellas. It was through Mary Dessi, the only daughter of Lilly's sister Caroline, that Dr. Haas was introduced to the Martorellas. Apparently, the good doctor was, in some way, related to Adrien Dessi, Mary's husband. When Gus and Louise realized that they were going to have their first child, Patricia, they needed a doctor. Mary introduced them to this very tall and handsome young doctor. Needless to say, Dr. Hass guided them through their first pregnancy without any troubles.

Two years later, after their second child was born—named Frank, after their grandfather—an event of nearly devastating proportions fell upon this young budding family living in the basement of 628 Avenue V. Frankie, the newborn son of Gus and Louise, was no more than six months old when he awoke during the night. Gus was on his way home from working a club date. Before he even entered the basement apartment he could hear his son screaming at the top of his lungs, apparently in extreme pain. At that moment, Louise was in a state of panic, having already had her son in her arms for nearly an hour with little or no success in comforting the boy. She screamed for Gus to call Dr. Haas.

Fortunately, Dr. Haas was home and immediately answered the

telephone, almost as if he sensed that some emergency might happen. Realizing the urgency of the call, Dr. Haas jumped out of bed, threw on his topcoat over his pajamas, gave his wife Eva a kiss on her cheek, and flew out the front door of his apartment. It was in the middle of the night and there was hardly any automobile traffic on the streets of Brooklyn; Dr. Haas arrived at Avenue V in ten minutes flat.

Meanwhile, Gus, overcome with emotion, had already passed out on the bed. The good doctor instructed Louise to lay out a bedsheet and blanket on the kitchen table. The doctor lifted Frankie from his crib. The baby was in utter agony and still screaming at the top of his lungs. By some miracle Dr. Haas was able to calm the little child down. Upon careful examination it was determined that Frankie's appendix was about to burst. The good doctor rushed the little patient to Coney Island Hospital just in the nick of time to have the appendix removed. Frankie was saved.

After a few days of hospital care, the loving and immensely thankful parents were able to collect their son and bring him home. Gus didn't know how to thank Dr. Haas for saving his son's life. So, he thought that perhaps, since he could play the piano, he would offer the doctor his services by giving his two children piano lessons free of charge. The following Monday, at about mid-morning, unannounced Gus went into the doctor's office on Ocean Avenue. The doctor was momentarily surprised to see Gus and asked, "What are you doing here at this hour of the day?" Gus replied, "Can I just have a moment of your time? I'll make it quick." The doctor ushered him into his private office and asked him, "To what do I owe the nature of this call?"

Gus got on his knees before the good doctor and thanked him so much for saving his son's life. He then proffered his services by offering the doctor's two young children free piano lessons. Dr. Haas stood up from behind his desk, smiled, and came around to lift up Gus from the floor. He said, "See that portrait of my wife, Eva, hanging on the opposite wall? She is a graduate of the Juilliard School of music and plays piano quite well. She's already giving the children music lessons." Dr. Haas then put his arms around Gus and said, "You don't owe me a thing. It was simply a routine house call. And we were very lucky." As Gus gathered himself together to leave the office, the doctor called after him nonchalantly. "Mr. Martorella?" Gus turned expectantly. The doctor continued while writing in his pad, "Have Louise come in later in the week for her routine exam." Gus thanked him again, placed his hat on, and departed.

Dr. Haas would continue as the family doctor for many more years. About four years later he would come to the rescue of another member of the Martorella family: That fateful time, it would be Anita.

Anita had a difficult pregnancy when bringing John, her firstborn child, into the world. Dr. Hass gave Anita a good deal of counseling and assistance during the nine months leading up to the moment of delivery. Even then, it took several hours of difficult labor before John entered the world. Dr. Haas stood by Anita's hospital bedside throughout the entire period, giving her aid and comfort and ensuring the health and stability of mother and child.

Chapter Twenty-Three

One by one, over the six-year period between 1947 and 1953, all of Clayton's six siblings would be married. The house on 628 Avenue V would turn into a way station, as one couple after another married and moved on into their own dwellings.

Gus and Louise were first to marry and start their family while World War II was still in progress. Sal and Jeanne followed suit not long after the war ended. How could Sal resist the subtle beauty of his wife-to-be? With her gentle smile, beautiful milk-white skin with just a touch of rose, and classical features atop a nearly perfect figure, she was the quintessential Venus de Milo. From 1943 to 1946, Jeanne was a dancer who performed as an active member of the famous Radio City Rockettes. She also danced in the Jewish theater and toured with the USO. Jeanne studied under the Russian master Anatole Vilzak. Later on in her marriage to Sal, Jeanne taught ballet at their home in Huntington, Long Island.

All seven offspring of Frank and Lilly were blessed with good looks, but also, more importantly, with good health. Clayton started life with the handicap of having contracted rickets at an early age. Thankfully, he recovered quickly. As the beneficiary of loving care from his two older sisters during his youthful years, Clayton grew into a healthy young lad.

On sunny afternoons after school, at times when Frank Jr. happened to be home, he and Clayton would play catch with a baseball and mitts by the side of the house. Frank Jr. and Clayton had a special relationship in that both loved the game of baseball. The love of the game was a legacy handed down by their father and uncles on the Martorella side of the family tree. During World War II, while Frank Jr. was in the Pacific, he was the hard-hitting, slick-fielding shortstop for his company team.

It wasn't long after his discharge from active duty that Frank Jr. met his beautiful wife-to-be, Ann. During the early stages of their marriage, Ann worked at the famous Macy's department store in Herald Square, which was where they first met. Their wedding would take place at Michelle's, an upscale restaurant in downtown Brooklyn. At Christmas, this lovely couple always treated Clayton to a handsome shirt or sweater, wrapped inside a beautiful red Macy's box. Clayton took great pleasure in opening that strikingly big red box, and he would notice Ann's sweet smile as she sat opposite him and next to his brother at the dining room table during family Christmas Eve dinner.

The empty lot on the south side of Neck Road and Ocean Parkway was the scene of so many youthful activities in which Clayton participated. There was football and steal-the-flag during the winter, and baseball in the spring and summer. Kids from all over the neighborhood gathered at this naturally formed dirt-filled infield diamond that sloped upward slightly into the outfield; tall maple trees enclosed left field, circled around center, and ended partway into right field. A strand of high bushes, hiding the Gelb Mansion on Neck Road, completed the contours of this exceptional place called simply "The Lot." This magical place was close to the neighborhood hangout throughout much of Clayton's youthful years, Bill's Candy Store, owned and managed by Bill and Neddy Tanenbaum. They were a loving couple who lived in back of the store, in a two-bedroom apartment on the first floor of a two-story prewar attached brick building.

The Migliaros continued to play an important part in the life of the Martorellas. Tony had become a well-known and respected hair stylist, applying his craft in the famous House of Shazame in Manhattan. In addition to styling hair for such famous celebs as Ava Gardner, Rita Hayworth, and Audrey Hepburn, as a special favor he would work on Anita and Barbara's permanents as well. He also palled around with Rudy and his friends. Tommy Migliaro became close friends with Frank Jr., and in later years, after they were both married and began to have kids of their own, their families naturally grew closer together. Tommy made a living delivering furniture for a major store on Avenue U that specialized in elegant home furnishings—always a useful presence among growing, prosperous families.

Eight-year-old Clayton had saved up a total of 29 dollars in his ceramic piggybank. This savings was from an accumulation of nickels and dimes from his weekly allowance for cleaning the dining room furniture. After three years of making ends meet, Rudy's bus business was beginning to provide a very nice profit to him and his three partners. One evening at dinner, Rudy announced that he was going to purchase a brand new 1949 cream-white Buick. Even though Clayton was still quite young, he loved automobiles and often played with a small collection of toy models. He thought to himself quietly and seriously, and finally decided that he wanted in on this transaction. He proceeded to break open his piggybank and hand over to Rudy 29 dollars in coins, so that he could also claim ownership of such a grand prize, a brand new shiny automobile. Needless to say, Rudy was not exactly jumping at the chance for a new partnership.

Not much later, Gus and John Termini suddenly decided to go into the photography business. John, the second of three Termini brothers, had a deep and abiding interest in photography, and he convinced Gus to join him in this venture. For Gus, prior to join-ing the Fire Department, it was a chance to earn some extra money to augment his income playing club dates on the weekends. Patricia, Gus and Louise's firstborn, who just turned four, and Clayton, already eight years old, became part of a photography experiment. One sunny Sunday morning, Patricia, with her lovely combed light brown hair and a beautiful smile on her face, and wearing her brand new pants outfit, and Clayton, dressed in a new grey checkered suit jacket and pants with a clean white shirt and a matching tie, posed for one of Gus and John's photos. Pat sat in Lilly's favorite newly floral-patterned sitting chair and Clayton was positioned standing next to her, there in the sunny living room of the house on Avenue V.

The photo venture turned out to be short-lived, as both John and Gus went on to bigger and more important things in their lives; Gus went on to save lives and property from the ravages of fire, and John studied engineering and, along with his brother Albert, went into the construction business, designing and build-ing summer houses in the Hamptons on Long Island. Nevertheless, the photo op turned out to be picture perfect, and it is still a memorable item among the Martorella family heirlooms.

Chapter Twenty-Four

The house on Avenue V hosted one great family party after another. "Let's celebrate Sal and Jeanne's engagement with a party!" the family's mystical muse seemed to command. Frank Jr. and Ann would be next. Then it was Anita and Jimmy, followed by Rudy and Terry, and concluding with Barbara and Pete. The entire clan of daughter-in-laws competed with Barbara and Anita over who was the fairest of them all. When it came to styling hair, Tony Migliaro, gladly, would be there to insure that all of these brides-to-be would look their very best. Naturally endowed, they were all beautiful people. It seemed all at once that, with the wave of a wand, Frank Sr. and Lilly's family doubled in size.

On Christmas Eves, Frank Sr. would continue to bring home live eels along with a variety of other exotic fish. Before the new era in the annals of religious ceremony in the Catholic Church, eating meat on Fridays and on Christmas Eve was forbidden. So, on such an occasion, there was no shortage of culinary accompaniments to compliment a finely prepared seafood dinner by none other than Anita and Barbara, who, by that time, had evolved into culinary experts in Neapolitan Italian cuisine. Still, they had to contend with the live eels jumping around in the kitchen sink. Shortly after dinner, Lilly would coax Clayton to stand next to her, by the Christmas tree, as they sang a few popular Christmas songs. Naturally, everyone else sitting around the dining room table would join in on the singing. During all of this merriment, Frank Sr. would be resting contentedly, discreetly smoking his favorite Havana cigar while sitting in his favorite chair on the porch at the front of the house.

Once in a while, especially on the eve of a popular holiday, Frank Sr. would tie one on. Amidst all his contacts and the comings and goings demanded of him daily, there were two favorite friends with whom he was truly comfortable: Strungone, the ice man and winemaker, husband to Lilly's sister Caroline, and Emilio, an automobile chauffeur to the deputy commissioner of the New York Sanitation Department. Late into the evening at one of the parties on Avenue V, the telephone rang. It was Aunt Caroline. Sal picked up the telephone to hear Caroline imploring, "Can someone please run over to my house to pick up Francesco?"

Sal and Rudy were sent to fetch their father. In the basement where Caroline fed her family and welcomed everyone, around the family table were seated Frank Sr., Strungone, and Emilio. They were humbly sipping espresso coffee and eating anisette cookies. Earlier in the evening, while everyone in this household was gathered and enjoying the moment, a sudden rumble was heard at the front door of the basement. All three compadres had stumbled down the three steps leading into the house. As the evening closed, order was restored. Frank Sr., Strungone, and Emilio were safely tucked into their own beds, within the confines of their own homes.

Emilio and Rosie were a joyful couple and close friends of the family. Often on sunny Sunday afternoons, Emilio and Rosie would pick up Clayton and take him to the Bronx Zoo or to some other outdoor venue. They hadn't any children of their own and were delighted to spend the afternoon with Clayton, who was only four years old at the time. Emilio had a moustache and generally dressed in a black suit and white open shirt. Rosie had soft graying hair, combed into a bun. She wore thin metal-framed glasses and brandished a warm sweet smile on her face. Frank Sr. valued their friendship and appreciated their kindness toward his young son.

Chapter Twenty-Five

It was 1951. Barbara had just graduated from Abraham Lincoln High School with a commercial diploma in secretarial studies and was about to start her first job with the Kellogg Engineering Company. Anita, two years older than Barbara, had already begun to work for the Metropolitan Life Insurance Company. The girls were attractive and very competent in fulfilling their secretarial responsibilities. They were fortunate to be working for two reputable companies.

Barbara couldn't wait to get her first paycheck. The money was spent before she even received it. Her salary disappeared in a matter of minutes, replaced with brand new clothing, a hat, and shoes. With Anita it was another story. She was a saver, always giving her father ten dollars after each and every paycheck. Barbara went through clothes and shoes like running water down a fast-flowing river. Anita, on the other hand, kept her wardrobe in pristine condition. Every inch of her clothing was cleaned and pressed. No matter what they did, though, the girls were beautiful. Clayton loved to tease them. When Anita would ask him who the better cook in the family was, he would answer that she was the best. When Barbara asked him the same question, he would answer that she was the better cook. Clayton was always the diplomat; after all, he knew where his bread was buttered.

For several years after the end of World War II, block parties were occasional popular events. The block party was the byproduct of a feel-good period. Neighbors came out of their cozy homes to share in each other's good feelings. Neighbors shook hands with neighbors. Amidst the fun and jubilation, an eighteen-year-old boy, Jimmy, met a sixteen-year-old girl, Anita. It was the beginning of a courtship that would eventually lead to a lasting marriage.

The Tolkins were next-door neighbors to the Martorellas, connected by a common driveway, and separated only by a chain-link fence. Steven Tolkin, who was a few years older than Clayton, sometimes joined him when he was playing stoop ball in front of his house. Clayton often annoyed Steven by bragging how good he was at catching the ball off the stoop. Steve's dad sold jewelry in the diamond district of New York and, for some of the Martorellas, he was the person to see when it was time to buy a diamond wedding ring. Often, after Clayton finished his paper route, he would meet with Steven's grandfather, Joe, at the entrance to the garage for a friendly game of checkers. Joe, a rather large, impressive-looking man, sitting on his stool, wearing a black yarmulke or a black hat and scratching his graying beard while pondering his next move, cut an imposing figure. On one occasion, Joe and Clayton actually played a game of checkers to an unprecedented stalemate. After pondering the situation for about a minute, Joe peered at Clayton with a stern look in his eye and then gave him a gentle smile. He reached out to shake the boy's hand and said, "Let's go inside and have some tea."

Murray and Booby Weinberg lived in the house just beside Dr. Rosenblatt's. Helen and Lucky Wright were a young couple who lived in the Weinberg's basement apartment, in the same manner as Gus and Louise occupied the Martorella household basement. They had two girls who were about the same age as Gus's children,

Patty and Frankie. Helen and Lucky had recently emigrated from Great Britain, so Lucky could work for a Manhattan bank. It was the charm and fluidity of living on Avenue V that brought these two sweet and innocent couples, the Weinbergs and the Wrights, together for a brief moment in time. Changing circumstances often force people to move on with their lives, and kind spirits have a way of coming and going in the blink of an eye.

Barbara Weinberg was a tomboy, only one year younger than Clayton. She was sharp and scrappy. By the time she graduated from grade school she had already skipped a grade and caught up to Clayton. He could never shake her loose. She followed him like a hawk. When he played roller hockey with his male friends, Barbara was always right next to him. The same was true for punchball and stickball as well. Only when he joined his friends in "The Lot" on Neck Road, around the corner, was he able to shake her. Barbara wore braces on her teeth, brandishing a cute smile and a cheerful quick spirit in her demeanor. She really was a genuinely lovely person, only Clayton didn't know it then.

The Weinbergs were a genteel family. Rita was Barbara's younger sister. She was less athletic, more feminine-looking, and quite attractive for her tender age. Harold, a third child, arrived several years later. On pleasant summer evenings, generally after supper, Murray would sometimes engage Clayton in friendly conversation while resting on his porch after a long day at the office. He was genuinely interested in what Clayton was up to, and sometimes offered him friendly advice, as a father would to his own son. After finishing her homework, Barbara sometimes came outside to join them in conversation. Booby, Barbara's mother and Murray's loving wife, also joined the gathering with glasses of lemonade to take the edge off a hot summer night.

Murray owned and managed a very successful clothing factory

in Long Island City, with a showroom in the Manhattan garment district. During Clayton's junior year at Abraham Lincoln High School, Mr. Weinberg even offered him a part-time job in his factory, with the idea that Clayton might consider learning the clothing business after he graduated from high school. At the time, though, Clayton was not interested in that line of work. His thoughts wandered more in the direction of playing sports and carousing with his friends. Unlike Barbara, who was bright and heading for college, Clayton was an average student, getting by with a modicum of school work and consequently graduating with a modest 76.51 percent grade average. Nevertheless, he did pass all of his Regents exams, so if he ultimately chose to pursue a higher degree, his options were still open.

Chapter Twenty-Six

With wedding bells in the air, home Tupperware parties were a common occurrence at 628 Avenue V. They presented a chance for Anita and Barbara to meet with their girlfriends over coffee and cake. Whether they filled the wedding trove with plastic containers, stainless steel pots and pans, or vacuum cleaners, the parties, for Clayton, were always a chance to share joyful moments with the neighborhood girlfriends of his two sisters. His ears became accustomed to listening in on the local gossip and his tummy looked forward to the wonderful sweet treats provided by his sisters and their bubbly friends. More often than not, Clayton was sworn to secrecy, or was asked to leave the room during the more intimate conversations. Of course, his lips were tightly sealed.

Lilly began to realize that her life was becoming more insular. Her daily activities were centered on maintaining her own health, looks, and well-being. Her husband and children were now leading lives that were beyond her control. From time to time Lilly would entertain her closest friends Molly and Josi at an afternoon tea in a local café on Avenue U. Apart from listening to the radio, her brief moments with her two dear friends were her only contact with the outside world.

After being single for many years, Molly, while attending a

church function at St. Edmund's, made the acquaintance of a middle-aged gentleman who was unattached. It was Ian Fitzgerald, a retired family physician, and he soon discovered the wonderful attributes of this dear woman. On one of Lilly's rendezvous for afternoon tea, Molly broke the news to Lilly that she was planning to sell her house, marry Ian, and move to Ireland, where her future husband still had family. In the same visit, Josi broke the news to Lilly that she and her husband Pino would also be moving on. They found a lovely house in the Poconos and would eventually retire to that more tranquil place. Neither development constituted good news for Lilly. Although the loss of her two closest friends came as a setback within the confines of her own world, Lilly would eventually discover new friends in her future grandchildren, with whom she could share her imaginative fantasies.

Through all of the pomp and circumstance taking place at 628 Avenue V, Clayton managed to carve out a little space for himself. Every once in a while a beautiful angel seemed to rescue him from the everyday trials and tribulations of that rather complex world. He fell in love with Mrs. Winant, his fourth grade teacher at P.S. 153. She had a special way of creating calm while imparting knowledge to all the fourth-grade rascals, including him. She had coiffed wavy black hair, in style with the times, and soft white skin with a touch of light red lipstick; she was medium height in two- or three-inch heels, and she dressed to perfection. Schoolwork was lively and never boring. World history and economics were her specialties. One student each week who did their best through classroom participation was given a prize. On the week that Clayton managed to rise to the top of the class, he received an orange-colored hardcover book about the economy of how things are made. For many years to follow he referred to this book as if it were his Bible, but more importantly it always reminded him of

Mrs. Winant's kindness. With all of the distractions in life, this fourth grade feel-good experience remained with Clayton for many years to come, and impressed upon him the importance of getting an education.

In that same year, 1952, Clayton would turn eleven in March. On Mondays and Wednesdays, at lunchtime, he would walk over to Coney Island Avenue to the corner hobby house, only a couple of blocks from school, to sit in on a Bible story group. The group included a few elderly folks along with some young mothers and their small children. They came to this storybook oasis in anticipation of learning their next biblical chapter. It was a captive audience. The leader was a young gal from Des Moines, Iowa.

It was not clear which group or faith she represented, but she always told a biblical story with dramatic flair and skill in a way that held Clayton spellbound for a full thirty minutes. Her story for the day ended with just enough time left for him to return to school for the afternoon session. The lady was about fifty years old. She wore her graying hair tied in a bun, atop a plain but kind-looking face with no lipstick. She effectively utilized a green felt rectangular board, approximately four feet in height and six feet across. She also had a very large collection of biblical figures made of cloth, representing a who's who of characters from the Old and New Testament. To enhance the drama of life in olden times, she used cardboard pieces representing horses, lions, chariots, wagons, and carts, with caves, mountains, a coliseum, a forum, and other stirring backdrops in a never-ending saga of life in the old world. These descriptive stories were, for Clayton, a kind of elixir that kept him curious and excited about human history and the origins of the ever-perplexing world around him.

Chapter Twenty-Seven

The big day was fast approaching. In a span of just one year, from January 1952 to January 1953, Anita, Rudy, and Barbara all entered into married life. The older six of Lilly's seven children were to soon fly from her nest, to start homes of their own, far beyond the comforting accommodations of 628 Avenue V.

Gus and Louise continued living in the basement of Frank and Lilly's house for nine full years. Their three children were born and raised in the Martorella basement apartment before the family moved to Haring Street in the Marine Park area of Brooklyn.

Sal married Jeanne and soon after they bought their first house on Fillmore Avenue in the Marine Park area, just around the corner from Gus and Louise. Later on both families would abandon Brooklyn in favor of the larger and seemingly more attractive environs of Long Island. Over time, they would pay dearly for this added space and tranquility in the form of progressively growing real estate taxes.

Hank and Ann married and moved into Ann's beautiful brownstone home in Bay Ridge, Brooklyn. They raised two lovely children, Franc and Donna, in their stately house.

By that time, Rudy was fully engaged in growing his own bus business. Anita and Barbara, after finishing high school, started working in the corporate world as very capable secretaries, skilled in stenography and office management, having acquired a take-charge persona from the homemaking and management lessons imparted to them by their loving father.

Anita had been dating Jimmy for a few years before they decided to tie the knot. She, being the beautiful young lassie that she was, had a number of suitors who were interested in hitching their wagon to her star. But it was Jimmy Oddo, all along, who would win her heart in a lasting and loving marriage. At a young age Jimmy lost his younger brother to leukemia. On top of that tragedy, he also lost his father only one year before his marriage to Anita. Early on, Jimmy had become the breadwinner in his own house. The Oddos occupied a semi-attached white stucco house on the left side of East 7th Street, beside three apartment buildings leading to the corner of Avenue V. Palmina (in Italian, Barniba), Jimmy's mother, worked as a seamstress in the garment district of Manhattan. Jimmy acquired valuable mechanical skills while working in a machine shop until he was drafted into the army.

Frank Sr. realized how much his two daughters contributed to keeping the family together through very difficult times, but he also loved them and wanted the best for them in starting their own families. To show his support for the coming nuptials, Frank Sr. wanted Anita's wedding to take place at the Riviera, his sister's catering hall in the heart of Coney Island, and perhaps the best in all of New York. Antoinette's son Andrew had taken over the reins from his father and was determined to present to the world at large a first-class catering experience. Anita and Jimmy would have a European Continental wedding to remember.

Chapter Twenty-Eight

Our Lady of Grace Roman Catholic Church was founded on January 6, 1935, in a local store on Avenue X and West Street in Brooklyn. Six months later, on June 28, Reverend Salvatore Cafiero was appointed pastor and commissioned by Brooklyn's Bishop Malloy to build a church. On March 8, 1936, ground was broken and construction began. On September 27, 1936, the first Mass was offered, led by Father Cafiero at seven a.m. At the time, the congregation consisted of 908 candidates (parishioners). By 1940 an extension was added to the church's mission-style red brick construction. Several steps ascend up to the main sanctuary of the church which was, and still is, located on Avenue W and East 4th Street. A bell hangs at the apex of the building, under a symmetrical arch.

As a child, upon waking up on Sunday mornings, Clayton could hear the clarion call of the church bell, summoning the local parishioners every hour prior to the start of Sunday Mass. For Clayton, it evoked a special feeling of renewal. As a testimony to the neighborhood's growing, predominantly Italian community, in 1942 the final mortgage payment for the church building was completed, followed by a celebration at the Knights of Columbus Club in downtown Brooklyn. On December 8, 1945, a dinner was held at the Hotel St. George celebrating the end of World War II that September and the gradual return of the troops. During the following year the wood floor of Our Lady of Grace Church was covered by asphalt tile. In the sanctuary, in back of the marble altar, a triptych of panels was installed with the saintly image of the Virgin Mary at its center. Additionally, new stained glass windows were dedicated to the 36 local servicemen lost in World War II.

For more than a full year in advance, the Riviera was booked solid every Saturday night. The only available date was Sunday, January 20, 1952, due to an unexpected cancellation shortly before a scheduled event. Since Frank Sr. insisted on Anita and Jimmy's wedding reception taking place at his sister's catering hall, that Sunday was chosen as the day of the wedding. Our Lady of Grace Church was the natural choice for where Anita and Jimmy would be wed.

The week prior to the big event was one continuous fanfare. 628 Avenue V was converted into a combination beauty salon and fashion house. Tony Migliaro spent nearly every evening in the dining room and kitchen cutting, styling, and shaping ladies' hair. At first it was Anita, and then Barbara, followed by Delores (Tony's sister), Ann Schiano, and Ann Stecco. Ann Schiano was Anita's best friend who lived on East 8th Street, near the Martorella house. Ann Stecco was a first cousin to Jimmy. The bridal party consisted of Barbara and Carlo (Jimmy's closest cousin). They were the maid of honor and best man. The groomsmen were Frank Schiano (husband to Ann), Jimmy and Anita's best friends, Tony Migliaro (always near and dear to all of the Martorellas), and yet another Frank (this one a close cousin to Jimmy).

The coffee pot was perking day and night, all week long. There were never enough Italian pastries and Kornfeld's bagels on hand to satisfy the cheerful palates. For Clayton and his two cohorts,

Patty and Frankie, it was party time.

Anita's wedding dress was being constructed, from the silky laced veil to the fashionable white shoes, by Jimmy's cousin Sarah who lived nearby. Sarah and her two sisters were well-known for their dress designs and fulfillment of ballroom dresses and gowns suitable for all occasions. Over the ensuing years of her marriage to Jimmy, Anita would be the beneficiary of some beautifully styled dresses and two-piece suits crafted by Sarah. With the exception of Anita's bridal gown, all of the other gowns and tuxedos were rentals. Between Avenue U and Kings Highway, there was no shortage of very fine women's and men's clothing stores.

Apart from Caroline and her husband Strungone, the Vallefuocos would not be attending Anita's wedding at the Riviera. There was still a deep divide between Lilly's family and the Martorella's. Ben and his wife Barbara would have attended the wedding, but Ben's employment in the State Department's Office of Strategic Services kept him out of the country on foreign assignment. After the war, Sal and Jeanne Martorella and Ben and Barbara Vallefuoco would continue their close friendship for many years thereafter. Sal and his uncle Ben would become golfing buddies.

It was three o'clock in the afternoon and Our Lady of Grace Church was jam-packed with family, friends, and local folks interested to see the neighborhood's next newlyweds. Neighborhood weddings seemed to occur in those days on most weekends of the year. When the church bell rang prior to the big event, it was like the announcement of a newborn baby. A church wedding was a cheerful, come-as-you-will moment. At three o'clock, women always flocked into the church wearing curlers, dressed in their everyday house clothes to have a look at the latest beautiful bride.

Three limos arrived in front of the church that sunny Sunday in

January. One by one, the bridal party and the immediate family were ushered out of their black vehicles by their respective chauffeurs. One of the parish priests greeted this most beautiful group, coaching them as they assembled at the foot of the church. The bridal party ascended the church steps, led by the twin flower girls (the lovely seven-year-old twin daughters of Jimmy's Uncle Leo), followed by the maid of honor. The bridesmaids came next. The groom, best man, and ushers were assembled in order at the foot of the altar, awaiting the arrival of the bridal chain. During the previous week, the entire ceremony was dutifully rehearsed several times over.

When Anita (the beautiful bride) and her handsome father, Frank Sr., entered the front door of the church, the organ music changed from "Ave Maria" to "Here Comes the Bride." All eyes quickly shifted from the front altar toward the back entrance of the church. The procession of beautiful women marched down the center of the aisle in a slow but steady prescribed manner while the onlookers gazed at this wonderful entourage of fair ladies. One might catch a glimpse of a smile from one or two of the bridesmaids as their eyes momentarily peeked at the crowd standing at attention along the two sides of the aisle. Excitedly, the procession slowly marched to the altar.

The magic moment had come. The bride and her father were the last to make this slow journey toward the front of the church. Clayton was the young boy who trailed the bride, making sure that the long bridal dress followed the bride without any wrinkles. Anita would accept nothing short of perfection. Once all were assembled on the altar, Father Cafiero proceeded to administer the pledge of marriage and accept the vows of Anita and Jimmy, the bride and groom. They were declared man and wife. The handsome groom then kissed his beautiful bride.

As the bridal party left the church they were of course showered with rice, the bulk of which was, naturally, tossed upon the heads of the bride and groom. Apart from the clanging sound of the church bell, it seemed that every car horn in the neighborhood was ringing cheerfully, adding acclamation to this joyful event. What more can be said but that it was a memorable moment in the family life of the Martorellas, commemorating all of the hard work, angst, and joy borne upon the proud, resilient shoulders of Frank and Lilly.

Chapter Twenty-Nine

There were three hours of extra time from the close of the church service at three in the afternoon until the bridal party was due at the Riviera for picture-taking at six in the evening. The bridal party was directed to go to the bride's house at 628 Avenue V. When the three limos arrived at Anita's home, like running water, a crowd of neighborly good-wishers quickly gathered around the house to catch a glimpse of the bridal party as they scurried into the house for some good cheer.

The reception at the Riviera began at eight o'clock in the evening. Antoinette opened the lounge downstairs, one half hour earlier than the usual seven o'clock starting time, in order to accommodate some of the early guests. It was only a few steps down from the main ballroom to the lower level, home to the Art Deco lounge. Luigi Cetano, the accordionist, discreetly circulated around the room, serenading the guests as they came into the lounge and settled onto the circular black-and-white Art Deco sofas at the center and the cushioned settees which ran along the two side walls.

In the Art Deco lounge, the bride and groom could choose whether to have carved ice figures of angels or swans at the libation table. Three-ounce crystal glasses of gently spiked pink fruit punch were served by a well-schooled, tuxedo-clad waiter. Finely prepared hors d'oeuvres of crusted shrimp, stuffed, baked little-neck clams, small, bell-shaped puffs filled with seasoned mozzarella cheese, and other delicious samplers were served on gold-plated trays by wandering waiters wearing white gloves and pleasant smiles.

At the back of the lounge, standing behind the coatrack counter was Tony Lieto, husband to Maggie's daughter Leticia. He was a six-foot-two Adonis with jet-black hair and an engaging smile to match his good looks, the quintessential tin soldier of Victor Herbert's famous musical, *Babes in Toyland*. In addition to hanging up coats, he sold Cuban cigars and packs of Lucky Strikes, Chesterfields, and Camel cigarettes to the invited guests.

After an hour of dancing and mingling, the good patrons ascended the carpeted stairs to the main ballroom. While the invited guests were being prepped for the main event by the master of ceremonies, the bridal party was being pampered in one of the two adjoining rooms at the front entrance of the hall. It was picture-taking time again, and the whole family certainly had plenty to smile about.

Two waiters were assigned to the bridal party while they were taking pictures in the very comfortable side room at the entrance to the main ballroom. The balcony was on the second floor, on the inside part of the entrance to the hall, above the bridal party room and business office. A thin staircase, behind the business office, led from the ballroom up to the balcony, where the sixteen-piece dance band and a special guest table for the occasion were assembled. Andy Zack, short for Zaccarino, was the only child to Antoinette and Zaccarino Cavitola; he had his own booth from which he and his father could view the entire proceedings of the evening. Antoinette was in charge, totally, of the kitchen. Not a single morsel of food came through the kitchen's swinging doors and into the dining room without her approval.

Gus sat in on piano for a few of the popular dance tunes that were requested. Some of the Sinatra numbers were among Anita's favorites, and the Ed Casso band played them brilliantly, earning them great popularity among local storeowners and restauranteurs. By eight o'clock in the evening nearly everyone was seated at their respective tables which were arranged around the generously spaced rectangular dance floor. Live music at the Riviera was one of the main ingredients that went into a one-of-a-kind wedding experience. The master of ceremonies, John Apicella, requested, "Please rise with your glass of champagne, for a toast to honor Anita and Jimmy Oddo, the bride and groom." As the colorful strobe lights focused on the beautiful couple floating into the room and onto the dance floor, the band in the balcony played the snappy Sinatra tune "Fly Me to the Moon."

The Riviera prided itself on offering a "Continental Wedding," led by the master of ceremonies and two captains—one for the wine stewards and the other for the waiters. On the night of the grand wedding, the people who responded by invitation numbered a little over two hundred, just about the maximum capacity for the dining room. It took eight experienced waiters to handle this number of people, with the captain pitching in when necessary. Each waiter was dressed in a standard black tuxedo and wore white gloves while serving. The captain wore a slightly more sophisticated tux. In addition to directing the waiters, his main purpose was to keep the guests in good spirits.

The captain of the four wine stewards was responsible for introducing the various wines being offered for the evening and following through with any special requests coming from more discerning patrons. His tux was similar to that of the captain of the waiters, but he also wore a shiny silver key that hung from his shirt collar. It was the symbolic key to the wine cellar. The wine stewards wore the same tuxedo pants as the waiters, but their jackets looked more like laced toreador vests. Not only the bride and the groom, but everyone present, sensed that they too were special guests of the house.

Let's not forget the royal treatment the Riviera's staff accorded to the guests' discerning palates. The tables were set with black, gold-trim decorative plates of the finest quality. The first serving was an antipasto salad served on smaller white dishes. The offering consisted of a bright red pimiento filled with finely cut salad and covered with two fresh anchovies. On one side were three slices of Genoa salami and on the other, three slices of provolone. The remaining two sides were garnished with two large green and black olives, laid opposite a stalk of celery on the other side. On each table was fresh, crispy Italian bread with butter and cruets of oil and vinegar for garnishing the antipasto. In the kitchen, each serving of antipasto was individually prepared on separate plates. Every waiter would fill on his tray the appropriate number of plates to be carried to his respective table, to in turn be given to each individual guest of the bride and groom.

The soup came next. It was a mild broth containing tiny pieces of macaroni, finely cut pieces of carrot, fresh parsley, and something else—a secret ingredient which only Antoinette and her brother Louie knew, and shared with no one else. It was a special offering indeed. The warm soup was served out of silver tureens and wheeled out on carts, with the soup dishes stored underneath.

What is an Italian wedding without pasta? The manicotti, perforce, came next—two mouthwatering macaroni crepes, filled with a light creamy ricotta cheese, fresh parsley, and melted mozzarella cheese, covered with a fresh homemade light marinara tomato sauce and a touch of basil mixed in for good flavor. The Parmesan cheese, of the finest quality, was already on the table resting inside two shiny silver bowls. In between every two tables was a work station where silverware and sundry items and utensils were stored. Wine was also endlessly served from these stations.

The main course was the half chicken, oven-baked to perfection and served with two creamy soft and delicately deep-fried potato croquettes, filled with melted mozzarella cheese, alongside boiled fresh peas, onions, and tiny sautéed pieces of liver covered with mushroom gravy. Liquid spirits were served throughout the evening. As the wedding celebration was winding down, the evening dinner was topped off by an extraordinary Luigi Alba wedding cake. Two miniature figures of the bride and groom were, of course, gently placed on the top layer. The bride and groom were obliged to cut and serve the first pieces to the members of their own bridal party. The remaining four layers were wheeled into the kitchen, to be equally distributed to the rest of the night's more than two hundred guests. Never a single slice of this exquisite delicacy was wasted or left behind.

While the cake was being cut and served, Leona, Jimmy's first cousin from Endicott, New York, stepped up to the microphone and announced that she was about to sing two arias, one from *La bohème* and the other from *Carmen*. The bride's brothers Gus and Salvatore would accompany her. Leona's captivating voice held her audience in an eternal moment of love and tranquility.

The band followed up with a lively tarantella. By that time the entire crowd was ready to bounce onto the dance floor. Some of the Martorellas who'd been working in the kitchen came through the swinging door and into the ballroom to join in the festivities. Even the commissioner of the Department of Sanitation and his lovely wife were seen dancing in the mix. When a circle of revelers took shape, the bride and groom were ceremoniously led to its center. The floor rumbled with dancing feet. In an atmosphere of untiring good cheer, the house band happily agreed to play for another hour.

Chapter Thirty

It was close to midnight when Frank Sr. whispered to his son Rudy that the time had come to take Clayton home. Clayton remembered that his mother wanted him to bring her a slice of the wedding cake. Before leaving, he slipped into the kitchen and asked his Uncle Dominick to give him a healthy slice to take home for Lilly. Antoinette also slipped a few miniature laced, glazed almond party favors into a bag to take with him. She then gave her young nephew a hug and a kiss on the cheek, and said, "Go home, figlio mio."

Rudy dropped off his brother at the house and made a beeline right back to the wedding, as the night was still young. Clayton entered the house and quietly put the wedding cake into the refrigerator. It had been a long and exciting day, and Clayton was tired. He instantly fell onto his bed, still wearing his tuxedo. A few moments later he heard a high-pitched voice call out to him, "Claynta, Claynta: Come to me, vieni qui." It was his mother.

Coming out of a brief slumber, Clayton slowly gathered himself and quietly walked into her room. "Let's have a piece of that wedding cake that you promised to bring home," said Lilly. Clayton went into the kitchen and prepared two small slices of this still fresh and delicious wedding cake. He also boiled some water for a cup of Lipton tea which he sensed that his mother would like with her dessert. Lilly set up her small night table next to her bed. They sat for a moment without saying a word. "Was she beautiful?" Lilly asked. "Yes, she was," Clayton responded. She continued, "Did Gus and Sal play at the wedding?" "Yes. Jimmy's cousin sang two songs from an opera."

Clayton asked his mother if he could quickly take off his dress clothes and put on his pajamas. "Why?" she demanded. "I feel uncomfortable," he replied. "But you look so handsome dressed in your suit," She said with a smile. She continued, "Go on, I'll wait for you to come back." When Clayton returned to her room, his mother held before him a rather large black-and-white picture of herself dressed in a beautiful full-length wedding gown with a thin laced, embroidered veil, held together atop her head by a small framed tiara encircling her classical face. She was simply beautiful. But it was only half of a picture. The other half was cut away. Clayton hesitated to ask, but did so anyway: "What happened to the other half of the picture?"

After they spent a moment together in silence, Lilly said, "There was an accident and the other half of the picture was destroyed." "What happened?" Clayton asked. She said, "Let's not talk about this anymore tonight."

The house was empty on this festive evening and Clayton was feeling quite alone. His mother asked him if he would like to sleep at the foot of her bed. He nodded affirmatively. She tossed him a pillow while making some extra space at the opposite end of the bed. The lights went out as these two lonesome souls drifted into their own world of dreams.

Chapter Thirty-One

After the horrific bombing both in Europe and in the Pacific, it was incumbent upon the United States to foster a program of reconstruction for these devastated parts of the world. The Marshall Plan was designed to put American dollars and physical energy toward accomplishing this goal. The G.I. Bill was also signed into law to send returning American soldiers back to school. It also provided a kick start toward the great American movement of home ownership, transferring the many American families from the more crowded inner cities into the greener pastures of suburbia, thus allowing millions of working-class citizens to fulfill the American dream of owning one's own piece of real estate.

Sal Martorella was a direct beneficiary of the G.I. Bill. He put himself through night school in his quest for a law degree. Shortly after his marriage to Jeanne, Sal purchased their first house on Fillmore Avenue in the neighborhood of Marine Park, Brooklyn.

Six months after Anita's wedding, Rudy would follow suit. Not to be outdone by his sister Anita, Rudy and Terry would have their wedding at the famous Beekman Tower, inside the mid-Manhattan hotel bearing the same name. Anita and Barbara were two of the bridesmaids among the many beautiful people forming Rudy and Terry's bridal party. It was a grand wedding that would pave the way for this young couple in their journey toward greater wealth and prosperity. Rudy was handsome and debonair and Terry was a tall, beautiful blonde dressed in an elegant bridal gown. Of course Tony Migliaro coifed Terry's hair, and every strand was elegantly combed. Her charming smile, combined with an engaging personality, completed the picture of the perfect Hollywood couple.

Apart from Clayton, who was still too young for girlfriends, much less a spouse, Barbara was the last Martorella to marry. Barbara met Pete at a family dinner hosted by Delores Migliaro at the Migliaro household. It was love at first sight. Marco Migliaro had married Ann Dalton, the sister of Florence Dalton, and Florence was Pete's mother. Peter Charles Donnelly (Pete), a son of a long-standing Irish family from Sheepshead Bay, had served in the Marine Corps throughout the four-year campaign in the Pacific. Along the way he won himself the Purple Heart along with numerous medals for bravery and heroism. He was the real deal. During one of many battle engagements, Pete sustained severe combat injuries, and in one instance word came home to his dear mother that he was missing in action. Pete, alongside his stranded platoon, was able to camouflage himself in an underground tunnel inside a small Japanese-held village until Marine reinforcements were able to retake this territory.

The wedding took place at Gargiulo's Restaurant and Catering Hall, in the heart of Coney Island, and in the neighborhood where many of the Martorella clan still lived. Barbara and Pete were a beautiful couple. Wedding catering was new for the Gargiulo family, but the affair had a first-class look and feel. Frank Sr. pulled out all the stops to insure that a wonderful time was had by all. The wedding also marked a rare moment when all the members of the Martorella, Vallefuoco, and Migliaro families put their differences behind them and attended a beautiful event with pleasure. The Daltons and the Donnellys were also in full attendance. Many of Frank Sr.'s political friends and colleagues attended the wedding as well.

The five-piece band at Barbara's wedding was not quite as large as the house band at the Riviera, but the musicianship was just as good. There was no shortage of Irish jigs and Italian tarantellas to ease everyone into a dancing mood.

At last, with the exception of Clayton, Frank Sr.'s youngest child, all the Martorella children were signed, sealed, and delivered in marriage. Frank could now walk with his hands behind his back while smoking a Havana cigar in a brief moment of happiness and tranquility. His job as father and family patriarch was nearly completed. Once again, though, Lilly was not in attendance. She was in no mood to be seen in public.

Chapter Thirty-Two

The house on 628 Avenue V had suddenly become a quiet sanctuary. Gus and Louise moved out of the basement apartment and into their first house on Haring Street, around the corner from Sal and Jeanne. Patricia, Frankie, and their youngest, Joanie, were all born in the basement apartment. The timing was perfect; Barbara and Pete, the newlyweds, moved right into the space vacated by Gus and Louise, and they promptly began their family.

A brand new black-and-white television was the latest addition to the household on Avenue V. With six Martorella children married, only Frank Sr., Lilly, and Clayton were left occupying the first floor of the house. Most evenings they found themselves in front of the TV. Lilly sat in her favorite floral decorative chair at the far side of the living room. Frank Sr. sat on the porch, settled into his very soft and comfortable easy chair. Clayton generally occupied the long couch next to Lilly. The TV was suitably placed in the southwest corner of the living room, ideally located so that all three could watch television at the same time.

Clayton was ten years old when he received a brand new Schwinn Black Panther bicycle at Christmas. It was complete with a red horn box beneath the center bar, chrome fenders over rather thick tires, and a bullnose shock absorber at the front just below the center of the handlebar. He rode his bike everywhere in the neighborhood. It gave him a strong sense of freedom and independence. In addition to playing baseball around the corner in "The Lot," Clayton could roam over to the Mellett Playground between 13th and 14th Streets on Avenue V or head up East 7th Street to play with other friends. Steven Termini (Fat Stevee) and Bobby Gelfat were his closest friends and would often travel with him in search of new adventures.

Clayton's first real job began with neighborhood deliveries of the Brooklyn Eagle newspaper. He worked out of the East 9th Street branch located between Avenues U and T, and, in a relatively short period of time, Clayton was promoted to stationmaster. After school, he delivered papers to his customers daily; in addition to completing his own route, he often picked up one or two other newspaper routes, replacing the regular paperboy whenever he called in sick. Clayton received an extra fifty cents per covered route.

Clayton's customers received excellent service and were always treated kindly. At the end of each week, usually on Saturday, Clayton collected the money for the past week's delivery, and usually received a rather nice tip. As a result, for the first time he had real money in his pockets and could do as he liked. At Thanksgiving the following year, Clayton brought in the most new customers in a contest that rewarded him with two turkeys. With a great deal of pride, Clayton presented, to each of his two sisters, one freshly killed turkey.

By now, Barbara and Pete were comfortably lodged in the Martorella basement apartment and Anita and Jimmy were settled in their semi-attached, stucco-built home on East 7th Street, just a short half-block walk from the house on Avenue V. There were many mornings when Barbara would join Anita, each of them pushing their own baby carriage with a newborn resting quietly inside, as they made their way toward Avenue U for some light shopping. Barbara's firstborn was a girl, whom she named Patricia, and Anita's little boy was named John. This was a very happy moment in time for Clayton's two wonderful sisters.

Rudy and Terry settled into an apartment in a new building on Kings Highway, close to Ocean Avenue. A year later John, their firstborn, arrived.

Rudy and his business partners were poised to make their big move, taking the Veterans Bus Corporation, with its fleet of ten buses, to Floral Park, Long Island. By a stroke of luck, hard work, and perhaps some political maneuvering, Rudy and his partners won the bid to service the Sewanhaka School District. At first, the bus count grew to fifteen. Over the next few years, though, the school district expanded to include New Hyde Park, Elmont, and Floral Park Memorial High Schools, as well as two junior highs and a couple of parochial schools, quickly bringing the bus count up to 45. It took some creative financing and help from General Motors to facilitate the growth from fifteen to 45 buses and to properly meet the needs of the expanded school district. Rudy and his partners decided to change the name of their business from Veterans Bus Corporation to the Long Island Bus Company. A nearby coal depot, set alongside railroad tracks, had been closed and converted into empty space, and this empty tract of land provided enough parking space to accommodate the company's entire fleet of buses, along with a maintenance and repair shop.

Shortly after Long Island Bus Company began operating, Rudy and Terry bought their first house in Bellmore, Long Island. Once settled into their new home, Terry gave birth to their second child, Joy, a lovely little girl. Rudy and Terry were the first among the young Martorella families to purchase a home on Long Island.

Over the next couple of years the bus business would prove to be quite profitable, and Rudy and Terry were able to leapfrog from Bellmore to Dix Hills in Huntington, Long Island. This was a more posh neighborhood. The house was newly constructed to mark this rising young family's entry into an upper-middle-class community. The two-story colonial house was located on two acres of terraced land and came with an in-ground swimming pool encased by a spacious concrete-and-wood deck and a private cabana.

Shortly after Rudy and Terry moved into their new home, Sal and Jeanne were invited to visit with them for a weekend. The fresh clean air, the beautiful shrubs, the open airy look of each room inside the house and, of course, the in-ground swimming pool was simply breathtaking to the visitors. Jeanne insisted that Sal meet with a local real estate agent to find them a house in the same neighborhood. It happened immediately. A recently built ranch-style home on an acre of land was located literally around the corner from Rudy and Terry. It was a done deal. They would all be neighbors for many years thereafter. Sal would begin his daily trip from Dix Hills, Long Island, to the Kings County Supreme Courthouse in Brooklyn.

Suddenly Lilly felt somewhat disappointed and abandoned as two of her sons were far away. While Frank Jr. and Gus were still living in Brooklyn, they were preoccupied with families of their own and would only come by occasionally to visit with their mother on Avenue V. Lilly was in some ways comforted by having her two daughters close by, but Barbara and Pete, with their three beautiful children and a fourth one on the way, would soon move on to Long Island as well. Lilly took solace in the fact that she could always see Anita's house from her front porch window. To Lilly, it meant that at least one of her children would be there to look out for her in her old age.

Chapter Thirty-Three

Clayton continued to skip along through life. During his youthful years, Clayton found himself engaged in a variety of activities, weaving into and out of the lives of his two sisters and his own parents. He was on call to give a helping hand to his sisters and his parents when needed. He babysat for Barbara and Pete when they needed to go shopping for food, or when they, on occasion, went to the movies at the Mayfair Theatre on Avenue U. In the early years of their marriage, in order to save some money, Jimmy would take on various household projects. On one such occasion, Clayton assisted Jimmy in making brand new kitchen cabinets.

Barbara served as the homemaker in her family, and her specialty was Irish stew. To a rich tomatoey cooked sauce, she added fresh garden peas, bitesize white potatoes, onions, and tender cut pieces of beef, all prepared to the peak of perfection. For Anita, who was likewise the homemaker of her household, a Mediterranean style of cuisine was more to her taste, including homemade manicotti that simply melted in your mouth with every bite. Added to that tasty morsel were cut pieces of baked chicken, surrounded by braised potatoes, garnished with cut broccoli rabe in olive oil, and sprinkled with just a pinch of parsley, salt, and pepper. Frank Sr., Lilly, and Clayton were among the beneficiaries of these tasty meals.

Clayton played and followed baseball with a youthful passion. He joined the altar boys of Our Lady of Grace Church just to play baseball with them. Father Rosario J. LoGotto was the priest in charge of the altar boys. Before becoming a priest, he was an exceptional baseball player and played on a triple-A team, connected to the major league Detroit Tigers. Every Friday afternoon this dedicated priest would "fungo" fly balls to some 30 eager altar boys in an adjoining lot next to the church. New York had the special privilege of hosting three major league baseball teams, the Dodgers, Giants, and Yankees. The guys at Bill's Candy Store on Neck Road would go back and forth arguing whether Duke Snider, Willie Mays, or Mickey Mantle was the best center fielder in all of baseball. Of course if one was from some other major baseball city, names such as Stan Musial, Ted Williams, or Hank Aaron could be added to the list of immortal baseball players.

Clayton was glued to the television screen, watching one baseball game after another. His favorite player was Roy Campanella, catcher for the Brooklyn Dodgers. As a young boy, Clayton played the catcher position on his church team. Frank Sr. was a Yankee fan and often joined his son in watching a ballgame on evening television. For Frank Sr., however, viewing baseball on television took second place to watching Westerns on Channel Thirteen or a good detective series, such as *Dragnet*, on Channel Two. Lilly preferred the *Ed Sullivan Show* on Sunday nights at eight o'clock. On Saturday nights, all three viewers filled the living room with laughter as they witnessed the comic antics of Sid Caesar and Imogene Coca's popular *Your Show of Shows* comedy hour and a half. It was a great time for American popular entertainment, and a lovely and relaxing time for the Martorellas who remained at 628 Avenue V.

Chapter Thirty-Four

Sooner than anyone in the family expected, time seemed to be running out for Frank Sr. Diabetes was catching up with him, and in 1957 he was forced to take early retirement from the Sanitation Department. It was difficult for Frank to go from leading a very active life, filled with diverse people and challenging situations, to an almost completely sedentary existence. Yes, he still had his gardening to fall back on. Sometimes one of the boys would bring him out to Long Island for a weekend to help with their gardening needs. Barbara and Pete, with their lovely family of four children, would, from time to time, invite either Frank Sr. or Lilly separately for a week at a time to their house in Wantagh to help with their gardening chores or just to give them a chance to breathe some country air. For some reason, Lilly took a liking to Barbara's husband Pete. Perhaps it was his Irish wit and charming smile or his twinkly eyes that caught her attention.

In 1959, as Clayton was about to graduate from Abraham Lincoln High School, his father became seriously ill. His general health was rapidly declining and he was living with a great deal of pain. Frank Sr. entered Long Island College Hospital for treatment, but shortly thereafter he experienced a painful death from uremic poisoning due to kidney failure. He had suddenly and unceremoniously come to the end of his life; and, given the abruptness of his father's death, Clayton acutely felt the uncertainty of sudden loss. In his later teenage years, Clayton began to distance himself from his father's sphere of influence, perhaps as a means of coping. With the passing of the ensuing years, Clayton came to truly regret not spending more time with his father. Nine years later, Clayton would find a second father and mentor in Hans Geering, his father-in-law and father to his lovely and loving wife, Danielle.

For the moment, Lilly and Clayton would carry on together at 628 Avenue V for several more years. It was a quiet time for the older generation and a moment just before the start of an active time for Clayton. It's a good time, perhaps, to place a period or ellipsis on the Martorella family history before continuing with Clayton's story, a story that, for now, can wait for another day.

Interlude

The Roaring Twenties and the Depressive Thirties witnessed the nation's Melting Pot at full steam; the shining star of Americana continued to dim to a small glow as Old Glory marched off into World War II.

The garden varieties of the Mob captured the daily newspaper headlines across the country. The Italian, Irish, Jewish, Dutch, and other mafias laid claim to their own piece of the bootlegging and gambling turf. A breach of territory by any aggressive member of the family generally resulted in a shootout. Funny money flowed from the tenement streets of New York City on up to the pockets of Wall Street financiers, underground businesses, crooked politicians, judges, and anyone else who had their hand in the till. The Gravesend–Sheepshead Bay–Coney Island neighborhood of Brooklyn staked out its own fair share of funny money as well.

Through all of this madness and chaos, Frank Sr. and Lilly, for all of their faults, managed to bring into this world and foster seven wonderful, upstanding children. The legacy of Frank Sr. and Lilly continues through the children of their children. Clayton's eighteen nephews and nieces are full-grown and have made notable contributions to their own families and to the America of today. Thanks to Frank and Lilly, the farmer and the beauty queen, new buds from their original tree continue to grow and flourish as ever more beautiful flowers.

Frank Martorella Sr.

Lilly Martorella

Above: Carmela and Salvatore Martorella Sr.

Below: Christina Vallefuoco, c. 1920

Above: Martorella family farm, c. 1912. Back row: white horse, Frank, Carmela, Salvatore, neighbors. Front row: two of Frank's younger brothers

Below: Entire Martorella family at an event held at the Riviera, possibly for Frank's promotion to Brooklyn borough superintendent, 1935

Sal and Gus in front of the house at 628 Ave. V, 1942

Louise, Patricia, and Gus, 1946

Frank Jr., Rudy, and Anita with dancing partners, 1947 Halloween party

Patricia and Clayton, with Lilly's favorite living room chair, 1949

Above: Sal and Jeanne at the entrance to the Riviera, 1950

Below: Martorella family at Anita's wedding, Jan. 20, 1952. Back row: Rudy and Terry, Mary (Terry's mother), Sal. Front row: Ann and Frank Jr., Clayton, Louise and Gus, Frank Sr.

Above: Anita and Barbara at Anita's wedding, Jan. 20, 1952

Below: Anita and Jimmy, bride and groom

Anita and Jimmy, bride and groom, at the Riviera, Jan. 20, 1952

Above and below: P.S. 153 at 1970 Homecrest Ave.,
Clayton's elementary school

Above: Anita and Jimmy's house on E. 7th St. between Ave. U and V

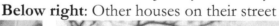

Below left: Anita and Jimmy's driveway
Below right: Other houses on their street

Above: The Tolkin and Weinberg house on Avenue V

Below: The apartment building across from 628 Avenue V

Above: Dr. Rosenblatt's house, with double garage, on Avenue V

Below: Left side of Ocean Parkway, facing Neck Road from Avenue V

Above: Formerly, Weber's corner grocery store

Below: Formerly, Bill's Candy Store, left of the white doorway entrance

628 Avenue V

Above: Martorella family farmhouse, E. 7th St. between Ave. Y and Z

Below: Southerly view of Ocean Parkway from Ave. V.
What was once a horse bridle path has given way to a sitting area

Above: Our Lady of Grace Church, E. 4th St. and Ave. W

Below: Our Lady of Grace Church entryway

Above: Corner of Stryker Court and Stryker Street

Below: As above; home to much of the Vallefuoco family since 1913

Above and below: Various views of Stryker Court and Stryker Street

Above and below: Abraham Lincoln HS, West Ave. and Ocean Parkway, where all Martorella kids attended, except for Frank Jr. (Brooklyn Tech)

Above: Ocean Parkway leading into Surf Ave., Coney Island

Below: Nathan's Famous, on the corner of Stillwell Ave. and Surf Ave.

The famous Stillwell Terminal, where four train lines complete their routes. In 2019 it will be 100 years old

Clayton Martorello

Above and below: Riviera caterers, established 1920 on Stillwell Ave., two blocks north of Nathan's Famous

Above and below: Our Lady of Solace, family church in Coney Island

ST. GILES FOUNDATION
New York, NY

The St. Giles Story: Over a Century of Service to Children

The House of St. Giles the Cripple was founded in 1891 by Sister Sarah, an Episcopalian nun.
Located in Brooklyn, it was one of the country's first hospitals to concentrate on orthopaedic care and treatment for children. From its earliest days, St. Giles was concerned not only with the hospitalization and surgical treatment of children but also with their rehabilitation and education while in the care of the hospital 97 sometimes for extended periods due to polio and cerebral palsy.

After several moves to larger quarters, in 1916 St. Giles opened a new hospital at 1346 President Street and the corner of Brooklyn Avenue. Coincidentally, that was the year of the great polio epidemic, and the new facility quickly filled to its capacity of 100 patients. A separate convalescent home, "St. Giles in the Fields," had been built in 1903 at Garden City, Long Island, and it too filled to capacity.

From the 1920's through the mid-1950's, polio was the most dreaded childhood disease and one of the most difficult to treat. Victims of polio required more individual attention than all other St. Giles orthopaedic patients combined. For many of those years, St. Giles also ran the second largest outpatient clinic among all of the children's orthopaedic hospitals in America.

In 1954, Salk vaccine was discovered, followed by Sabin oral polio antitoxin in 1960. This led to an almost immediate decline in polio cases and a steady falloff in the patient count at St. Giles. As polio became less and less prevalent, the need for our Long Island convalescent home diminished and it was sold in 1973.

After 1975, the polio patient population in the U.S. became so small that the rated capacity of St. Giles Hospital was lowered considerably. Concurrently, the hospital faced new capital outlays ordered by the New York State Department of Health, a national trend away from small, specialized hospitals, and steadily rising operating losses. After careful analysis and consultation, the decision was made to close the hospital and transform St. Giles into a charitable foundation. This was done in 1978.

As a foundation, St. Giles has retained its original mission of serving disabled children while it has simultaneously expanded its reach and effectiveness over a far broader spectrum of juvenile diseases and disabilities than ever before.

St. Giles Hospital, where a young Clayton spent a few months recovering from a severe case of rickets

Part Three

Alone and On My Own

Chapter Thirty-Five

Mama (Lilly) passed away on March 16, 1967, two days after my twenty-sixth birthday. If Mama had passed any time before my twenty-sixth birthday, I would have had to spend two years in the army. At that time in my life, I was set on a different trajectory. But for the moment, let's backtrack a few years, to 1958.

It was during the springtime semester at Abraham Lincoln High School when my neighborhood friend Arny M. convinced me that I should try out for the football team. He was one year older than me and entering his senior year the following fall. He had been on the team for a year. He was a short outside defensive linebacker and loved the hitting and tackling aspects of the game. For me it was a different story. As a young boy I enjoyed the free flow of the games that were played on Avenue V or East 7th Street. It was two-hand touch, three players on each side attempting to run a successful pattern to the opposing goalpost and a touchdown. It was a game of head fakes, quick feet, and beautifully completed passes. We could play for hours, sometimes into the evening under the street lights. My passing game was often spot-on.

I played baseball the same way. It was the skill and beauty of the game that excited every fiber of my being. For me, competition was always a secondary consideration. Sure, it was nice to win, but making a great catch, hitting the ball out of the ballpark, or getting a clean hit is what gave me that sudden thrill of the moment. Variations of baseball included punchball, which involved hitting a pink rubber ball (called a "Pennsy Pinky") with a clenched fist and smacking the ball with the bony part of the four fingers, just above the finger nails; stickball or three-sewer ball, which utilized a pitcher, a catcher, an outfielder, and, of course, a batter, again played with a Pennsy Pinky rubber ball and a stickball bat; and softball, which required nine players on each side and was usually played on a concrete surface, inside a neighborhood ballpark or schoolyard.

In 1958 Coach Vince Gargano had a seasoned football team heading into the fall semester. In the springtime or the off-season, he was always looking for younger talented players to augment the ranks of his varsity unit and to build a foundation for future teams. I was one of about seven players competing for the quarterback position. Arny convinced me that, since I had a pretty good passing arm, I should try out for the team. When I witnessed a six-foot-six Jack Boyle, the assistant coach, throw a football nearly the length of a football field, I was in awe, and I said to myself, "I'll give it a go."

Going into Hell Week, during the last ten days of August and two weeks from the start of the next football season, we were one hundred strong, trying out for 33 positions. Once again, I was against stiff competition, trying out for the quarterback position. Other than playing baseball in a summer league during the late spring and early summer—and, I might add, at a rather low-key level—getting into the fray of this heightened competition was very new but challenging to me. Suddenly, I felt that I wanted to be one of the 33 players to avoid the cut and make the football team.

I was not a contact football player. I had seen too many broken arms and legs while growing up around sportsmen and did not wish to be included among those statistics. I enjoyed football for the sport itself, minus the contact. At the time, high school players played both offense and defense. The players who really loved contact gravitated toward defense. I stuck to quarterbacking. I had quick hands and an ability to call plays off of a T-formation. Within a 30-yard range, I could hit my receivers with a good degree of accuracy. Heading into the 1958 football season, I was the third-string quarterback, responsible for calling plays with the third-string unit. They were mostly players who would be coming back the following year, barring injuries. Lincoln's was a seasoned team of mostly high school seniors who had been coached by Vince Gargano over the previous three years.

All the hard work during the summer, in addition to surviving Hell Week, was well worth the effort as we stormed out of the clubhouse, through the near end goal post, and onto Lincoln Field, in front of five thousand cheering fans. I had that warm feeling of ecstasy filling my very being as we uniformly drilled through our warm-up exercises and made our way to the sidelines, just before the start of the game. That game was the coming-out party for head coach Vince Gargano and assistant coach John Boyle. Prior to the tenure of that coaching duo, Lincoln had already built a reputation for a strong football team under Gargano's predecessor, Coach Kahan.

At the time, we were a team of mostly Italian and Jewish players, with a sprinkling of other ethnic athletes who grew up in the general area of Gravesend. Names such as Della Pietro, Parisi, Freed, Steinberg, Goldberg, the Muccillo brothers, and O'Keefe filled the ranks of the 1958 Lincoln High football team. That group of wonderful athletes went on to win the city's Public Schools Athletic League (PSAL) football championship, having an undefeated season and giving up only two touchdowns to all the opposing teams. The high point came in the first or second Saturday in October. On a snow-covered field that fall day, Lincoln triumphed over a perennial Brooklyn Tech football powerhouse by a score of 33 to 0. I even had a chance to run a few plays with the third-string unit during the fourth quarter, when the game was out of reach for the opposition. I believe that year, nine of the mostly senior Lincoln players made the All-City football team.

The following year was a time for rebuilding the football team. I, along with two younger quarterbacks, worked with the new young crop of players to maintain a credible team. However, we ended the season with a two and five record. In all the games, the scores were close and we were competitive. The Madison game was the one exception. That was the first city high school game to be televised, and Marty Glickman, the well-known New York Giants football radio announcer, called the game. In earlier years, Marty was a three-letter man from Madison High. I had the game of my life as we triumphed over Madison 24 to 0. As I recall, I believe that I even threw a touchdown pass during that game.

Well beyond the game itself, the euphoria of the moment gave me confidence in myself to go on with my life, wherever my path would take me. I was a late bloomer, having grown about three inches between my junior and senior years of high school, ultimately ending up measuring five feet nine inches tall. Soon after the football season had ended, I began working at the Riviera, my aunt's catering hall, on weekends. Upon graduation, I thought it was time to find a steady job and continue going to school at night, perhaps at City College. But that endeavor was short-lived.

After my father's death, I suddenly realized that I had spent very little quality time with him. I had become so caught up with the emotions of being a teenager and did not realize how much he had wished to share in my coming of age. My sister Anita, who was already married and settled into her family life, had suggested, at the urging of my father, that I continue my education after high school. On several occasions, she had whispered to me that Dad would buy me a car if I started college.

But it was not to be. Not long after I graduated from Lincoln High School, my father passed away. At that moment in my life I felt deep remorse. I sadly realized that my father would have liked to be closer to me, especially during his final days on earth. My mother was living in her own little world. Amidst all her personal conflicts, she too felt some remorse over the loss of her husband. At that point in my life I just couldn't imagine myself in my father's shoes. It was a lack of compassion that I truly regret.

After my father's death, Mama and I occupied seven rooms in the large house on Avenue V. Mrs. Lerner was the only one living upstairs, having recently lost her husband, and with all her children fully grown and out of the house as well. My sister Barbara and her husband Pete had recently purchased a detached gingerbread house in Wantagh, Long Island, leaving the basement apartment empty. With two girls, a boy, and a forth child on the way, the Donnellys required a larger domicile. For quite some time after my sister Barbara moved to Wantagh, the basement apartment remained empty.

Some of my closer friends were on the move. Edward Kwasnewski was finishing up his studies at City College and would eventually settle for a job with the US Customs Service. Fat Stevee became a full-time butcher and would eventually buy his uncle's butcher shop in Long Island City. Bobby Gelfat would hook up with my high school football friend Frankie Hunt and join the Marines, signing up for a six-month stint of basic training, with a required five-year reserve obligation. Their choice of doing the extended reserve duty took the place of having to fulfill a two-year full-time military obligation. It was 1960 and America was engaged in a cold war with Russia. There had also recently been a crisis brewing with Lebanon, in the Middle East. Fortunately, that crisis and intervention was short-lived, and no further US military action was ultimately necessary.

I was thinking of joining the Marines along with my two buddies, but when Dad passed away I became the only child living with my mother, which exempted me from required military service. So I changed my mind about joining the Marines. After two months of job hunting, I found an entry-level position at the Bankers Trust Company on 14 Wall Street. I also took the initiative of registering for two evening business classes at CUNY's Baruch School of Business.

Though I had spent a few raucous evenings in the Big Apple during my late teenage years, viewing Manhattan as a working adult was a truly new experience for me. The financial canyons of Wall Street, shadowed by the massive concrete and grey-stoned buildings, felt like the columned tombs of ancient Egypt. However, the daily eight a.m. sea of humanity entering the city each morning filled this graveyard with a lively spirit of renewal. Initially, at least, the hustle and bustle of Manhattan instilled new life into my young bones.

I went through the customary ritual of being interviewed, accepted into the ranks of new employees at a large, iconic institution, and receiving an orientation on how I could advance in the banking business, starting from the ground up. Over time, with continued schooling, I could advance up the banking ladder in pursuit of a successful business career. Just like that, I was in, hook, line, and sinker.

I received the formal office tour during the first month of my employment. An office manager guided me through the bank's back rooms. It started with a look at the bank's adding machines, then moved on to the rows of filing cabinets that maintained an accurate and orderly recordkeeping system, and concluded with the correspondent desks, accompanied by the dedicated typing pool. I was charged up and ready for action, with the thought that someday I could become a senior bank executive.

I began my career in the auditing group and was initially deposited into the bank's basement. My team of initiates was assigned the task of counting and tabulating securities. In effect, we were counting someone else's money. There didn't seem to be any end to that endeavor. After two months of counting, tracking, and logging those endless waves of securities, boredom began to set in to the core of my very being.

Attending night school wasn't any better. After working eight hours during the day, attending classes for three more hours twice a week seemed a bit much. There I was listening to two middle-aged part-time male instructors, from the daytime corporate world, discussing the finer points and subtleties in reading balance sheets and income statements. To me, it was like learning a foreign language from some other planet. The other subject was marketing, the principles of selling widgets and ratchets in the pursuit of profitability to fill the coffers of some large company. Usually, halfway through the second class of the evening, at about nine thirty, I had to struggle with all my might just to keep my eyes open. I realized pretty quickly that I was ready to move on.

With barely three months under my belt, I gave notice to the powers that be that I was leaving the banking business. Coincidentally, on the final day of my employment, while I was taking lunch in the bank's crowded employee cafeteria, a pretty-looking young gal asked if she could sit across from me. I was alone with only my thoughts of what to do next with my life, when that lovely distraction came upon me. She was perhaps five foot two, on the short side, with straight, thin-cropped blond hair and a sweet smile to complete that lovely portrait. Without even a thought, I nodded. We sat at a table for two, in a corner of the crowded cafeteria.

She proceeded to unwrap her sandwich from a wax paper bag and to bite in while sort of staring into space. As I was sipping my own bowl of house-prepared vegetable soup, I summoned up enough courage to ask, "A penny for your thoughts?" She smiled and said, "Just daydreaming, not really thinking of anything." As it turned out, that also happened to be her last day at the bank. She had grown tired of typing all day long with not much else to do.

During our conversation, she said that she lived in the Bronx with her mother and father in a two-bedroom apartment. As we continued to play down our brief banking experience at Bankers Trust, we began, almost without realizing it, to gently touch each other's heartstrings. Without even a thought, I suddenly asked if I could see her home. She gave me a yes, and we agreed to meet each other after work, at the front entrance of the bank.

Having been caught up in the moment, neither she nor I thought to exchange names. It was only later that evening I learned her name, Catherine. It was the beginning of December, when the days grow shorter and the nights stretch out as the bright sun gives way to the grey of nightfall. Catherine lived just above Tremont Avenue on the Bronx's west side.

Together, we walked up four flights of stairs and into a two-bedroom apartment where she lived with her parents, recent arrivals from Scotland. I was warmly welcomed to stay for supper, which turned out to be a wonderful, flavorful meat-and-potato stew prepared by her mother.

After supper, Catherine gently led me to her bedroom, where

we could share a private moment. Her parents quietly settled into the living room to catch the evening news, followed by their favorite TV program. At dinnertime, I had learned that her father worked daytime hours at the central branch of the US Post Office in Manhattan. After going through rough times, barely scratching out a living during and after the wartime years, Catherine's parents had moved from Scotland to America in search of a new and more secure life.

The conversation between Catherine and me skirted around our growing attraction for each other, leading to an embrace and a bit of kissing. It wasn't the kind of culmination the movies and television might have led young people to imagine, of immediate ecstasy requiring a brisk camera pan to a silken window shade. No, it was more of a tender embrace between two young people finding a measure of love for one another at a special moment in time.

I left the warm household at about eleven p.m. I carried with me a deep affection for that lovely girl, who simply walked into my life on our last day at the bank. Perhaps it was the long distance between the Bronx and Brooklyn by train, or that I was young and wrapped up in my nineteen-year-old concerns and anxieties, but somehow I never called Catherine back for a date.

Shortly after my departure from Bankers Trust, I decided to drop my classes at CUNY. At that time in my young life I did not have the patience for routine work and school. I wanted something that was more adventurous and challenging to me. Ever since I'd received my Schwinn Black Panther bicycle at age ten, I yearned to see the wider world beyond Nat and Abe's Deli, Kornfeld's Bakery, Dominic's Grocery Store, Weber's Neck Road corner grocery, and Bill's Candy Store—as welcoming and delectable as those neighborhood landmarks were. A college education, I decided, could go on the back burner, while I pursued the more animated life out on the streets.

Chapter Thirty-Six

The Mayfair Movie Theatre, on Coney Island Avenue and Avenue U, was an ostentatious building for mid-20th-century Brooklyn, giving neighborhood folks a feeling of opulence and a sense of what it was like to have material wealth. In my teenage years I sometimes found myself sitting in the balcony of the theater, next to a girlfriend, kissing, touching, nothing serious, while watching a favorite Lana Turner movie. It was sheer nirvana. Of course, following such entertainments, the manners and mores of the time called for a weekend confession and Sunday communion, posthaste.

Heading into my late teens and early twenties, I discovered Bernie's Diner on Coney Island Avenue, between Avenues U and V, just around the corner from the Mayfair Theatre. It was the perfect place to chill out after a good movie, or just about any time of the day or night. I enjoyed eating great short order food cooked on the stove top grill and served at the comfortable booths, which included coin-operated popular music selections at each table. The buzz of lively conversations, from the counter to the booth, added to the local ambience. From time to time, one could even wager a bet on a major boxing match or some other sporting event. Most of the patrons kind of knew each other. Even the short order chefs engaged in conversation with the dining crowd. And sometimes the conversation was somewhat brisk and colorful.

Kings Highway, between Ocean Parkway and East 16th Street, was another neighborhood hot spot. One could find just about anything along that neighborhood strip. There was another fancy movie theater, the Jewel Theatre, on Kings Highway between East 7th and 8th Streets. At Neil's Clothiers, with enough cash one could measure up for tailor-made suits. And Dubrow's Cafeteria, on Kings Highway at the corner of East 16th Street, was the main stop along that golden avenue. Extra-large, with no shortage of excellent delicatessen cuisine, Dubrow's was Kings Highway's cornerstone, and became a go-to stop for presidential and gubernatorial campaigns, sports press conferences, and even TV and film settings.

Among the endless conversations that took place at Dubrow's, I came upon an old friend from high school, Georgie G. When I told Georgie about recently becoming unemployed, he suggested that I call on the Publishers Guild, on East 23rd Street in Manhattan. Georgie G wore the latest tweeds, with shirt and tie to match. He said I could make a lot of money selling magazines, and, given his outfit, I believed him. He treated me to a first-class pastrami sandwich, coffee, and a delicious slice of chocolate layer cake. Having recently parted company with Bankers Trust and finding George seemingly rolling in dough, I decided to give it a go.

The following Monday morning I dressed up in my finest Klein's department store–bought suit from my brief banking days, and hopped onto the Brighton Beach Line train to Manhattan. I said to myself, "Could this be my lucky day?" I entered a sixteen-story Gothic-style slender building, located at the middle of East 23rd Street, between Park and Madison Avenues. There was a crowded café located at the street level of that Arcadian building. I took the elevator to the ninth-floor headquarters of the Publishers

Guild. The Guild occupied the entire floor: the large front room was for the salesmen; order processing, payroll, and additional clerical staff were efficiently located behind the front offices; and there were two extended offices which were occupied by the principle owners, Sam and Saul Kaplan.

I was warmly greeted on arrival by Jacques Darcel, the flying Frenchman. He wore a tweed suit with a light brown cashmere scarf loosely wrapped around a fashionable shirt and tie. Without further ado, he said, "Let's get a cup of coffee downstairs." I suspect that he knew I had arrived for an interview. Upon entering the café, we were immediately surrounded by young, good-looking, well-dressed salesmen. They were mostly Jewish and many were from the old neighborhood in Brooklyn. Georgie was among them and talked a mile a minute with many of the other salesmen. They were a cheerful bunch, full of energy and ready to start a new day in their various territories.

"Where are you from?" "Whadda-you know?" "How-ja-get here?" Quick questions came from these curious enquirers carrying black leather satchels and making ready to hit the streets. They were mostly friendly. One salesman, Jeff, blurted out to Jacques, "Don't whisper sweet nothings in his ears." As if on cue, Jacques then whispered into my ear, "Don't believe a word of what he says. He can sell you the moon." I remained speechless. Taking it all in, I concluded that I was witnessing a one-of-a-kind happening. Jeff blurted out to one of his colleagues, "I'll cover Bellevue tonight." Another salesman, Barry, replied, "I'll head over to the Village today." Again, Jacques leaned closer to me and said, "Let's head back upstairs. I'll show you the ropes."

We ascended back up to the ninth-floor front office and sat down upon one of the soft couches that lined the walls. Behind the couches were shelves and racks of the latest magazine covers which the salesmen availed themselves of in keeping their portfolios of sales props up to date. We settled down on one of the couches and promptly began putting magazine covers into plastic see-through folders. Jacques gave me an order form that included some fifty different magazine titles. They featured the more popular covers, like *Mademoiselle*, *House & Garden*, *Mechanix Illustrated*, *Esquire*, *Sports Illustrated*, and *Field & Stream*. Then he went into one of the back rooms and returned immediately with a handsome black leather bag. He unzipped the bag, revealing a large Webster's Twentieth Century Unabridged Dictionary.

When opened, the bag was laid flat on top of a nearby desk. Jacques began to demonstrate the niceties of owing a brand new Webster's Twentieth Century Unabridged Dictionary. It contained more than two thousand pages of words, etymological listings of words in eight different languages, the latest maps in color, and many other back-end features. What actually sealed the deal, for prospective customers and, frankly, for me as well, was that one could easily lift up the dictionary by as few as ten or twenty pages, at the middle of that massive 8½-by-11-inch hardcover book, without it ever falling apart. The best part of the sale was that the prospective customer could become the proud owner of that jewel of a book free of charge. There was just one stipulation to the offer.

Jacques explained that one need only choose any three out of fifty different popular magazines and subscribe to them one, two, or three years, depending upon which titles were selected. The weekly magazines, such as the popular *Cue*, a television and weekly events magazine, was a one-year subscription. A monthly, such as *Esquire*, might require a subscription of two or three years. Perhaps ten or twelve folders featuring the most popular magazine covers would be neatly tucked into a side pocket of the same bag. Those bright, colorful, suggestive covers enhanced the salability of the offering. The total cost was $39.95, which included shipping and handling. The salesman received a three-dollar deposit with the order, and the customer paid $1.95 upon receipt of his or her free dictionary, which alone appeared to be worth more than the entire order of magazines. The customer received 35 envelopes in which to send in a dollar per week for 35 weeks, to pay off the balance due.

The dictionary was shipped from the Publishers Guild warehouse in Chicago, Illinois. The salesman kept the three-dollar deposit and was entitled to an additional five dollars and fifty cents upon completion of the order. Once several weekly one-dollar payments were made by the customer, the salesman would then receive his commission balance, which came in the form of a weekly check. I couldn't wait to go out to my own territory and start making sales.

For me, the project was an instant success. After my first few sales pitches I realized that I had the gift of gab. As Jacques, my sales mentor, advised, "You have to create the sale." The combination of magazines and the wonderful gift of the dictionary suited my personality to a T. After only a week or so I walked up to the second floor of a small office building in the Bronx, somewhere along Tremont Avenue, into a room filled with several engineers and architects. I introduced myself, gave them a flamboyant pitch, and demonstrated all the benefits of owning this excellent dictionary. Because of that effort, I was rewarded with no less than five cash sales. I left that gold mine of an office with two hundred dollars in my pocket. For the moment, at least, I was in seventh heaven.

I suddenly realized that I could walk into so many different places, pitching to all types of people, young and old, male and female, tall and short, fat and skinny. I had only to find the hot button for each customer and the sale would follow. I set myself the goal of writing at least 25 orders per week. It wouldn't be easy, as I was in the company of hard-driving salesmen and their managers who shared the same goal as me, all striving to become rich and, by extension, reaping the benefits of the good life.

Stuie Bloom was the area manager of the eastern region. He was also the top dog under the Kaplan brothers, the owners of the Publishers Guild. The area managers of the other two regions across the country, central and western, also reported to Stuie. Stewart Bloom (Stuie) was young, about ten years older than me. He was medium build, about five feet ten, good looking, with blond wavy hair to match an engaging smile.

Stuie Bloom was fully in charge of sales production, yet he still took the time to go out to the territory with his immediate crew of three or four sales reps to bring in new business. He led by example. He was well-dressed in suit, shirt, and tie, went skiing on weekends with his beautiful wife and two children, and always projected a successful image. There were other very good-looking, successful managers in the eastern region as well, primarily working in the Long Island and tri-state areas. They included Barry Craig, Bob Falkowitz, and Jeff Bloom (Stuie's younger brother and my immediate supervisor). I aspired to become a manager among that select group and have my own crew of salesmen working under me.

The goal was to make lots of money and to live the good life. Training my own group of salesmen like the other managers would afford me the opportunity to collect an override of no less than a dollar for each order my sales reps generated. Sure enough, within six months I indeed became a manager and began training and retaining my own sales group. I was a part of the pyramid, collecting a monitory override that channeled straight up to the top sales manager. By the end of my first year I had not one, but two crews of salesmen, with nine or ten people working under my guidance. In a relatively short period of time I made enough money to afford new handmade suits from Neil's Clothiers, on Kings Highway. I was twenty years old when I bought my first automobile, a 1961 white, two-door Ford Galaxie with red interior, for which I paid twenty-three hundred, cash.

With my new Ford I could transport my own crew of three or four sales reps into territory beyond the city limits. I discovered that, on occasion, other sales managers were willing to swap their territory with me in efforts to keep our juices flowing and to inject new energy into what otherwise could have become a stale routine endeavor. Before long I developed another team of sales reps, with its own manager reporting to me. For a time, while I might be working in Yonkers or White Plains, my other sales crew might be roaming in and out of buildings in an assigned area of lower Manhattan. I was making money all the time.

Direct selling is probably one of the most difficult forms of promotion. It is always one-on-one with the customer. There was often a great deal of distraction: people in a hurry to return to their job, a supervisor telling me to stop my presentation and leave the premises, and so on. I had to be able to create and close the sale quickly, which was never an easy task. Each week, sales reps were obliged to update their magazine covers, assembling ten or twelve colorful and provocative brochures as samples to entice the customers to select three magazines from a wide list of popular offerings.

I had to push myself to walk in to certain buildings—for example, a hospital. I would gingerly roam around on each floor, stopping here and there, to open my case and pitch my dictionary.

I would take pains to spread out the brochures on a table beside the dictionary. Hopefully a nurse or group of nurse's aides might stop and listen to my sales pitch. One or two might take me up on the offer. When there was interest, I would try to close (make) the sale quickly, yet convincingly.

Sometimes, I would walk away with three or four orders. Often, I would be ushered out of the building by a hospital security officer, coming up empty handed. At that moment, I had to take a deep breath and say to myself, "Oh well, on to the next open door." Selling magazines was not for the faint-hearted, but it was for the person who had the "get up and go" to make the sale and reap the substantial monetary rewards. The monetary goals and social rewards had no ceiling in the world of the Publishers Guild. For me, the new car, the fancy new handmade clothes, parties, dances, and, above all, the beautiful, well-dressed girls, were where it was at.

In my neighborhood, growing up in the 1950s and '60s was rather simple. Bill's Candy Store on Gravesend Neck Road, between East 7th Street and Ocean Parkway, remained our hangout. It was a guy's place. That's not to say that pretty young ladies were not allowed in. On the contrary, once a new fancy apartment building replaced our dirt-filled playing field ("The Lot") sometime in the mid-'50s, one pretty lass after another became a more than welcome sight.

Arguing and disagreement were commonplace happenings at Bill's Candy Store. Baseball player favorites, picking a winner at Aqueduct, sexy women, and so on, were only a few contentious issues from among a much larger list of daily topics. As with many hangouts, that oasis was a place to unwind from the travails of a busy day at work. We engaged in life's simple pleasure of friendly arguments that reflected our own tiny-eyed frosted windows.

My sister Anita and her husband Jimmy lived near Bill's, just one half-block from our house. Mom and I could see Anita's house from our front porch window. Anita shouldered the responsibility of ensuring that Mom and I were properly fed at suppertime. It was somewhat of an imposition unceremoniously put upon my brother-in-law, but he hung in there like a good soldier.

Like so many of the guys who hung out at the candy store, Jimmy was also a tradesman. He worked for the AT&T telephone company. He installed cable boxes and telephone wires, linking houses and apartments to telephone poles outside. Jimmy took a great deal of pride in his work, and he often worked overtime to earn extra income. In addition to looking out for Mom and me, Jimmy had the primary responsibility of taking care of his widowed mother, his wife, and his three growing sons.

For me, peddling the dictionary and selling magazines constituted a momentary period of financial success, but for my brother-in-law it represented a bone of contention. Jimmy took issue with my earning what he coined "easy money." After all, Jimmy did hard labor for his paycheck, and he was a good, steady provider and family man. I would have to say that I was a bit of a distraction to his well-balanced household. But I would add that my presence offered them a small window into an outer world that stretched beyond the local community.

My brother-in-law argued that I was making a quick buck and that my job would not last very long. To Jimmy, it was a flash-in-the-pan moment. I countered that he need not worry, as I was "earning an honest dollar and no bother or burden to his family." Jimmy and I also had different political views. I generally took the side of the less fortunate folk of the world, whereas he tended to believe that the underdogs were, on balance, freeloaders who had little drive or ambition to succeed.

The irony in our political argument was that he was a union employee and I was the entrepreneurial type. Often my sister Anita would side with me, to the annoyance of my brother-in-law. In the end, I usually found a way to calm his nerves by giving up some ground in our argument to regain his friendship and good spirits. After all, I did not wish to bite the hand that fed me. He was, in fact, a good guy and I genuinely liked him. To this day I believe he still treats me as if I am one of his children. At times, when we were on the same end of the social and political spectrum, we shared a few laughs while enjoying a hearty supper and sipping a fine glass of red table wine. No matter what little differences popped up between us, life was good.

Chapter Thirty-Seven

The late 1950s and early '60s saw the emergence and the continuing growth of Latin and rock 'n' roll music and dance. On Friday nights, the Hollywood Terrace in Brooklyn, located on New Utrecht Avenue, was where dancing magic took place. Across the country, the youth of America were swinging and swaying to such exciting rhythms as the mashed potato, the slow dance or foxtrot, the twist, the hully gully, the walk, and other trendy favorites of that era. But it was Latin music that captured the hearts of Brooklynites and others all around town in the Big Apple.

In the southwest corridor of Brooklyn—namely, Gravesend and Borough Park—the mambo and the cha-cha-chá became the dances of choice. Other clubs and hotels throughout the city, such as the Palladium, Taft Hotel, and El Caribe, also started to pick up on the Latin theme. The tastes and preferences at the time boiled down to Bill Haley & His Comets, along with Ben E. King and the Drifters, versus Tito Puente's "Oye Como Va" and the Latin beat. Onto this scene, enter my cousin Vinnie and his two beautiful sisters, Cookie and Toni. While I was making lots of money selling magazines and giving away bibles and dictionaries, my first cousin Vinnie was holding court at Brooklyn's Hollywood Terrace.

I first encountered Vinnie when we worked weekends at the

Riviera catering hall on Stillwell Avenue, in Coney Island. It was during my senior year at Abraham Lincoln High School. Vinnie was a few years older than me. He had recently finished a five-year hitch in the US Navy. On some weekends, before the evening weddings, Vinnie parked cars along the side of, and across the street from, the hall. While a wedding was in progress, Vinnie usually came into the kitchen to assist Uncle Louie with plating meals in between the large Vulcan ovens and the lengthy marble counter.

Both Vinnie and I could have had careers in catering if we had taken up our cousin Andy Zack's offer to send us to catering school. Andy Zack was the only son of Antoinette and Zaccarino, who were the owners of the Riviera. Antoinette was the sister of Sophie, Vinnie's mother, and of Frank, my own father. But catering wasn't in the cards for us; a couple of years after we worked at the Riviera, Vinnie and I found more lucrative means of making a living. At twenty, I was staking out a good living at the Publishers Guild, and Vinnie became involved in various business ventures. During his Navy tenure, Vinnie played baseball for one of their teams. Following his time in the Navy, Vinnie continued to play baseball for a semi-professional team in the Coney Island league. In my youth, I too played baseball in the Parade Ground League, but not at the same level as cousin Vinnie.

Vinnie was a natural ballplayer. He played centerfield, making every catch look easy while patrolling the outfield. He possibly could have become a Major League ballplayer if not for his first loves, the nightlife and beautiful women. He was a genuine matinee idol. Wherever he went the girls seemed to flock to him. On Friday nights, the Hollywood Terrace was where Vinnie held court.

If one could think back to the Golden Age of film, one might compare Vinnie's good looks to those of actor Tyrone Power. Vinnie was five foot nine and nicely built, but not muscular. He possessed olive skin with a five o'clock shadow, black hair, thin but not too thin, and almond-shaped dark brown eyes, encased by dark prominent eyelashes. His eyes along with his sensuous lips smiled at the same moment. Dressed in a fashionable black, almost tuxedo-like suit, white shirt with matching tie, and black wing-tipped shoes, Vinnie came to the Hollywood Terrace to dance and dazzle the fine-looking young ladies.

Friday nights at the Hollywood Terrace featured not one, but two bands. The principle band was Latin. From one week to the next, a leading band of the moment would appear in full force. One week it might be Tito Puente and his big band, the next it could be Machito or Mongo Santamaría and their accompanists. There would also be a second, lesser known but still excellent American band to complement the Latin musicians. A dancing crowd religiously attended the Friday night sessions at the Hollywood Terrace. There was no doubt that cousin Vinnie was the very best dancer among a crowded field of dance connoisseurs.

As soon as Tito swung into his signature mambo beat, Vinnie would glide onto the floor with his partner. Almost from the start he would swing and sway with not only his original partner, but with one or two other fair ladies who would join in, forming a circular dervish pattern. Vinnie was the center of it all, twisting and turning all three beautiful divas at the same time. To coin a phrase, "He was poetry in motion." Often, his two beautiful sisters, Cookie and Toni, joined him on the dance floor.

Cookie, more so than Toni, closely resembled, in charm and good looks, her brother Vinnie. She had the added beauty and grace of a tall and slim model. Her best and most frequent attire was a tight-fitting black dress, falling to slightly above the knees.

The dress was décolleté, sitting just slightly above her breasts. In perhaps two-inch heels, Cookie was a perfect five-foot-seven complement to the handsome Vinnie. Her beautiful, engaging smile, with reddish pink lipstick, twinkly eyes, and coiffed black hair, had the neatly dressed men queuing up for a follow-up dance, in hopes that one of them could gain her favor. Of course, I always felt special when I could slip into a dance with either Cookie or Toni.

In between dances, when the bands changed from Latin to American dance, the bar business flourished. The choice of beverage was usually scotch and soda or rye and ginger. One could naturally request something other than the standard drink, such as a dry martini or a daiquiri, or even some other exotic mixed drink. However, few in attendance would get that carried away. At the Hollywood Terrace in 1962 hard liquor drinks were always the beverage of choice over a bottle of beer or a glass of wine.

Chapter Thirty-Eight

Days and nights seemed to fold into each other seamlessly. On most work days I started out "on territory" in the early morning, and maybe made a quick sale before the sun reached its zenith. A little later I might settle down with a tasty Gristedes sandwich, on the steps below the arch in Washington Square, in Greenwich Village.

On another day, I'd make my sales pitch over and over until my mouth went dry and I had no fuel left in my tank. I sometimes strolled around lower Manhattan, hesitating about whether to enter one building or another. On one such day, with nothing in my pockets and the afternoon growing gloomily greyer, I suddenly decided to call it a day. Out of the blue, a lucky moment arrived like a ray of light entering my very being.

In the 1960s, Greenwich Village was one of the places in lower Manhattan where the day seemed to flow smoothly into night as the good folks, poets, and troubadours moved from the open-air square into the warmth of the many cozy cafés. Art Ford's and the Champagne Gallery come to mind as two hangouts I visited in those days for some psychic relief. But on one such occasion it was the Village Vanguard, at 7th Avenue South and Perry Street, where my wanderings led me. At five o'clock in the afternoon I happened into the Vanguard. My mouth was dry as a bone from pitching my dictionary all day long with nothing to show for my efforts.

At the bar I ordered a scotch and soda, with lots of ice and a lemon peel. I rested my sales kit on the stool next to me. "What's that in your black bag?" a sweet feminine voice called out from behind me. I suddenly turned my head toward the voice and away from the bartender who was serving me my drink. She had flaming red hair, beautiful blue eyes, and a great smile. She wore a sleek, tight, pleated white dress that fell to just below her knees.

It was Meg Myles, a popular jazz and mood singer who was the top bill for that day and the ensuing weekend. She ordered a chilled glass of vin rosé, repeated, "So what's in that bag, sweetie?" and she proceeded to sit next to me. I gently opened my bag and began my sales pitch. The bartender stood quietly for a moment, not quite sure whether to command me to close my bag and leave. I felt a bit skittish as I gently continued giving my sales spiel to this beautiful Venus de Milo. "What do I have to do to get one of these?" she asked. In an instant, I signed her up. She instructed me to send the dictionary to her favorite niece, living in New Jersey, and the magazines to her Brooklyn apartment. She then asked the bartender to give me four ten-dollar bills to seal the deal.

A moment later the actor and comedian Don Adams walked over to our spot, gave Meg a gentle kiss on her cheek, and asked, "What's this all about?" Meg told Don, "You should buy one of these for your kids!" After I delivered a shortened sales pitch, he cut me off and said, "I'll take one too." Both Don and Meg agreed that I should hang around for the eight o'clock show and have supper, compliments of the house.

We sat at the bar for a while longer. They wanted to know where I lived and how I could make a living selling magazines. It was going on seven o'clock when they left to get ready for the eight o'clock set. The bartender said that I could sit at one of the side tables close to the stage and a waitress would come by to take my order.

I looked forward to seeing Meg Myles perform one of her more popular songs, especially her signature piece, "Love for Sale." Don Adams shared equal billing on that particular weekend, although he was the more popular of the two performers, having gained notoriety from his recent comic detective television series, *Get Smart*. I, of course, felt quite privileged to sit there as their honored guest at the Village Vanguard.

And my day was not yet over. No sooner had Don finished his opening line when a jetsetter tapped me on the shoulder and asked if she could join me. She had a clean yet frumpy look about her. She wore a loosely fitted flowery dress that fell down to about three inches above her ankles. Her blondish hair, with some dull grey streaks mixed in, streamed down to slightly below her pronounced bust, sans bra. She had a pretty face: clear white skin, steel grey eyes, and a friendly smile. Along with the audience, which had filled the room by the time Don Adams was halfway through his shtick, we two continued to laugh and chatter.

Lucinda was her name. Toward the end of the show Lucinda leaned over to me and whispered into my left ear, "Let's blow this place; I have another spot I'd like to hit, the night is just beginning." This sudden request caught me by surprise, yet I said to myself, "Why not?" I asked the waiter for a check, which was for the extra couple of drinks. I paid the tab, leaving him a nice tip for his fine service. I nearly forgot my satchel as we were leaving the café and did a turnabout to collect my livelihood at the table. As I left the café, Lucinda was sitting in the driver's seat of a late 1950s two-door Aston Martin coupe, with the top down. "Hop in killer, we're off to another party!"

We drove from the West Village to an underground club on the Lower East Side. She parked her car nearby and told me to leave my satchel in the trunk. We had to walk down a few steps to enter an expansive basement bar and restaurant. The place was packed full. It was essentially a mixed young crowd of beautiful people, dancing up a storm on a dance floor that surrounded a circular bar. The colorful jukebox was belting out one of the catchier Marvin Gaye swing songs, "How Sweet It Is." As Lucinda clasped my left hand, we were swept toward the bar by some of her spirited friends. Toni, Francine, Tommy, Julie, Lucinda, and I were suddenly engaged in lively conversation, and the drinks kept coming.

"How are you darling?" one asked, and another exclaimed, "Lucinda, where did you find this handsome fellow?" Toni and Francine began swinging and Lucinda took my hand, pulling me onto the dance floor. Life was good, and the crowd was too: colorful, spirited, moving, and, above all, friendly. I felt so immersed with everyone. It was a wonderful feeling. I completely lost all sense of time when Lucinda noticed that I was beginning to feel and look a bit tipsy. She decided that we had better be moving on.

Before I could regain my bearings, we were sitting in her convertible. She asked me where I lived. I replied, "In Brooklyn." I told her my exact address on Avenue V. She said that she lived in Brighton Beach. She added, "Let's get you home!" It was two in the morning as we were cruising south on Ocean Parkway. My eyes closed. When we arrived in front of my house, Lucinda parked the car and shut off the engine. We just sat quietly for a few minutes, then she asked, "Did you have a good time?"

As I came to my senses, I found myself staring into the face of a beautiful free spirit direct from the heavens. It was a special moment for me and I said to Lucinda that I had never been with a more cheerful group of friends. She told me that I was a good sport and that we'd get together again sometime. She leaned over and kissed me on my lips and said, "Get some sleep!" I closed the car door, walked into the house, and never saw her again.

Life is short and times are fleeting.

Chapter Thirty-Nine

I hit the bed with a thud. As I sank into the mattress I began to feel total relief from the spent energy of a full night and day, or was it day and night? I couldn't remember as the lights went out. It was ten or eleven the next morning when I awoke to a voice calling me, "Claynta! Claynta!" It was Mama. "Get up! Get up! Are you okay? Vieni qui, come! I made you some toast." I called back, "I'm coming, Mama." My pajamas were wet with sweat as I slipped out of bed. I scampered into the bathroom to relieve myself and jump into the shower to make a fresh start for a new day.

For a moment, we sat at the kitchen table and said nothing. I looked at her and smiled. I said, "I'm going to start a new life, no more magazines." There was a stoic look on Mama's face when she asked, "What are you going to do now?" I didn't have an answer, but I knew that I had grown tired of pitching magazines every day. With some resignation, Mama suggested that I should be like Gus and Frank, my two married brothers, and get a job in the Fire Department. I responded that I did not want to become a fireman, but that I would do something. I remained in the house all weekend pondering just what I would do next.

The following Monday, I decided to dress up and head into Manhattan to the Publishers Guild. I walked into the office on

23rd Street as if I were about to start a new day "on territory." But instead of heading out I walked into Stuie's office and sat with both Jeff and his older brother. I said simply that I no longer had the desire to continue selling magazines and that I was willing to turn over my two crews of salesmen to Jeff. They spent the next hour trying to convince me to stay on, offering me more territory and more responsibility. But I had already made up my mind to break with selling magazines while I was still ahead of the game.

After two years of success in sales, I handed in my satchel and began a new chapter in my young life. On that same morning, I left the Publishers Guild and headed over to Central Park for some fresh air and to rest my head in the gentle arms of Mother Nature. I couldn't stop thinking while I sat on a bench, watching the birds and the squirrels scamper about. Mothers were wheeling their baby carriages, bikers were biking, and all sorts of people were walking on the winding footpaths heading toward various parts of this wonderful, bustling city called New York.

Several possibilities crossed my mind as I pondered what to do next with my life. Over the previous two years I had earned a lot of money. And, while I had also spent a lot, the frugal side of me had thought to put a few shekels into my bank account. I still had my relatively new Ford Galaxie and I was feeling pretty good. Working for the Publishers Guild had been my first real full-time job, but, at the ripe old age of 21, I was ready to face new challenges and experiences in my life.

While taking a brief pause from full-time work, I could help cover expenses some weekends by waiting tables at my aunt's catering hall, the Riviera, in Coney Island. My cousin Vinnie had, for some reason, stopped working at the Riviera and was, it seemed, engaged in some business in which he was making lots of money. Vinnie had begun driving a new Cadillac Eldorado. My uncle

Louie, assistant chef to my dear aunt at the Riviera, told me that Vinnie had opened up either a beauty salon or a health spa. It was not clear to me exactly where his money came from. But I knew that he was still holding court as a dancer at the Hollywood Terrace and playing baseball locally.

Mom was slowly getting used to my being around the house on a regular basis. Every few days she would give me a shopping list for a few items, written down in red crayon on a brown paper bag. I continued to give my sister Anita ten dollars per week, and occasionally more, to cover my evening meals at her house on East 7th Street. My neighborhood hangouts were still usually Bill's Candy Store and Bernie's Diner, where I could always find some local conversation, day or night, among kindred spirits.

Emilio's grocery and delicatessen was located between Avenue V and Neck Road, a stone's throw from my house. It was a family store with upstairs living quarters for Emilio and his four children, two boys and two girls. Unbeknownst to me, Emilio lost his wife while his four children were still young. Emilio (Milio) had many talents. His deli was open every day from dawn to dusk, and he made the greatest hero sandwiches.

Nicky was the eldest of Milio's four children. He was in his mid-twenties and he positioned himself as his father's right-hand man. He was tall, rather stern-looking, and was responsible for counting the hard-earned pennies from the grocery business. Angelina, two years younger than Nicky, was already married and had started a family, living nearby and working part-time in the store as well. Then there was Eugene, who was tall, well-built but on the heavy side, and two years younger than me. He had a cheerful, cherubic face and was usually quite playful in his manner. He was also an All-City middle linebacker for the Abraham Lincoln High School football team. Dolores was the youngest of the four children and resembled her brother Eugene in her good looks, stature, and cheerful demeanor.

Milio was a healthy 60-year-old stud. He ran his grocery store and deli like a pro, and his business had become an integral part of the neighborhood. The kids, the families, the apartment dwellers, and the store merchants all knew him by his first name. He was a smiley, likeable person, a character truly indicative of his southern Italian lineage. In his more youthful years Milio was a champion speed bike rider who competed against some of the best cyclist in the world, in the Coney Island Velodrome. Since his speed bike racing days had ended, he had taken to pot bowling.

I had been a regular patron at Emilio's ever since I was a teenager, as the store was only a stone's throw from my house. One day while I was waiting for Delores to whip up a ham-and-cheese hero, Nicky grabbed my arm and pulled me to the back of the store. He whispered, "Come on by tonight at about eleven. We're going over to the Avenue X bowling alley to watch my dad bowl." As he let me go, he added, "Bring some money!" This sudden request caught me by surprise. I left the deli wondering whether I should or shouldn't show up.

After spending the rest of the day debating inwardly what to do and speculating on what kind of patrons were likely to be there, I decided to meet Nicky at the store at eleven, as he requested. We drove over to the bowling alley in my car. When we entered the large sports complex, I noticed that all twelve bowling lanes were filled with the Thursday night league bowlers concluding their matches. At midnight, the alleys would be closed to the regular patrons, but a little later they reopened to the pot bowlers, who gradually drifted in between twelve fifteen and one a.m.

Milio was already warming up when we sat on the benches behind him at his self-appointed lane. Before I could blink an eye, other people had gathered around Nicky and me, some standing. Shorty Byrnes approached Milio and said, "Let's get started!" Nicky took me aside and whispered in my ear, "Bet on my father tonight, he's on a hot streak."

We sat back down among the gamblers. One of the patrons, I think Tommy D., said, "I'll put up fifty on Shorty." Nicky whispered to me to go ahead and take the bet. With some slight hesitation, I agreed to cover the fifty. Milio bowled a 252, beating Shorty by fifteen points. By the time the night ended, at about three in the morning, I walked out of the bowling alley up by 125 dollars.

Over the next three weeks, every Thursday night found Nicky and me at the same spot. In no time at all, I found myself ahead approximately one thousand dollars. For me it was a small fortune, made the easy way. At the conclusion of each bowling match, I, along with Nicky and friends, celebrated our good fortune over a pre-dawn breakfast at Bernie's Diner. I then meandered on home and fell into my bed for a satisfying sleep that lasted for the entire day that followed.

Each week I kept telling myself that that lucky streak could not last forever. Sure enough, on the fifth Thursday night, the moment of reckoning arrived. There were two consecutive games in which Milio had bowled a 240 and a 250, only to be beaten by scores of 252 and 300, the latter constituting a perfect game. That night, I was relieved of 200 dollars. The next week, when Nicky asked me to come with him, I declined. I suspected that Milio's lucky streak had ended and I was not about to give back any more of what I had already gained. For me, all of that monetary good fortune was a onetime happening. I decided to quit while I was ahead of the game.

During less exciting moments, especially on Sunday evenings, I genuinely enjoyed taking part in lively poker games, though for lower stakes than were played by the bowling crew. Friday or Saturday nights were generally reserved for going dancing. My close friend Jimmy Syracuse and I, either in his Pontiac Bonneville convertible or in my Ford Galaxie, would make the rounds at the various dance clubs: the Hollywood Terrace, Palm Shores Club, or, on Saturday nights, the Taft Hotel in Manhattan. Sometimes we went dancing with our latest girlfriends, and other times, if we were lucky, we would connect with two new lovely gals, hopefully to lead to some kissing at Plumb Beach, followed by a late-night breakfast at, where else, Bernie's Diner. Gentlemen that we were, the ladies were always escorted back to their respectable homes. Life was good.

My year of full-time unemployment would not be complete without several visits to either Aqueduct or Belmont Race Track.

Every Tuesday, Uncle Louie, or "Creepy" as he was affectionately known by close family and friends, would join his crew of cronies at Pop's Place, on Mermaid Avenue in Coney Island, facing the Atlantic Ocean two blocks north of the boardwalk. They'd leave the restaurant in a chartered bus, making a beeline to the track. Just before noon, with plenty of time left before the first race at Aqueduct, Creepy and his friends would settle into their familiar spot near the finish line on the track's ground level. On one such Tuesday, Uncle Louie acquiesced to my heartfelt wish to tag along with his friends.

On that occasion I wanted to demonstrate my analytical skills at picking the right horse in the race. Uncle Louie formally introduced me to some of his closer pals among the neighborhood's many race track aficionados. First and foremost there was Tony Fats, then Captain Schmohawk ("Bobby G."), and lastly Ignatius, also known as "I'da-had-it Iggy." As the day progressed, I met a number of other local gambling personalities of the Gravesend–Coney Island area.

I settled down on a bench near the finish line and proceeded to lose myself in the daily racing form, the *Morning Telegraph*. There was still ample time before the start of the first race. After a few minutes had lapsed, I lifted my head out of the newspaper and proclaimed to all those who were willing to listen my picks for the first two races. After I stated all the reasons why Marymount Miss and Keep Pitching should arrive at the finish line first, those two horses, I declared, were surefire hits right at the top of my list. "The kid's nuts," cried Tony Fats to Creepy. "Both horses are long shots; they can't possibly come in first. Keep Pitching is an old grey mare who won't even make it to the finish line." Creepy huddled over me and whispered, "Are you sure you know how to read this paper?" "She can do it," I whispered back. "There's good breeding in her and Eric G. is having a strong meet at this track. He's the leading jockey on this tour. I'm going to the window to play my double."

Perhaps you could call it beginner's luck. There I was screaming and shouting, with just a small prayer mixed in, as Marymount Miss came thundering past the other horses, crossing the finish line a half-length ahead of the second-place finisher. It paid 65 dollars to win.

I went back to the drawing board (the daily racing form) to convince myself that Keep Pitching was the right pick for the second half of the double. Suddenly a sharp, cutting voice came from behind me and asked, "Who-do-ya like in the second race?" It was Ignatius, better known as I'da-had-it Iggy. I proudly and emphatically volunteered my pick, giving that veteran of the race track my learned reasoning for my selection.

Regardless of the condition of the track, the second race, as with almost all races, would go off as scheduled. It was billed for eight furlongs on a fast track, coming off an early morning drizzle which had turned into a bright, sunny spring-like day. At first glance, Keep Pitching resembled an old greyish-looking mare with a few white spots. I didn't think she would be able to go the distance. I admit I had some last-minute reservations about my pick. Yet, when the race was over, it had happened again: I had my second winner. She came down the home stretch, passed everyone, and crossed the finish line two lengths ahead of the field.

I stood at the finish line glued to the fence that separated me from the track itself. I was in a state of ecstasy, mesmerized by my winnings of 25 dollars that flashed up on the tote board. The daily double, a prize paid for picking the two consecutive winners of the first two races of the day, paid $1125 for my $2 bet. Suddenly, the entire Coney Island crew was upon me, with Creepy leading the pack. There I was, this young stud, shouting out to all, "The drinks are on me!"

Who could guess, as the day wore on, that I would be on a hot streak? It was one of my luckiest days ever, at least up to that time in my life. On that Tuesday, I picked five winners in all. Creepy and I took a limo home instead of the usual dollar-and-fifty-cent bus ride. I treated my uncle to a full-course meal at Carolina's in Coney Island, one of the truly fine Italian restaurants in the neighborhood. After such a grand day, I returned to my corner hangout on Neck Road for another round of boasting to the locals.

Chapter Forty

From time to time, when I felt the need to make some money, I would stop by the Riviera, my aunt's catering hall. During the week, three of my aunts on my father's side of the family, Maggie, Sophie, and Antoinette, worked daily, preparing the fresh food for the upcoming weekend weddings.

One day might be spent in preparing sumptuous hors d'oeuvres, the next in preparing trays of homemade manicotti, a delightful pasta entrée. Then there were the trays of half-chickens that were neatly arranged like soldiers ready for battle. My uncle Dominick was there to deal with the different food vendors who delivered the various ingredients during the week. Uncle Louie was the sous-chef, responsible for neatly placing the trays of goodies in the large-sized refrigerators down in the basement.

At five foot two, Uncle Louie barely cleared the four-and-a-half-foot-high marble-covered cooking counter. One could scantly see his eyeballs just above the counter line, hence his nickname, "Creepy." He was poetry in motion, and a master at his craft. Every manicotti and half-chicken was perfectly aligned on large trays that would travel from the cooking counter to the walk-in fridge and, finally, to the huge Vulcan ovens on wedding days.

I was told by some of my relatives that Uncle Louie was quite the dandy in his time. On the dance floor he cut a tango or a foxtrot in a Fred Astaire–like manner. He was admired by his friends when seen dancing with a beautiful blonde or redhead, women who were usually much taller than he. It didn't matter. Much like Vinnie, his younger nephew, Louie demonstrated a smooth style of dance and a winning smile to go along with a pair of bedroom eyes under a wave of jet-black hair.

I recall that on the same evening I hit it big at the race track, Creepy, with a few extra dollars in his pocket, managed to hook up with Millie, a sometime-girlfriend of his from the neighborhood. Both Creepy and Millie reached middle age together with some semblance of order in their everyday lives. Every now and then, particularly when Uncle Louie was flush, he and Millie would come together and reminisce upon days of old while sharing the same bed for an evening.

Creepy lived in a one-room upstairs apartment above the Riviera. Antoinette and her husband Zaccarino lived upstairs as well, but in a more spacious apartment. At one time Creepy decided he wanted to get married, but only if he could continue living above the Riviera. His sister unequivocally nixed this request. So, of necessity, and perhaps also quite a bit by choice, Uncle Louie continued to remain a bachelor and a loyal sous-chef right up until his departure from this world.

Chapter Forty-One

In or around 1961 Aunt Nicoleta, known as "Aunt Nick," opened up a luncheonette on Avenue M, just to the west of Nostrand Avenue, a couple of stores over from the corner. She purchased it from her younger sister Theresa, who tried to make a go of it but had strong opposition from her husband Tom. Tom was not happy living in Brooklyn and yearned to move back to his home turf in northern California. At that same time, coincidentally, Aunt Nick, having lost her husband Jack a few years earlier, was on the lookout for a new business enterprise, so the familial exchange was auspicious for both sisters.

In her youthful years, Nicoleta, along with her husband Jack, operated a successful café and bocce court out of their home on the corner of Stryker Street and Stryker Court, a block or so east of McDonald Avenue and south of Avenue W. It was a money-making enterprise that helped pay the bills of the entire Vallefuoco family who had all settled into the same neighborhood. Together, Nick and Jack had five children—four boys and one girl. In her mid-sixties Aunt Nick had to still provide food and shelter for her daughter Rozzeria, her youngest son Benny, and Rozzeria's three children, Christina, Roy, and Nickylin. Benny took over as the bulwark of the household after Jack's death, providing a strong presence of masculine stability.

Benny, at age 23, was a year older than me. He was blessed with good looks, about five foot ten, and a bit on the heavy side. He was on balance a rather good-natured fellow and had a difficult time saying no to his mother. His older brothers were already married by then, with families of their own. His sister Riz was a single mom with three children to feed. Mentally, Riz had her good days and bad days and could be quite unpredictable when it came to working in the luncheonette. Vincent, two years older than his brother Benny and just finishing his two-year military obligation, wanted no part of working in the store.

The bulk of the physical management of the business fell onto Benny's shoulders. With only rare moments of feeling put upon, Benny took this responsibility in good spirits. It was in that period that he and I became good buddies. Benny became a part of my coterie of close friends, and we shared some good times together on the dating circuit.

After Aunt Nick purchased the luncheonette from Aunt Tess, Tess and her husband moved back to California and opened a delicatessen in Half Moon Bay, just south of San Francisco. When Aunt Nick took over the place on Avenue M, she kept the front part of the luncheonette dedicated to the original family business of serving primarily breakfast, lunch, and late afternoon snacks to the local folk and school children who came by before school or at lunchtime. Some of the local customers and merchants of the various Nostrand Avenue shops popped in throughout the day as well. Benny, Riz, and one or two hired hands prepared milkshakes, soda, coffee, tea, meatball heroes, spaghetti, and soups, but no pizza. The place was set up to accommodate about 25 or 30 people at a time, with seats along a candy store–type counter and three or four booths that could seat four people each. Candy and magazines were sold at the front of the store. From time to time Gil Hodges, the New York Mets baseball team manager, would stop by for a treat with members of his family. They lived nearby on Bedford Avenue.

In the fall of 1963 Aunt Nick and I decided to start our business of making frozen rice balls at the luncheonette. Together, we purchased a brand-new large refrigerator/freezer and set up shop at the back of the luncheonette. We devised an egg-based white rice mixture, prepared in advance and kept in large bowls inside the refrigerator until the filling was added. The filling consisted of a mixture of cooked ground beef and peas, Parmesan cheese, and parsley, all immersed in a finely simmered tomato sauce. Each ball of rice was formed with the aid of an ice cream scoop. The rice ball would pop out of the scoop and into our hands, and with our thumbs we'd make a wide opening to allow for a hearty teaspoon of the beef and cheese mixture to go inside each ball. Each rice ball was closed and rounded, rolled in Italian-style breadcrumbs, and then deep fried, 30 to a pan. Five of these rice balls filled each package, which was then kept frozen for next-day delivery. We made a meatless rice ball as well, with mushrooms and mozzarella cheese replacing the ground beef.

I was able to procure a New York State Board of Health seal and printed labels to place on each package. My good childhood friend Jerry Schacker, who worked in his father's printing business on Lafayette Street in lower Manhattan, printed the labels, showing five brown rice balls on a plate, below our corporate name of M&T Enterprises (after "Martorello & Turiano," Nicoleta's married name).

Within a short period of time, I managed to string together a growing number of mom-and-pop grocery store accounts in the Gravesend and Bay Ridge areas of Brooklyn. Danza Supermarket, with stores in three locations, was our largest customer. Lucy, the wife of my Uncle Joe on my father's side of the family, introduced me to her parents; they ran a grocery store on lower 5th Avenue in the Bay Ridge section of Brooklyn, and they turned out to be my best customers.

After six months of making rice balls by hand, we decided we had to either automate the process and upscale our operation or pack it in. If we expanded the business, we would need to find a separate and larger location. Newly designed equipment would be required to mass-produce our packages of rice balls. On a small scale people were buying and eating our delicious rice balls, and the business was making a modest profit, so it seemed like it had a shot at growing into a formidable business.

The venture, however, was not to be. Aunt Nick's son Vincent wanted no part of the enterprise. After serving two years in the army, Vincent decided to pursue a college degree. He was a more private person than the rest of us and, apart from living at home, he had very little interaction with the family. Benny, who was the backbone of the family luncheonette, wanted no part of the rice ball business either. I could not expect Aunt Nick, who was in her late sixties and suffered from severe arthritis, to handle the production end of the business without help from at least two of her sons and Riz, her daughter. Although the frozen rice ball business showed some promise of growing into a successful operation, Aunt Nick and I had to abandon the short-lived venture due to lack of assistance. It was a sad moment for both of us, but life goes on.

In the course of a year I had managed to deplete most of the savings I had accumulated from working at the Publishers Guild. I sold my 1961 Ford Galaxie for $1300, my last source of income in my twenty-second year. Nearly penniless, I saw that it was again time for me to look for a steady job.

Chapter Forty-Two

The school bus business had expanded rapidly after my brother Rudy won the bid to service the Sewanhaka School District in Long Island's Nassau County. From its humble beginnings in 1951, the Veterans Bus Company of Brooklyn, New York, had expanded from ten to 60 school buses, had moved to a much larger depot in New Hyde Park on Long Island, and became the Long Island Bus Company. With no other job prospects on the horizon, I decided on a whim to give my brother a call in the hopes that he might hire me as a bus driver for his ever-expanding business. He told me that I could come on by, and that Eleanor, his trusted bookkeeper, could also use an assistant in preparing the weekly payroll. He'd even let me use one of the company vehicles to go back and forth from Brooklyn to Long Island, until I could buy my own car.

If I was going to drive a bus, I would have to learn how to drive one. I could practice with a couple of the full-time drivers. I took a liking to Bruno and Willie from Brooklyn. Bruno lived in Bensonhurst and Willie in East New York. Both young men were married and with children. They worked for Rudy in the early days when the company was formed and chose to remain there after the company became LIB. They were experienced drivers, good natured, and they played pinochle with two or three other drivers in between their school runs. They taught me how to handle floor shift gears and maneuver the bus, especially when parking in and out of the schoolyard. Before I could go to the Long Island Department of Motor Vehicles to take my test for a Class 2 license, my brother told me to drive a school bus out of the parking lot of the depot and to continue driving it around the block, backwards. "What?" I spluttered. "Yes," he insisted, "backwards." With some trepidation, I managed to complete that task, and I ultimately succeeded in procuring a Class 2 license.

In his effort to improve the bottom line of his business, Rudy began, with the approval of the bus drivers' union, hiring part-time female drivers. It was an ideal situation for women who had children attending school and husbands working full-time jobs. It was an opportunity for housewives to make some extra money for the family. Long Island Bus still needed some full-time drivers to cover some of the midday and weekend charters, so there was still work for me to do. Also, some of the women were easy on the eyes and made driving a bus a rather pleasurable experience.

Rudy was in the process of expanding the business into Suffolk County. Not long after I began driving a school bus, LIB won the bid to incorporate the Farmingdale School District into the already successful operation in New Hyde Park. Suddenly the number of buses grew to nearly two hundred and Rudy's desire to build a new facility, office building, garage, and parking lot at a prime location in Farmingdale became a reality. I was given the opportunity to dispatch 60 school buses out of the New Hyde Park location. That presented quite a challenge for me, though I gladly accepted it. Along with the sudden increase in responsibility came a modest jump in salary. With that extra bit of savings, I was able to purchase a used car, a 1958 powder blue Oldsmobile, and once again I was feeling quite good about my situation in life.

My brother had his hands full just trying to make an ongoing success of the Farmingdale operation, but he still had to divide his time between Farmingdale and the old location. That placed more responsibility on me for the day-to-day operations. As a dispatcher and branch manager, my job was to skillfully arrange the daily school bus routes for each bus driver. That responsibility included rescheduling the routes of drivers who, often at the last minute, called in sick. It was no easy task. The 1960s were not a time of cell phones and GPS. When a bus broke down, one or two standby drivers who were sitting in the office would be dispatched to pick up the remainder of that route. At times, I had to quickly redeploy a driver who finished his or her route to go back out and cover one or two runs where children were still waiting to be picked up.

To do my job effectively I needed to be friends with everyone: the bus drivers, the mechanics, the union shop steward, and the public, consisting of parents and students. Each day the buses had to complete the full run—the show must go on. Often, for me there was no lunch break, and quitting time saw me leave the office a couple of hours beyond the norm. As management, I did not receive overtime pay. On some Friday nights, I would be in the office until eight or nine o'clock trying to distribute weekend charter runs to the usually full-time drivers, who often played the seniority game in competing for the more favorable destinations. I often played salesman in trading off one week's work for another in order to gain the cooperation of the drivers. It was certainly difficult, but sometimes the challenge of making everything perfectly fit into place could even turn out to be fun.

For me, the experience and the challenge in working with so many different personalities and, for the most part, winning them over afforded me a great deal of satisfaction. I realized that I genuinely liked working with people. There was Carl Gutterman, the shop steward, a burly, demanding sort of chap, who kept reminding me that I had to play by the union rules. There was John Werthmann, an old-timer, who always kept his bus neat and clean. He was tall with greying hair and wore thick-rimmed glasses. He kinda looked out for me. He was often Johnny-on-the-spot, the one I could count on to pick up a last-minute emergency school route, and sometimes even to bring in coffee or a donut to boot. Then there was Pat Fiorentino, the lady's man, who kept trying to impress the fair ladies of the day. Terry Mazzola and Dotty Hauk were two leading ladies who drew some attention from the wandering eyes of LIB men, including me. They were always smartly dressed and sexy in tight black pants and blouses to match. I think I had a momentary crush on Terry, especially her wavy black hair, ruby red lipstick, and bright dark eyes. She almost always threw me a flirtatious smile whenever she came into the office to pick up her school run. Still, needless to say, both ladies were happily married women.

By 1965, ten years after my brother Rudy and his three partners started busing teenagers to their local high schools in south central Brooklyn, the company had grown from a fledgling operation of ten buses to a large fleet of two hundred, serving several school districts in both Nassau and Suffolk counties. During that time, Rudy successfully bought out all three of his original partners and replaced them with a couple of minor outside investors. Rudy remained the sole major stockholder of Long Island Bus Company.

To me, Rudy's greatest strength was, and still is, his skill and ability to find solutions to perplexing problems. This skill set afforded him the entrepreneurial ability to start and develop successful businesses. More importantly, I always had the feeling that Rudy had my best interest at heart. It goes back to when I was a child, when I had to overcome a bout of rickets, a childhood bone disease. When I was rehabbing at St. Giles Hospital in Brooklyn, it was Rudy who came to visit with me in his Model T coupe, sharing with me a handful of red grapes. Over the ensuing years he periodically popped into and out of my life with warmth and concern for my well-being. It is a special bond we have always had, right up to this day. Some of his curiosity and business skill to some degree has rubbed off on me and, in turn, on my own two sons, who to this day are quite successful in their own endeavors.

Rudy arrived to work each morning, formally yet modestly dressed in suit, shirt, and tie. One or two days each week would always be spent at the New Hyde Park bus depot, observing that things were running smoothly. He'd spend the remaining days of the work week holding court at the newly constructed Farmingdale depot. In running a bus business one had to understand the rules of the political game. With the care of a watchmaker, Rudy had to make sure all the intricate pieces fit when working with local politicians, school administrators, and union representatives; not to mention, bank managers, bus manufacturers, and his own workers. School contracts frequently came up for bid, compelling Rudy to be spot-on in his negotiations with all those entities. Rudy had a special way with people and could find the hot-button issue between management and labor that would help him attain favorable terms and concessions. In the school bus business, always, the show must go on.

As a successful business man, Rudy was able to attain for his wife Terry and his two children, John and Joy, all the trappings of the good life. He and his young family moved from a starter house in Bellmore to a newly built luxury home in Dix Hills, Long Island. It came with an in-ground swimming pool, a sweeping wooden deck, and a cabana. They attained upper-middle-class status, the American Dream. The house itself was built as a two-story colonial, boasting a modern eat-in kitchen just off the swimming pool deck. It also featured an ornate living room, designed mostly for viewing and an occasional piano concert. There was also a more livable dining room, for everyday use. I believe there was a bedroom on the first floor and of course several more comfortable bedrooms on the upper level, with accompanying bathrooms as well. The house rested upon terraced land, upon which there was a well-tended grass garden of flowers, trees, and shrubs, cared for by Rudy himself. Among his many skills, including sailing and flying, Rudy also possessed a green thumb.

After World War II, my brother Sal went back to school and became a successful lawyer and a close confidant to Rudy, his younger brother. Upon visiting Rudy's beautiful house in Dix Hills, Sal and his wife Jeanne fell in love with the tranquil setting. At Jeanne's urging, Sal found a local real estate broker and enlisted him to find a house in the same neighborhood. In the blink of an eye, Sal and Jeanne were suddenly neighbors of Rudy and Terry, and their lives were suddenly anchored in a sprawling, single-level ranch-style home on two acres of well-manicured land. Sal also enjoyed gardening. The living room in Sal's house boasted not one, but two baby grand pianos, one for Stephen and the other for Philip, his two sons who would eventually grow up to become concert pianists. Sal continued to play the violin into his mid-sixties, when his life ended abruptly from a bout with cancer of the lower spine.

At LIB I was back on track and making a steady living, dispatching school buses daily out of the New Hyde Park depot. The 1958 powder blue Oldsmobile I was sporting was in relatively good condition. It took me back and forth to work from my house in

Brooklyn to Long Island Bus. It was once again nice to have a set of wheels for my after-hour activities. So once again, life was good.

From time to time, at the urging of Mama (Lilly), I would take the wheel and drive her to visit one of her children living in Long Island. By 1965, four of Lilly's children—Sal, Gus, Rudy, and Barbara—were settled into their own homes out on Long Island. Frank Jr. lived in Bay Ridge, Brooklyn, having moved into his wife (Ann's) brownstone house, while Mama and I still lived in our seven-room house at 628 Avenue V, only a half a block from my sister Anita's house on East 7th Street.

I was Mama's official chauffeur. Often, on weekends, we drove to Long Island for planned family visits—of course, by invitation only (only kidding). We might visit with Rudy and Terry, spending some time at the poolside and enjoying the summertime weather. The prime reason for visiting with family was always to check up on Lilly's grandchildren. As with most Italian mothers and grandmothers, Lilly wanted to satisfy her curiosity in knowing that everyone was being fed properly and that all were looking healthy. Seeing John and Joy scampering about, diving into the swimming pool, and generally looking well put a smile on Lilly's face. She would not hesitate to let Rudy and Terry know if she detected any irregularities in the air, even though her own health in our urban neighborhood was generally less than perfect.

At Sal's home, just around the corner from Rudy's, Lilly would be treated to a classical music concert. Lilly's eldest son Sal, on violin, and his two young sons, Stephen and Philip, both on piano, eagerly entertained their loving mother and grandmother.

My brother Gus and my sister Barbara lived only a town apart from each other, in Seaford and in Wantagh, Long Island. For Mama, those visits were also a twofer. Gus and Louise lived in Seaford, along with their five children, Patricia, Frankie, Joannie,

Bobby, and Pauli. They owned a modest split-level ranch-style home, with a full basement. Working as a fireman at Brooklyn's Sheepshead Bay firehouse, Gus had to travel to work whenever he was on duty. On Sunday afternoons Gus played piano in Johnny Mullay's sixteen-piece band at the Roosevelt Grill in New York City.

Outside the upper echelon of society, most homes on Long Island were modestly built in response to a growing lower middle class during the post–World War II era. Settlement on Long Island, as with many suburban communities throughout the United States, was the fulfillment of the American dream of home ownership and a slice of the good life. The kids could play on family-friendly streets and their parents could barbeque on their backyard patios over pleasant summer weekends. Trips out to the island with Mama were always a scenic pleasure.

Barbara and Pete Donnelly moved from their basement apartment at 628 Avenue V directly into their lovely brick gingerbread Tudor house in Wantagh. It was a smallish A-frame house with a large attic room where their daughters Patty, Barbara-Ellen, and Cathy slept. Their son Peter, named after his father, occupied a bedroom on the ground floor. There was a master bedroom at the front of the house and a living room, dining room, and small eat-in kitchen at the back end of the house, overlooking the grassy lawn and small family vegetable garden.

Perhaps it was Pete's cheerful repartee that captured Mama's sensitivities, or the cheerfulness of the four young children, or even the three little canines that scampered around the yard and into and out of the house—whatever it was, Mama felt more comfortable there than anywhere else. Sometimes she would spend a full week visiting with Barbara and her family. Any other visit with children and grandchildren would be for a single day only, with a return home by nightfall. With Barbara, Pete, and the kids out at Wantagh, I think Mama truly found solace.

Chapter Forty-Three

For me, life was like playing a game of poker. Every time I won a hand, I gained more confidence in myself, and felt that I could see more clearly both the risks all around me and the path that I could forge ahead. Moreover, once I saw what success was really like, I didn't need to lose back all my winnings before I could appreciate what I had. As with my winning streaks at the race track and at the bowling alley, I could intuit when it was time to walk away without disappointment. I always understood the value of quitting while ahead, to be better prepared for the next adventure, with the full benefit of retaining my successes from the last.

When I decided to break from one moment in my life and move on to the next, I somehow knew, by instinct, when to give up the ghost. Just as quickly as I had arrived at the LIB, it was time to move on.

It hit me like a ton of bricks. Word went around the neighborhood that my cousin Vinnie, the matinee idol, the son of my Aunt Sophie on my father's side of the family, had died of a heart attack. "How could that be?" I asked myself. He was only 35 years old. What seemed even more frightening was that he'd apparently expired during a baseball game. He had just caught a fly ball in center field for the third and final out of the inning, trotted into the dugout, leaned back against the wall of the dugout bench, closed his eyes, and never woke again. When I stopped by my cousin Bunny (Camille)'s beauty salon on Avenue M, not far from my Aunt Nick's luncheonette, she sat me down on one of the salon chairs and broke the sad news to me.

Bunny and I were born a day apart in the same month of March, in the same year, 1941. She was also very attractive, possessing the same Mediterranean good looks as my cousin Vinnie and his three sisters. She possessed the added asset of a very sweet and tender spirit, an inheritance from her loving parents, Uncle Salvatore (Toddo), from my father's side of the family, and his wife, my Aunt Viola. Bunny and I were both greatly saddened by Vinnie's passing. Over the previous few years, Bunny and I had taken a liking to our cousin Vinnie.

I left Bunny's beauty salon, got into my car, and headed straight down Nostrand Avenue into Sheepshead Bay, where I stopped at the Palms Shore Club for a drink and a bit of lunch. I couldn't eat much of anything as I sat on the back deck, sipping my scotch and soda and viewing the various sailing craft passing by.

I quietly sat for I don't know how long, thinking of so many wonderful moments of my life up till then. It seemed like yesterday when Vinnie and I happily danced the night away at the Hollywood Terrace. In that period, I occasionally stopped by Aunt Sophie's house on a Sunday afternoon and had dinner with Vinnie and his three beautiful sisters. The last time that I saw Vinnie he was actually living with a lovely young lady who had two small children. Together, they were one beautiful family. I miss them all. To this day I wish I could still find even one of his sisters. The last I heard, Cookie married a rather wealthy man and moved to

Staten Island. Toni had met someone from the neighborhood and moved to Nevada, disappearing into the glitter of Las Vegas. After Vinnie's death, I unfortunately fell out of touch with nearly every one of my aunts, uncles, and cousins on my father's side of the family.

I wasn't quite sure where Vinnie had been going with his life. From outward appearances, he seemed to be living the good life. There was the green Cadillac Eldorado, the beauty salon, the flashy clothes, the fair ladies—and finally, at the age of 35, he seemed to have found the one gal who could bring his life together and steady the ship called Vinnie. Yet it was not to be, as the dark figure of death came upon him on the ballfield.

As I sat at the table overlooking the waters of Sheepshead Bay, I asked myself, where did I fit in to all of this? I was 24 years old. I'd done a few things with my life, but so far they hadn't seemed to add up to very much. Barbara Weinberg, my childhood tomboy girlfriend, had gone on to college and become a schoolteacher. Among my male friends, Frankie, from my football days, had gotten married and had a daughter, Bobby G. was about to marry a pretty gal from the Philippines, and Fat Stevee had married a nice Italian girl some time ago, as his family had expected. He bought his uncle's butcher store in Long Island City. Cousin Benny, from Aunt Nick's luncheonette, was hanging with some gal who raised German shepherds.

So where did that put me?

Not too long before Vinnie's death, my brother Rudy had asked me if I wanted to become a junior partner in the bus business. I could run a new depot housing about 30 buses. I gave it some thought and concluded that I did not want to tie my horse to that hitching post and manage buses for the rest of my life. Mama's wish that I become a fireman continued to fall on my deaf ears. I began to realize that gambling for a living, although it had some romantic appeal to me, would not prove a viable path to my future. At that moment I really had no one to mentor me. I was truly on my own, with my own thoughts as my only ally.

Going back to school had crossed my mind a few times before, but there, at the ripe old age of 24, I asked myself, "Am I too old to go back to school?" When I was peddling magazines in the study hall and cafeteria of Pratt Institute in downtown Brooklyn during the night sessions, I engaged with many adult students who were much older than me. I thought to myself, "Perhaps I can go back to school? I think I'm ready for a change in my life." I needed to know who I was and where I should be going.

A few days after my musings at the Palms Shore Club, I found myself casually walking along Park Row in lower Manhattan, opposite City Hall. In front of those massive attached concrete buildings, at 41 Park Row, was a sign that read, "Accepting new applicants to Pace College." I walked through the main entrance of the building and into a room filled with people, desks, and typewriters. I filled out a simple form with the usual personal information about myself which included what I had been doing of late. After the document went through several hands I was greeted by a receptionist who led me into a backroom office, to be seated before the desk of Dr. Benjamin Ford.

Opposite me sat a gentle man. He wore a friendly cherubic face, and was neatly dressed in a suit, shirt, and colorful matching tie. Dr. Ford greeted me with a kind, friendly smile below a thinly coiffed head of white-blond hair. He had already reviewed the briefly written history of my past six years since graduating from high school, as well as my completed application. With some curiosity, Dr. Ford asked me why just then I decided to go back to school. I responded that I needed to fill a void in my life. There was more to life than just going to work. I wanted to learn more about myself: who was I and where would I be going with my life? I had thought about these feelings for some time and I had concluded that by going back to school I would likely find some answers.

At that moment in time, if I had to compare myself with anyone, it would be Marcello Mastroianni's character in the popular Italian movie *La Dolce Vita*. After sloshing in the waters of the Trevi Fountain and then embracing the beautiful, blond Anita Ekberg, who was dressed in a timeless tight-fitting silky black gown beneath a cascade of water, and finishing an entire night of partying from sundown to sunup, he sat, the next morning, at a petite table in front of a nearby café sipping an espresso and staring into space with an incredulous look. That scene, and that look, felt very familiar to me at my own crossroads in the theater of life.

After taking a short placement exam, I came back to Pace for another interview with Dr. Ford, who, by the way, was also chairman of the History Department. After six years away from an academic environment, my exam results were not too flattering. My composition skills in answering a couple of thought-provoking questions showed some promise, but I needed some remedial grammatical work.

During my interview, Dr. Ford explained that I could begin taking courses at Pace as a qualifying non-matriculated student. I could choose a few courses, totaling no more than twelve credits for each semester. If I were successful in completing 24 credits in two consecutive semesters with a B average or better, I could become a matriculated student at Pace College. At the time, I was working one day a week at Long Island Bus Company, helping

Eleanor with payroll. With that modest income I qualified for a small education grant from Pace to help offset a small portion of the cost of attending college.

Being in the midst of that academic atmosphere, seeing students coming and going amidst the hustle and bustle, I left Dr. Ford's office suddenly feeling energized and looking forward to my first day of class in September 1965.

Chapter Forty-Four

My classroom experience started with Mrs. Joan Cushing's English 101. We began with Edith Hamilton's classic textbook *The Greek Way*, alongside the recommended reading of Mary Renault's *The Bull from the Sea*. Mrs. Cushing's classroom was filled daily with lively discussions of Greek classic literature, as well as comparisons with the current daily life experiences that many of her students carried into her classroom. Nestor Del Campo, from Argentina, and I were the two elder statesmen she called upon to share our worldly experiences for the benefit of the other, younger classmates who were recent graduates from high school. Although my grammatical skills were somewhat rudimentary, I made significant progress in my remedial English class, and I even managed to win a writing contest during my first semester.

With the continued encouragement of Mrs. Cushing and the college classroom environment, I began to absorb a few of the great works of antiquity. Sophocles, Euripides, Aristophanes, Boccaccio, and Shakespeare were just a few of the great writers who began to have an enormous impact on my thinking.

Professor Lurier, my early Western European history instructor, was another strong influence in my continued effort to gain more academic wisdom. The moment you walked into his classroom, you were greeted with a warm smile coupled with a firm request that you put down your pen or pencil, close your book, and just listen to his lecture. He always began his story with a poignant question pertaining to a specific period in history that he chose to impart to his students. He would set the stage at a critical moment in time—a turning point, or when a new invention arrived—and then he would captivate all of us with an action-packed story. Rarely did any of us want to interrupt his narrative, reliving the moment as if we too were a part of the story. The Greek war sagas, the emergence of Alexander the Great and Aristotle, Julius Caesar and the Roman Empire, the Byzantine world, and the era of feudalism were key moments in time brought to life inside his classroom.

For me, it seemed that both Mrs. Cushing and Professor Lurier took a modicum of interest in my curious desire to learn more of what they both had to offer. In my four years at Pace, I took several of their respective courses. To this day, I still envision sitting in on one of their lectures. Professor Lurier passed away a number of years ago, in the year 2000. However, it is still possible that Mrs. Cushing is alive somewhere in Great Britain, married to Professor Eastman, who, in addition to teaching English composition, was also the chairman of the English Department.

Studying architecture with Professor Callison for one semester introduced me to the great structures of antiquity and the Renaissance period of Western Europe. At that same time, as luck would have it, I happened to find a box of black-and-white photographs, the "University Prints" from Cambridge, Massachusetts, in one of my bookshelves at the college. Those fine reproductions of art and architecture proved a great text for gaining a visual perspective on the study of the classical and feudal periods consecutively. From time to time I still refer to them in my continued literary and historical readings relating to those pivotal moments in the evolution of Western civilization.

In addition to what I considered to be my core courses, I registered and completed classes in philosophy, psychology, logic, and a host of other related subjects during my first two years of college. I was quite comfortable in my new surroundings in academia. That emersion into the realm of new ideas, coupled with an exchange of opinions among my schoolmates and my professors, gave me a better understanding of who I was and where I would be going. I had no intention of returning to my past life on Neck Road. Even in the days when I was peddling magazines in the cafeteria of Pratt Institute in downtown Brooklyn, I had wondered what it would be like to be back in school again.

In my early days at Pace, I was still living at home with Mama. My sister Anita and I continued to look after her, making sure that she was eating properly and maintaining her strength, but she was gradually losing her battle with the dreadful pain of arthritis throughout her body. I was still, for the most part, having my dinnertime meals at my sister's house, nearby on East 7th Street. Often Anita would send one of her three wonderful sons over to Avenue V, with a packaged dinner in hand for Mama.

At 628 Avenue V we took on a new tenant to live in the basement apartment. Wendy answered an ad we had placed in the *Daily News*. She was slightly under five feet tall, skinny as a rail, with stringy brown hair, and she smoked like a chimney. However, she worked at Pips on the Bay, a comedy club located on Emmons Avenue, across from Lundy's and next to Randazzo's Italian seafood restaurant. Apart from providing us with a very modest rent, Wendy knew that I could use some extra money. She introduced me to George and Marion Schultz, the owners of Pips. Having had experience as a waiter at the Riviera during my late teenage years, I was a good fit to cover the entire room of the club on Friday nights. It turned out to be a good source of income while I continued to attend my daytime classes at Pace.

As an added bonus to making money at Pips, from week to week I had a firsthand, upfront look at the aspiring young comics, such as David Frye, Joan Rivers, Rodney Dangerfield, and Stanley Myron Handelman. I got to see them work out their material behind the stage before going in front of a friendly Friday and Saturday night audience at Pips, in the calm, seaworthy environment of Sheepshead Bay. Life was good.

During the second half of my second semester at Pace, I discovered that I could pick up a part-time job working in the Pace Library—but first I had to pass the litmus test of Henry Birnbaum, a short, cheerful, and rosy cherubic soul, neatly clad in suit, white shirt, and a colorful bowtie. In a brief pre-hiring interview, he stressed the need to be accurate, precise, on time, and quiet within the cloistered confines of the library. This seemed like an easy request until I met up with Walter Sobon, a younger and somewhat more mischievous student then myself. He was thoroughly ensconced in the library and eager to show me the ropes.

On my first day, Walter introduced me to Bruce Bergman, the assistant to Henry Birnbaum. Bruce was a friendly sort of person. He was neatly dressed, in a rather pastel color of clothing, and tall, with some white strands blended into thinning blond hair. He walked me around the library, pointing out the many sections organized by subject matter where returning books should be filed. The library was actually undergoing a reclassification program to convert, at that time, from the Dewey Decimal System to the Library of Congress System, a major undertaking.

For some reason, Walter seemed to find working in the library quite amusing. On my first day on the job, Walter pointed out that Bruce wore fluffy pink slippers. Mrs. Gibia, a smallish, nicely dressed woman in her early fifties who wore thick silver-rimmed glasses and a nice smile accentuated by a soft, lightly coated pink lipstick, stood guard at the front desk, checking in returned books as the students passed in and out of the front entrance. Sometimes Walter would snatch a book from the cart before Mrs. Gibia would be finished cataloging it, forcing her to yank it out of his hands and to then quietly shoo him away from her desk. I must admit that from time to time those little episodes made me chuckle. I had to watch that those moments of joviality did not put me out of favor with library management. The Pace Library, while reserved and quiet for student research and enquiry usage, was a friendly and helpful space for all in the college community.

Chapter Forty-Five

Life has a way of playing tricks on humankind. This is not a profound statement, but it's one worth remembering from time to time.

In thinking back on my high school days and shortly thereafter, I recall the comings and goings of my aunts and uncles on both sides of my family. Working weddings at the Riviera, my aunt's catering hall, the rice ball business, the concessions in Coney Island, and the Dodgers baseball games at Ebbets Field were magical moments in my life. As if by a wave of a magical wand, by the time I reached my midlife years the past had given way to all the present-day responsibilities of raising my own family, and my connection to all those relatives all but ceased to exist. Today, in my old age, I ask myself, "Where have they all gone?" The answer, of course, is that you can't get them back. However, new magical moments present themselves every single day, if you remain open to their presence.

Death is quick. My aunts and uncles seemed to have disappeared going into their mid-seventies or early eighties. One or two managed to live a bit longer. My own father left me when I was eighteen. He was 61. Like a puff of smoke, suddenly he was gone. Mama lingered on until 1967, two days after my twenty-sixth birthday.

It happened so quickly. I still wonder if we as a family took Mama to Kings Park or to Pilgrim State Hospital, on Long Island. I think it was Pilgrim State. At that moment in time, from the other side of an opaque glass door, I can still recall Mama slowly and quietly waving to me for the last time.

Shortly after Mama's passing, the house that I lived in for 26 years of my life, at 628 Avenue V, was sold. After placing an ad in the *Daily News*, my sister Anita and her husband Jimmy found a buyer for the house. Sal, my eldest brother, a fully-fledged lawyer, took care of the paperwork, quietly bringing to an end the storied life of Frank and Lilly, my dear and beloved parents.

Chapter Forty-Six

The back room of the Pace College library was a real happening. Henry Birnbaum, the director, assembled a very talented group of professional librarians along with some very hard-working Pace students, forming two teams in the effort to convert the system of storing and categorizing library books and manuscripts from the Dewey Decimal to the Library of Congress System. Our merry two teams of workers made a significant contribution to that worthy endeavor. Fortunately, I got to be a working member within that wonderful environment during the summer of 1967.

Group A was headed by Mr. Lee. He was a thin, soft-spoken man of Asian descent who occasionally saw the human, comical, or light side of a testy situation. He was on the short side, wore thick-rimmed glasses, and came to work each day dressed in a light white cotton and blue denim striped suit, white shirt, and matching tie. As with most good librarians, consistency was his hallmark. The same could be said for Group B's Marie Lennema, of Estonian descent.

Marie Lennema oversaw Group B. I believe she was still single. She was perhaps 30 years old, petite and pretty in a pale-faced sort of way. Her manner of dress was simple: tailored grey skirt, white matching blouse, and a simple necklace. She wore a sweet, friendly smile adorned with a thin veil of light pink lipstick.

Each team contained a varied cast of characters. Team A consisted of Mr. Lee, me, and five others. Walter, my cheerful and fun-loving prankster friend who never failed to capture some mishap in the regular course of workday activities, was onboard. There was also the beautiful Kelly O'Rourke, with green, emerald eyes and straight black hair. She was perhaps 40 years old and single, and dressed smartly, with enough sex appeal to easily garner some male attention. She was a full-time employee and too full of life to allow anyone the pleasure of tying her down in marriage. Three other part-time students filled in the gaps of a normal eight-hour day.

Ms. Lennema's team was similarly made up of seven top-notch workers. First and foremost there was Doris Faye, already a third-year English major at Pace and one of the leading female actresses in the popular Drama Department headed by Dr. Joseph Miranne. Rosemary Cunningham, the sweet, petite Irish lassie from Brooklyn, Juliette Thee, the girl with the flaxen red hair, from Poland by way of Paris, Danielle, a student scholar from Switzerland, and two additional undergraduates filled out the ranks of Team B.

Juliette was accepted to Pace and granted 30 credits for courses she'd completed during her Parisian studies. Danielle came to the States by way of a friend who lived in Long Island. She brought with her an interpreter's degree from the University of Geneva, Switzerland, for which Pace College granted her 80 credits toward a degree in American literature. Juliette and Danielle became good friends after meeting for the first time at Pace.

Then there was Charles. He was in his late twenties. An assistant librarian at Pace and a close friend of Bruce Bergman, he was given the go-ahead to throw a midsummer office party for all the back-office personnel engaged in the reclassification project.

Charles and Bruce shared a handsome brownstone house which Bruce owned, located in the Park Slope district of Brooklyn. It boasted a million-dollar view of lower Manhattan. Charles was a friendly, happy-go-lucky chap charged with transmitting, reviewing, and spelling out the requirements of the front office of the library. He was the cheerleader to each group, giving praise and, at the same time, valuable critique throughout the important reclassification of Pace Library's unending stream of books and manuscripts.

I thoroughly enjoyed mending and labeling the many books that fell into my purview for repair. These were the ones that were considered keepers. Many non-accredited older and worn-out books were either replaced or discarded. I took great satisfaction in hand printing the gold or silver titles on the spines of books, especially the complete works volumes of many great authors. I often felt as if my task put me in touch with antiquity.

Daily, each team competed to see which would end the day with the higher total of reclassified books, complete with index cards. Usually, Team A, of which I was a part, would take the early lead and continue to be ahead throughout the day. By day's end, however, shortly after Danielle turned in her statistics, Team B would finish slightly ahead of Team A, much to my chagrin and frustration. I couldn't quite figure out how Danielle managed to correct and retype so many categorical index cards. It seemed as if she were performing magic: combining brain, hand, and eye coordination, she was quick, quiet, and untroubled.

On one or two occasions, during our one-hour lunch break, Mr. Lee took a few of us to his favorite Chinese restaurant near Pace College, not far from Chinatown. It was on such an occasion that Walter and I took the opportunity to engage in conversation with Juliette and Danielle. At the time, except for Walter, we were all heavy smokers. Juliette smoked Gauloises, a Parisian, heavy non-filtered cigarette. It came in a chic, powder blue paper packet. Danielle smoked Lucky Strikes. Since I smoked a similar-tasting brand, from time to time, when I was out of cigarettes, I would ask her for one. The first time I spoke to Danielle, at that Chinese restaurant, was over a Lucky Strike moment.

Our days at the library generally included the usual back-office chatter about many of our shared personal stories. The women often complimented each other over what they were wearing. I decided to take the opportunity to bring in some designer clothing that happened to have "fallen off a truck" and somehow found its way into Bill's Candy Store on Neck Road. They were small, everyday items, consisting of woman's bras and panties as well as Leonardo Strassi blouses, some of the more special items to come our way. For me, it was a chance to make a few extra bucks. It was 1967, an unforgettable moment in time, as my being took root within the friendly confines of 41 Park Row.

Chapter Forty-Seven

Midway through the summer of 1967 Danielle extended an invitation to her close friend Juliette, and, by extension, Walter and me, to a weekend party thrown by her and her two female roommates, Judy and Linda. Judy, from Michigan, was a culinary student interested in trying out some recipes for hors d'oeuvres. The fête was for Linda, a sophomore student at New York University (NYU), who was celebrating a one-year engagement to Ted, a salesman working for one of the men's fashion houses in New York's garment district. Danielle was given the go-ahead to invite a few of her friends from the library.

Danielle and her two roommates shared a rented apartment on West 97th Street, overlooking Riverside Drive. The bedrooms were small. The shared kitchen was of normal size, containing a dining table for four, a small cooking counter, a four-burner stove, a small refrigerator, a sink, and some shelves with enough flatware to accommodate three people. They would rely on paper plates and plastic cutlery to cover any partying group that consisted of a larger number of people. There was a small bathroom with a combined bath and shower. The living room, large and panoramic, was the apartment's main attraction. Being three stories up from ground level, it boasted of three floor-to-ceiling windows, offering a magnificent view of the Hudson River by night, and occupants could watch boats of all sizes traveling up and down the water-front. Apart from being a wonderful sitting area day or night, it was a great space for a party.

The party took place on a fairly warm Friday evening at the beginning of July. The milky blackness of night served as a cheerful background to the shimmering lights of the boats passing by on the Hudson. The food was nicely presented and very tasty. The recorded music was varied and very satisfying to both those who wished to dance and those who were simply good listeners. Among such a college crowd in the 1960s, conversation varied from romantic movies and plays to sublime philosophical thoughts, politics notwithstanding.

We listened, talked, and danced the night away. We also latched on to Bob Dylan songs straight from the poetry den of Greenwich Village, danced to the slow steady foxtrot of the Five Satin's "In the Still of the Night," and concluded with the classical music of Mozart and friends.

At the end of the evening Danielle offered her goodbyes to her friends from the library. I was the last one to leave. For an instant, I suddenly stopped at the open door of the apartment and turned around to face our kind host. Danielle was wearing a sleek three-quarter-length pale green dress which fell slightly below her knees, with a pleasantly curved neckline. Her hair was a thinly coiffed blond mane that curved around her face and fell to her waistline. This portrait came with a cheerful smile. Without any fore-thought, I asked this lovely co-worker from the Pace Library if she would accompany me to Charles's party the following weekend. This quiet angel, with cheerful blue eyes framed by very fine eye-liner, said, "Yes." As I drove home to Brooklyn in my 1958 powder blue and silver chrome Olds, I thought to myself, "What was it that spontaneously made me ask Danielle for a date?"

244

The following weekend's party, as with all things Charles had a hand in, was a success. He served up fine white wine with some very tasty hors d'oeuvres, consisting of sautéed shrimp served on a toothpick, bitesize pieces of cooked liver wrapped in bacon, tiny tasty cheddar cheese puffs, and various other delectable items. Later in the evening, at around ten, we were treated to some delightful Italian and French pastries, complemented with a fine red wine and the option of nicely brewed coffee.

We were about twenty in all, which included a few neighbors who were close friends of Charles. Bruce had been away for the weekend, so Charles was free to entertain as he so wished. Spirits were high throughout the evening. It turned out to be a wonderful party and for me a joyful experience.

At about eleven o'clock or so Danielle and I decided to take a breather from all the dancing and conversation. We also felt a bit tipsy from perhaps a little too much wine. We discovered a back bedroom where some of the overflow of jackets were lying on a bed. We gently put them on a nearby chair and proceeded to lie down next to each other.

I asked Danielle a few questions about her family—where she grew up, how she came to America, and so on. She, in turn, wanted to know what I was doing besides going to Pace. I explained that I grew up in Brooklyn and that I was presently working as a waiter at Pips on the Bay, a small comedy club café in Sheepshead Bay. We continued to fill in more details for each other until slowly we trailed off into a soft sleep, she with her left hand resting gently on my right one. It was my first date with Danielle.

Above: Clayton, age 20, with new 1961 Ford Galaxie ($2300 cash!)

Below: Jacques, Danielle, and Clayton go to the Zurich magistrate

Above and below: With Marinette too, heading to the Zurich magistrate

Above and below: Danielle and Clayton's wedding day, June 18, 1968

Above: The beautiful bride

Below: Danielle's father, Hans

Above and below: Danielle in 1969

Above and below: Helene, Tante Frieda, Danielle en route to Canada

Above and below: Danielle and Clayton trek in the Alps, Spring 1970

Danielle and Clayton in Alpine paradise, Spring 1970

Above and below: Helene, Hans, Frieda, and Danielle at rest

Above: Jacques and Elizabeth

Below: Christian and Marinette with young Cathy. We were all so young!

Above: Danielle and Raphael hiking in Vermont, 1976

Below: Danielle and Fabrice with Mlle. Spondly and Helene, 1974

Above and below: The Martorella family, 1973, at Gus and Louise's house in Seaford, Long Island. All seven siblings in one place, with all the spouses except Barbara's. Fabrice was one year old. It seems Sal, in bow tie and tux, had a violin gig with the L.I. Symphony that same night

Part Four

Alone No Longer

Chapter Forty-Eight

D anielle came to the United States from Switzerland for the first time when she was sixteen years old, as a foreign exchange student, under the American Field Service (AFS) program. She stayed for one full year, hosted by a warm and friendly family living in Clearwater, Florida. Danielle acquired a good command of the English language, having taken several required classes during her studies in Zurich. As a sophomore student at Clearwater High School, she quickly adapted to life in the States.

After one year of living the normal, active life of an American teenager, Danielle returned to her home country with a warm feeling from living with an average, middle-class, all-American family.

Danielle was an A student from the day she first entered school as a kindergartener. As she grew up, she discovered that she had a gift for languages and mathematics, two subjects where she consistently scored either a five or a six on her report cards, putting her at the top of her class. Danielle's acute analytical skills and her high standards in academia were likely acquired from her loving father, Hans Geering, a champion chess player, open-minded thinker, and respected employee of the Union Bank of Switzerland (UBS) for 49 years.

Danielle's mother, Helene Kreyanbuhl-Geering, came from Lausanne, Switzerland. Even though her maiden name was of Germanic origin, Helene grew up in the French part of Switzerland, so she spoke and wrote primarily in the French language. Within the confines of her household in Zurich, Danielle, along with her older sister Marinette and her younger brother Jacques, learned both French and German as their native languages. All three children had a gift for languages and could speak English fluently as well.

After a one-year stint in Florida, Danielle returned to her native Switzerland, where she finished her studies at the gymnasium and moved on to the University of Geneva. Danielle had begun her musical career learning the piano in her youth, but then switched to the viola, which became her instrument of choice. Between her tenure at the gymnasium and the university, Danielle participated in a Swiss youth orchestra.

Her orchestral experience took her to several European countries, where her musical company performed at pre-booked concerts. Italy and Spain were two of the principle countries where she played the viola during her late teenage years. Traveling with the youth orchestra enhanced her social relationships with her soulmates. It also gave Danielle some space to engage in some of her romantic thoughts and feelings at a tender young age.

At some point in our discussions, Danielle expressed to me that she had been romantically involved with a young lad from Spain. The logistics of being from distant countries, as well as cultural differences, kept those two young lovers from ever marrying. Danielle also confided her concern that if she married a man from Southern Europe she might be subject to a domineering husband, a tendency which, for many a Swiss Miss, seemed prevalent in Mediterranean culture.

After graduating from the University of Geneva, Danielle linked up with Cathy, a college grad from Long Island, New York, who had taken some classes at the same university. She also connected with another gal named Catherine, who came from Strasbourg, France. She too had enrolled in some classes at Geneva. All three found positions teaching French to foreign students, mostly Americans attending a private school, in Lausanne. At that time, Danielle lived with her aunt, Tante Yvonne, who owned a house in Lausanne.

Not long after all three came together, Cathy, from Long Island, decided that she wanted to return to the States. She would ultimately convince Danielle to come with her. Secretly, Danielle had an urge to relive her life in the United States, having had a joyful experience when living in Florida as a teenager. Catherine, who was from Strasbourg, also wished to return to France to marry Alfred, her childhood friend who came from the same city and who had a successful dental practice. At the youthful age of 21, Danielle would begin a new chapter in her life.

Life in Bridgehampton, Long Island, was short-lived, although it was spent riding on the fast track. Danielle soon realized that Cathy was no pauper. It was high society all the way, and the days were spent horseback riding, swimming at the family club, and attending elaborate parties and social events on weekends. After a short while Danielle, coming from a humble Swiss environment, began to feel like a fish out of water. Besides, it was time to get back to the business of finding a college in New York that would accept her and give her some credit for her degree from the University of Geneva. Danielle wanted to pick up her studies in American literature so that she could return to Switzerland and pursue a career in education.

She combed the want ads in the *New York Times* for apartments for rent and discovered one listing by an Alan Margolis, offering a single-bedroom apartment located on Madison Avenue, on the east side, just below 42nd Street in Manhattan. Alan's family owned the apartment building, a three-story unit with six apartments; one of the apartments he occupied, and the other five were rented. He had an older brother who was a forensics specialist in the Los Angeles Police Department, and a second brother who was a doctor in Atlanta. He also had two older sisters, who lived, respectively, in Israel and in Brooklyn. Alan, a confirmed bachelor, was a few years older than Danielle, a bit on the heavy side, and an opera lover. He claimed that his recently deceased mother had been an amateur opera singer. Alan was a native New Yorker with a career as a State Social Services administrator. After an initial interview, Alan realized that he found the perfect tenant in Danielle. She was cultured, musical, young, and eager to attend school in the Big Apple.

Soon after taking up residence in her new abode, Danielle began her search for a school that would accept her Swiss diploma and place her in a program that would lead to a degree in American literature. In the fall of 1966, Danielle began her new student tenure at Pace College. Pace had granted Danielle 80 credits, and with that head start she managed to attain a degree only two and a half years later, with honors. In the meantime, she had a life to live, and in living that life she learned to stretch a dollar to the limit to make ends meet in New York City.

Chapter Forty-Nine

I n the normal course of events, and most often in the youthful years of one's life, magic and mystery are two elements that take a lively soul to a new place. At the age of 22, Danielle began her new life in New York City. In the fall of 1965, she moved into her new apartment on Madison Avenue. At that very moment in time Danielle met Hal, a young man who also rented an apartment in Alan's building.

It was romance by location for those two young lovers. Not long after they met and shared their life together in the magic corners of Manhattan, Hal finished his studies at NYU while Danielle was just beginning her own curriculum at Pace. Almost as soon as they had come together, sadly, they suddenly broke up their romance. He decided to return to Long Island, where he would find a job and go on to marry his neighborhood sweetheart.

Danielle was heartbroken, momentarily living under a dark cloud. Fortunately, she turned to her new friends from Pace College and, more importantly, to her dear cousin Margrit, who had recently moved to New York from Zurich, Switzerland. At the time, Margrit was in her mid-thirties and was an accomplished secretary. Her first job in the States was in the employ of the International Paper Company. She was single, attractive, and in search of new adventure in the United States. In the beginning she bunked in an apartment on 81st Street with her younger brother Hans, who had come to New York several years before she had arrived.

Margrit left IPC for a better paying position in Long Island City, Queens, as secretary to the owner of Waldes Kohinoor, a manufacturer of fasteners and zippers. She also enrolled in night classes at City College, in upper Manhattan, in pursuit of a degree in world philosophy, a subject that had interested her ever since she'd attended school in Zurich. Hans, meanwhile, had gained a reputation in graphic arts and partnered with others who were also engaged in the graphic arts business. His skill was in designing colorful, catchy pictures for consumer products which found their way into popular magazines and onto billboards. At the time, Hans was dating Ann, and he married her not long after Margrit moved in. Hans and Ann eventually moved to Lincoln Towers on West 66th Street, across from the Juilliard School of Music, so Margrit had to find new digs.

While Margrit was still living with her brother Hans on 81st Street, though, she engaged in a conversation with the proprietor of the grocery across the street from her apartment. The grocer asked her if she would like a newborn kitten. Back in Switzerland, Margrit had owned a cat while living in her mother's house. This petit chat, a sweet looking, innocent kitten, with light black stripes and a round, cheerful face, was like a needy child sent from heaven. She took him at once, without much thought for where they both might end up, and named the cat Sebastian. I'm not quite sure where the name Sebastian came from, but I think the name suited his restless and energetic temperament.

As Hans and Ann were soon to be leaving their place, Margrit made a connection with Ruth Gottlieb, an old friend from Zurich who worked as a skilled seamstress in the American wing of the

Metropolitan Museum of Art, on East 84th Street and Fifth Avenue, and was also employed as an aid to Vladja Maske, a concert pianist from St. Petersburg, Russia. Vladja occupied an entire floor in a building located on West 90th Street, between Broadway and West End Avenue. She had two baby grand pianos in her oversized apartment. The living room and dining room were combined to form a sitting area that could comfortably accommodate 30 to 40 people when there were recitals for Vladja's more accomplished piano students. There was a modest kitchen where Ruth could prepare some fine Swiss and American cuisine. Vladja occupied a large master bedroom. Ruth slept in a more modest bedroom, and eventually convinced Vladja to allow Margrit to stay in another.

I'm not quite sure how Margrit was able to convince Vladja to allow her to keep a cat in that rather luxuriant apartment, but she must have been quite a salesperson indeed, for Sebastian soon actively yet mysteriously roamed around in the space. The petit chat grew into an almost miniature tiger, and his presence lent an air of exotic curiosity and perhaps risk to the enchanting surroundings.

After Danielle moved into her new space on West End Avenue and 97th Street with her two female roommates, she connected with her first cousin on her father's side of the family, Margrit, through their shared love of classical music. Danielle played the viola and Margrit played the cello, and, along with Ruth on piano and another female friend named Dusty on violin, they formed a quartet that met once a week in the evening to play some of their favorite classical pieces.

Chapter Fifty

The summer of 1967 was a joyful time in my life. After Charles's party, Danielle and I began to date. We often hung out with two other couples, as we all enjoyed each other's company. My playful friend Walter began to date Danielle's new friend Juliette as well. Another Pace Library coworker of ours, Rosemary Cunningham, was seeing Gunther McKewen, who lived in New Jersey. For a brief period, we three couples shared in some fun times.

New York winter weather is unpredictable. One year can bring record-breaking snowfall from October through mid-March, while the next can be mild, with little snowfall followed by an early spring. The winter of '67 was bitterly cold, starting as early as September, with snow frozen to the ground for months to follow. I can recall trekking from Pace College in lower Manhattan to Danielle's apartment building on West 97th Street. The streets were layered with ice, like a Russian tundra filling my frozen thoughts. Often, Danielle and I walked hand in hand, she wearing a light brown three-button woolen parka with a hood, over a pair of cream white dungarees and a homemade Swiss woolen sweater, while I wore a dark heavy coat over corduroy pants or dungarees and usually a sweater as well. Danielle and I tended to wear boot-like shoes to protect our feet from freezing. We generally wore the same clothes repeatedly, in order to live within our limited budgets.

Danielle received a small financial stipend from her parents living in Switzerland. It was enough for her to buy some canned vegetables that were on sale, some pasta or rice, instant coffee, and a pack of Lucky Strikes, which she could make last for maybe three days. At the time, I was living with my next-door neighbor of many years on Avenue V, Mr. Cohen, in the second-floor apartment of the Weinberg house, since Mama's funeral. She had passed away in March 1967.

During the blustery winter of '67, Danielle was finishing her college tenure at Pace and preparing to graduate the following January. She and I continued to work part-time in the school library. I was then in my second year at Pace and, in addition to working in the library, on Friday nights I continued to wait tables at Pips on the Bay, in Sheepshead Bay.

Instead of sporting a new 1961 Ford Galaxie from my more lucrative days working at the Publishers Guild, I was driving a used 1958 Olds—a gas guzzler, though, of course, gas was quite cheap in 1967. Sometimes, on cold wintry nights, I stayed over and studied in Danielle's tiny bedroom. On one such occasion, Danielle was sitting at her desk, engrossed in writing a letter to her mother on aerogram, then a popular and inexpensive international paper form of written communication. For the moment, lost in her thoughts, she leaned forward to puff on a cigarette, and her long thin hair fell forward, touched a cigarette ash, and caught fire. I happened to be sitting next to Danielle, reading a book, but the moment I saw the flame, without even thinking, my hands came together and smothered the fire. Other than heightened anxiety for both of us, no damage was done.

Although I won a writing contest in my first-year English

comparative lit. class, under the guidance of my thoughtful and caring instructor, Mrs. Cushing, when writing class papers, particularly financial or economic summaries, Danielle stayed close by me, looking over my shoulder and instructing me as to the correct form and content. At last my guardian angel had arrived. While I wrote many of my English and history papers creatively, often the logic and sequence of the text turned out questionable. Danielle, with her five years of Latin study and her acute and skillful abilities with language, acquired from her schooling in Switzerland, gave me precious guidance that enabled me to satisfactorily complete my many required class projects.

Danielle played the viola, and hearing the work of her favorite composers sparked my abiding appreciation of classical music. Although Sal, my eldest brother, played the violin, and his two young sons, Stephen and Philip, were learning to play piano and would occasionally give me a free concert when I visited them on Long Island, I hadn't been ready yet to embrace classical music, much as I enjoyed their talents. When Danielle played, in a moment of relaxation, one of her long-playing records on her portable record player, I was suddenly transported by a new musical love. We listened to works of Bach, Mozart, Vivaldi, and other composers, played by the likes of Jean-Pierre Rampal, Maurice André, Clara Haskil, Cécile Chaminade, and many other wonderful musicians. Miraculously, a marvelous new world of music had come right to my doorstep.

In addition to blissful musical moments spent at Danielle's apartment, from time to time I had the pleasure of attending classical concerts at the nearby home of Vladja Maske. Once a week, perhaps on a Tuesday night, Danielle, Dusty, Margrit, and Ruth would come together, forming a string quartet to perform wonderful classical pieces for maybe two or three hours. This was music that gradually entered my very being, such that, to this day, it remains the music I choose to listen to on a regular basis. The only catch to attending those wonderful concerts, though, was that I had to share the experience with Sebastian.

As I mentioned earlier, Sebastian was that oversized tiger cat who had become Margrit's best friend. It was difficult for me to get comfortable in any chair or couch at those concerts, in what otherwise was a very cozy living space. I always felt the menacing presence of Sebastian, who either roamed or scampered throughout the apartment. I never knew when or where he might pop up next. I was constantly on guard, fearing that at any moment and without any warning Sebastian would land on my shoulders, poised to take a chunk of skin out of my precious neck. Needless to say, I did not attend those weekly concerts on a regular basis. However, I must confess, over time, as my neck remained intact, I did manage to warm up to that frightening house pet.

In the early fall, I met, for the first time, Danielle's mother Helene. Whenever Danielle was away from home, her mom missed her dearly and would come out of her comfort zone in Zurich to visit her daughter in the Big Apple. Not that Helene didn't have an innate sense for adventure; it was just that Hans, Danielle's father, was finishing his last year in the employ of UBS, and for the most part wasn't at all interested in traveling across the pond. That feeling would change in later years, but in the meantime it forced Helene to travel alone.

I am quite sure that Helene wondered about this peculiar fellow named Clayton Martorello. Where did he come from? Where is Brooklyn? And why hadn't her daughter made plans to come home after her studies and settle down with a nice Swiss lad, or at the very least come back to begin her teaching career in Zurich? Although Danielle loved studying the works of some of the great

American writers, her secret desire was to teach mathematics—although, at that moment in time, she felt sure that teaching mathematics in Switzerland was for men only.

During that getting-acquainted period, Danielle offered her mother the opportunity to see her boyfriend Clayton in action, by inviting her to Pips on the Bay on a Friday night. I gathered both ladies one Friday late afternoon and, in my then-trusty Olds, drove them from the Upper West Side apartment in Manhattan to the southeast side of Brooklyn, in Sheepshead Bay. By eight o'clock those two lovely ladies were comfortably sitting in two ringside seats, in time for the first of two evening shows. They had dinner on the house—hamburgers and fries—and genuinely laughed their way through two lively performances while I adroitly waited tables, covering the entire room by myself. The crowds were not large, so it was not too busy an evening, which afforded me ample time to still spend moments with Danielle and Maman.

On our way home that evening, Danielle's mom quietly whispered to her daughter that I had nice hands. I took that to be an auspicious sign.

Chapter Fifty-One

I was introduced to Danielle's mother as Jim (a derivative of James, my baptismal middle name). My own mother loved the name Clayton. Where or when she came upon Clayton is still a mystery to me and to the rest of my family as well. It is possible she heard the name while listening to one of the more popular melodramatic radio programs of the day. According to the good priests of Our Lady of Grace Roman Catholic Church, I needed a saint's name as a backup plan. Somehow James was chosen, and thus I answered to Clayton James Martorello. Where the letter "O" at the end of my family name came from, I'm also not sure, since my father and all my siblings have an "A" instead—Martorella.

As I grew older, answering to Clayton on the street began to seem unusual to me, since my neighborhood friends, from mostly Jewish or Italian ancestry, were given more common local names or nicknames. "Jimmy" seemed more normal to me, so, at an early, youthful age, I began telling my friends to call me Jim or Jimmy. In junior high school my brother Sal, the family lawyer, took steps to change my name legally to James Clayton, but the process stalled out at some point, perhaps because the official change seemed unnecessary when I was already called by so many different names. All my immediate relatives as well as my aunts and uncles from both sides of the family addressed me as Clayton; I can still recall my Uncle Dominick, from my father's side of the family, getting my attention in the kitchen of the Riviera by barking out in a commanding tone, "Clayton!!! Get the carts ready!" The Italian version of my name, favored by Mama, was Claynta. My brother Rudy and my two sisters, Anita and Barbara, often called me Cloots, to go with my role as their "baby brother," and that name and role have continued even up to my present age of 76.

From junior high school until I was 27 years old, when the Swiss authorities had a look at my birth certificate, I answered to the name of Jim in the outside world. After that, I officially returned to Clayton, although my in-laws from Switzerland, by force of habit, continued to always call me Jim.

Margrit, Danielle's cousin, also knew me exclusively as Jim. Throughout the period when Danielle and I were dating, Margrit often joined us for coffee, conversation, and dessert at a local café near Pace College or some other spot in the Village. After work hours Alan Margolis, Danielle's one-time landlord, would occasionally join us as well. He was a fan of the opera, and at times we might also go to an Off-Broadway play or a classical concert.

Margrit majored in philosophy at City College. During our impromptu gatherings, conversations usually evolved into an animated discussion over various philosophical differences of opinions. Pretending to be naïve, Alan often asked simplistic questions that appeared to have easy answers, but still led to differences between Margrit and myself. Danielle, as the voice of reason and saintly clairvoyance, usually could be counted upon to come to our rescue, in bringing our discussion to a resolution and giving all of us an exit strategy, allowing us to continue our discourse on another evening over café au lait.

Through cousin Margrit I learned about Danielle's family, from fascinating reminisces of family life in Switzerland. I learned that Hans, Danielle's father, had been an astute banker in the employ of the Union Bank of Switzerland since the age of sixteen. He was sponsored by his uncle Fritz Klarer, Margrit's father, who was a senior executive at the same bank. Hans's father passed away when Hans was barely four years old. His mother Mina, sister to Fritz, had to raise Hans and his three young siblings during difficult times.

Jacques, two years older than his brother Hans, would go on to an agricultural school of higher learning, which in turn led to a professional career in the field. Hans, meanwhile, honed his unique analytical talent in banking. Hans had two sisters as well: Frieda, who was very bright, self-sacrificing, and devoted to her siblings, and spent much of her life in the employ of the Nievergelt Stationery business; and her older sister Elizabeth, who furthered her studies at the university after spending several youthful years in the employ of UBS, where she demonstrated great skill in banking and business. Elizabeth eventually married Hans Nievergelt, an astute businessman from Oerlikon, and together they had a wonderful family of six children.

Uncle Fritz realized at an early stage in his nephew Hans's banking career that Hans had a keen intellect and an almost natural facility for learning foreign languages. In his youthful years Hans quickly learned all aspects of banking, and he journeyed to England, Italy, and France to engage with correspondents outside of Switzerland while in the employ of UBS. It was in Lausanne, Switzerland, where he first set eyes on the beautiful Helene, his bride-to-be.

Chapter Fifty-Two

I was gradually spending more time with Danielle, while steadily growing more distant from my former neighborhood friends.

By that time, Fat Stevee had married a beautiful Italian gal from across the ocean. After a grandiose wedding, the newlyweds settled down somewhere on Long Island. After learning the butchering business from working in his uncle's store in Long Island City, Queens, Stevee became a successful meat distributor, serving customers throughout the city. Cousin Benny continued to work with his mother, Aunt Nick, in the luncheonette. He dated a gal who raised and trained German shepherds for the police. Eventually, the luncheonette was sold and Aunt Nick moved to Florida to live with Christina, her granddaughter. Benny and his girlfriend moved to Phoenix, Arizona, and opened a laundry business. I continued to play softball with a neighborhood team in a Brooklyn beer league, and only occasionally popped in to Bill's Candy Store on Neck Road to catch up with my old cronies.

My intellectual curiosity continued to grow with each passing day at Pace College. Life with Danielle, Margrit, and friends put a new sunny spirit into my young bones. My curiosity and my thirst for knowledge had no boundaries, though I had to live within my monetary limits. Even so, I was a happy camper. Life was good. In that moment, I honestly felt that I was no longer alone.

I'm pausing here for an instant to take a snapshot of a place where I spent many hours of my youthful life, and where I was soon to remain no longer: the neighborhood mecca we all knew as Bill's.

On a Saturday in June or July, let us say around 1953 or '54, as the dog days of summer were approaching, the two top baseball teams in the Coney Island League were about to clash. All week long prior to the big game everyone in the neighborhood, from Dubrow's on Kings Highway to Bernie's Diner on Coney Island Avenue, was placing bets on either Tony Maniscalco or Sandy Koufax, Dairy Queen versus Nathan's. Sandy Koufax is probably still famous enough to need no introduction, but Tony Maniscalco was the son of a fishmonger who made the daily rounds about Neck Road, selling fresh fish from his delivery truck. Tony was a nicely built seventeen-year-old who possessed a great curve to go along with a lively fastball.

The game played out to a one-to-nothing score. Nathan's won on a tenth-inning home run. Even though he was on the losing side, Tony pitched the greatest game of his life. There was no doubt to anyone who patronized Bill's Candy Store that Tony Maniscalco was the hero of Gravesend Neck Road. As the unending pounds of fresh flounder peeled off the scales and into the hands of the local folk, one crusty old Italian fishmonger never missed a moment to extol the greatness of his son: "He's a-gonna make-a the big leagues some-a-day."

Ten years had gone by in a flash and there, for the last time, I wandered into Bill's Candy Store. Bill and Neddy were still there standing guard over their precious goldmine. Bill was happy to see me. He whipped up an egg cream, my favorite, and said, "It's on the house." I asked him how the old gang was getting along.

When I mentioned Tony's name, there was a subtle pause, a sigh, and sort of a hoarse cough in Bill's voice. A glance at Neddy's teary-eyed look instantly signaled to me that something wasn't right.

Bill asked, "Didn't you hear about Anthony?" I answered, "The last I heard was that Tony got married and had a couple of kids." "That's right!" Bill said. He continued, "They're two beautiful kids. They come into the store almost every day after school." Once again there was a moment of silence. I thought to myself, "God, what is it?" I looked up at Bill and said, "Come on then, tell me what's the matter." Bill replied, once again in a hoarse voice, "Tony . . . He suddenly got sick last year and died of cancer." Neddy was in tears as she leaned over the counter and cupped my hands with her own. She said, "It's not right, it shouldn't have happened to such a wonderful boy."

I left the candy store with some sadness in my heart. In a flash, so many memories raced through my head. As I turned up East 7th Street and walked toward my house on Avenue V, I realized that I could not turn back the clock. The lot on Neck Road had been replaced by an eight-story apartment building, and even Bill's Candy Store would soon disappear too, to be remodeled into some other venue. I realized, in that moment, that my life was about to go in a completely different direction. It had to.

Not even two years had gone by during my tenure at Pace College when it suddenly occurred to me that Danielle would graduate in January 1968. Upon graduation, she would return to Switzerland, her mother country. During that fall season, we could share a few precious moments together. The wonderful landscape of Central Park, and the variety of museum spaces, concerts, and Off-Broadway plays, gave Danielle and me a chance to know and become closer to each other and to learn about ourselves as we were and as we meant to be.

On a Sunday afternoon toward the end of September, at a time when summer was beginning to give way to the fall, I decided to cook a Brooklyn Italian meal for Danielle, her close friends, and her two roommates, Jill and Sarah, in their Upper West Side apartment. I borrowed some of my sister Anita's pots and pans along with her special meatball and tomato sauce recipes.

The occasion was Jill's birthday. The menu called for home-made tomato sauce, Anita's mildly seasoned meatballs, chicken cutlet Parmigiana, thin spaghetti, and a fresh green salad. The dinner was for ten people: Danielle and me, Alan and Margrit, Jack and Jill, Sarah and Peter, and Walter and Juliette. Sarah and Danielle bought a delicious chocolate cream birthday cake from Zabar's bakery on upper Broadway, not far from their apartment. During my high school days working at the Riviera, cooking in the kitchen had become familiar territory for me. On balance, then, with a decade of experience between those two times, the birthday meal was a success.

The one surprise for me was when I first came out of the kitchen to begin serving the dinner: sitting next to each other, there at the living room table, were Jack and Walter, both wearing the same black-and-white checkered cloth sport jacket. Coincidence or not, for a moment I thought that I was seeing double. Anyway, the meal was a hit with everyone. With a light Italian red wine to go with the meal, a good time was truly had by all.

The next outstanding culinary moment came when Tante Frieda's wonderful chocolate kuchen arrived in New York. I'm not sure if it was November or December 1967—that is, whether it was near Thanksgiving or Christmas—but Tante Frieda's once-a-year, family-famous chocolate kuchen arrived just before a weekend. On a Friday, a pink slip was taped to the door of Danielle's westside apartment. It read that she could pick up a parcel at the local post office. Her Tante Frieda had previously written via an aerogram that the kuchen was on its way to America.

Danielle declared to her roommates that she would like to invite them and their boyfriends that same Saturday evening for dessert. I slept over the night before and agreed to accompany Danielle to the post office the following morning. At about ten a.m. we arrived at the local post office, and, to our surprise, we discovered that it was closed for the weekend. That notice sure was a bummer. So what could we do?

In an instant, I took the pink slip from Danielle and asked her to wait for me at the front entrance. I nonchalantly walked around the block to the back of the building, and, as I suspected, postal delivery trucks were loading and unloading all sorts of packages. I approached one of the workmen with a fiver in my hand and gave him the pink slip with a request to somehow locate the kuchen.

I knew it was a longshot, but, sure enough, a few minutes later he returned with the treasured package in hand. Gleefully, I gave the man the five-dollar tip. I had a warm feeling of good fortune as I scampered back to Danielle at the front entrance with her package.

Danielle was in disbelief when I delivered the package to her. "How did you manage to get this kuchen?" she incredulously demanded. Without much ado, I explained that I simply tipped the worker and he found me the package. To my surprise, Danielle responded, "Jim! You were cheating!" For a moment, I had to collect myself before answering, "No! I just thought that I could take a chance of retrieving the package at the loading dock, in the back of the building." "This is not right! You shouldn't have done that!" she protested further.

In any case, we left the post office and walked back to Danielle's apartment, with Tante Frieda's kuchen in hand. On the way back, lost in our thoughts, we had nothing to say to each other. I wondered, "What was this all about?" I thought she would be delighted to have her chocolate kuchen. Instead, I was rewarded with recrimination.

I found out later that day, as the dense cloud of confusion lifted, that that type of transaction was simply not done in Switzerland. Danielle told me that I had cheated. If our relationship was to endure, which at that moment in time, with her graduation forthcoming, was not exactly a certainty, I would have to muster up some old-fashioned American pragmatism. I instinctively realized that I needed to forgo some of my old Brooklyn street smarts.

At the dinner table that same Saturday evening, Tante Frieda's kuchen was a resounding success. Danielle forgave me, and in that moment of forgiveness I realized that our approaches to life's testy moments were quite different. However, and more importantly, I knew that our friendship would endure despite our differences, and would continue to evolve in a positive way.

I also came to realize that Danielle and I were practical idealists. Our thoughts of life and humanity had to make sense to both of us for us to thrive. There was often debate in our relationship, but it generally ended in healthy compromise. Almost always, when Danielle would lean over my shoulder, she would exude her loving warmth and confidence in me as we confidently moved ahead with our life together.

We were the same height, five feet eight inches—but only when Danielle wore her flat ballerina shoes, which was almost always. Even if she wore a one- or two-inch heel, I always felt quite comfortable in her presence. She was slim and good-looking. Her hair was thin, light brown in color, almost blond. Her twinkly, steely blue eyes, much like her father's, were engaging, and above all friendly. Danielle's nose and mouth bore classical features and her face was peachy smooth. Her forehead was prominent and completely free of wrinkles.

Over time, I came to realize that Danielle, like a ballerina, had great legs that connected to her shapely hips and upper body in a seamless flow of beauty. Living on a limited student budget, Danielle usually wore a beautiful cloth-like miniskirt, of a blue and yellow floral pattern, that was very sexy in a tasteful way. On special occasions, such as a winter concert at Lincoln Center, Danielle dressed up in a classy, stylish cherry red two-piece wool suit, with the skirt falling to slightly below her knees.

With the exception of a thin eyeliner and a fine pink lipstick to cover her smallish lips, Danielle had little need or desire to cover her smooth skin with makeup. She always wore a beautiful gold Huguenot cross around her neck which fell to just below the open collar of a fine white cotton blouse.

As for me, I'm not quite sure what Danielle saw that led her to consider my prospects. My hair was brown and thinly textured, usually combed. At the center-top of my forehead, my brown hair folded to a widow's peak. I had a Roman nose, a bit wide at its base. The rest of my facial features consisted of brown eyes, a nice mouth, and smooth skin. I suppose, overall, I was not too bad to look at. Having played baseball and football, plus many other team sport activities, since I was a young boy, my body had an athletic tone, but I wasn't too muscular. I figured, whatever it was that led her to accept me as a partner, I'd be better off thanking my lucky stars than asking too many questions about it!

It was soon December 1967. There was some snow on the ground and it was quite cold. One evening we found ourselves meandering along upper Broadway, not far from Danielle's apartment on 97th Street, when we came upon a small secondhand jewelry shop.

Danielle was about to finish her studies at Pace and would graduate in January, one month later. She was a straight-A student with only one B in all her classes. That B came from a very nasty English lit professor. I still had two and a half years to go in my college program, and my grades were nowhere near as pristine.

On turning 25, Danielle would be returning to Switzerland at the finish of her studies. I, on the other hand, would still be engaged in my studies and likely clueless as to what my prospects would be. Our feelings about our future together were at times rather uncertain. I had never set foot outside of Brooklyn, and if there was to be an ocean separating us, suddenly it seemed like there might be no reason to continue our life together. Life poses its own conditions and often presents what appear to be insurmountable demands.

It seemed to me that since we came from two very different worlds, to which, apparently, we would each soon have to return alone, our friendship would also have to end. Yet there we were, peering through a tiny jewelry store window and spotting two simple but elegant gold-plated rings. We looked at each other and said, "What are we to do?" At that moment, we really didn't know. As if pulled along by some unknown force of gravity, we wandered into the shop.

I suspect that the jeweler with thick glasses and bushy eyebrows, seeing us staring at the rings in the window showcase, guessed that we were good prospects for making a sale. And he would have been right, because, before we knew it, those very rings were ours. After closing the deal, he complimented us on being a handsome couple and gave us his good wishes for a good life ahead.

We left the shop feeling warm and fuzzy, hand in hand.

Suddenly, as we stepped onto the sidewalk on Broadway, we spontaneously embraced each other and pressed our lips together, in a prolonged kiss. Around us, hands were clapping, like in the movies, and we gradually returned to earth. Just like that, we had decided to get married.

Chapter Fifty-Three

Fate and faith are powerful forces in the human experience. In the six months following our engagement, many events transpired in the lead-up to our wedding on June 18, 1968. First, Danielle graduated and returned to Switzerland. We corresponded constantly, with all our plans arranged for reuniting in Switzerland for the wedding after I finished my semester's classes. Second, the Swiss authorities needed to see my birth certificate. That was sent, neatly enclosed inside an aerogram. Upon receiving that document in Zurich, Danielle was shocked that I did not mail such an important piece of paper in an official, stamped envelope. I thought I was being economical. After a resounding response from Danielle, I was advised that other important paperwork should not be included in an aerogram. Aerograms were reserved for intermittent thoughts of friendship and love.

Margrit, Danielle's stateside cousin, suggested to me that after our marriage and upon returning to the United States we might consider housesitting in an eighteen-room English Tudor house in Bayside, Queens. The owner of the Waldes Kohinoor zipper factory in Long Island City, where Margrit worked as a private secretary to Mr. Waldes, wanted a couple to live in his mother's house for the summer while his mother would be staying in Czechoslovakia with his sister. As luck would have it, Danielle and I could live in that massive house rent-free, thus giving us an opportunity to hunt for an apartment where we could settle down while I could continue to attend Pace full-time. We of course agreed to that windfall arraignment. Again, as luck would have it, the elderly mother of Mr. Waldes decided to continue to live in Czechoslovakia for an additional year and a half, allowing Danielle and me to continue living in that wonderful house and enabling me to finish my college studies on a full-time schedule.

As further proof that saints and free spirits roam the corridors of our marvelous planet, Danielle's loving brother and sister, Jacques and Marinette, along with Danielle's parents, Hans and Helene, set the stage for an exceptionally wonderful wedding.

Up till our pending marriage I had never been on a plane, so suddenly finding myself on a flight to Zurich, Switzerland, by myself, no less, was quite an experience. When I arrived in Kloten Airport, as I was exiting the plane, I continued to follow some of the people on to another plane that would be traveling to Israel. I gradually realized to my great surprise that I was walking with the wrong group. Somehow, I managed to safely make my way to the arrival area where Danielle and Marinette collected me. At some point several years after our marriage, Danielle confessed to me that when I first arrived in Zurich she had her doubts as to who she was marrying. Driving back to Hirschgartnerweg 22, Danielle's house, having been apart for six months, we seemed like strangers to each other. For me, it was brand-new territory—and, by extension, a brand-new life.

Chapter Fifty-Four

Danielle's parents owned a three-story building that was home to six apartments. There were two families to each floor. On the right side were the larger two-bedroom units, and on the left were the one-bedroom units. Each apartment came with a spacious living room/dining room area, smaller sitting room, and a corridor that connected with all the rooms. There was a central stairwell that began in the basement, labeled "La Cave," and it ascended all three floors, ending at the attic ("galetas").

The building was one of two solidly built concrete and brick dwellings, surrounded and separated by carefully cut lawns, trees, and shrubs. The second, cornered apartment house was owned by Jacques Geering, Hans's older brother.

As Danielle and I walked on the cement block path leading up to the entrance door, there was Marinette smiling at us through her open kitchen window. She wore a cheerful smile and greeted us warmly as we entered the building. As we entered Marinette's home, she leaned toward me and, as was customary upon greeting, kissed me and then Danielle three times on the cheeks (left, right, left). That was a first for me. We then ascended to the top floor of the building, to Danielle's parents' home in the apartment on the right, and were greeted by Maman, Danielle's mother. Marinette and Maman had similar rosy cheeks, dark brown eyes, and a cheerful, sunny demeanor which, I was advised later, came from the French Swiss–Roman side of the family in Lausanne, where Danielle's mother grew up. After saying hello to Maman and once again exchanging a three-kiss greeting, we all sat down, Marinette included, around the kitchen table ("La Table") and enjoyed a wonderfully baked apfelkuchen garnished with raisins alongside a cup of café au lait. After our lovely dessert, it was bedtime for me. I slept for about six hours straight through the middle of the day.

I fell asleep just before ten a.m. and awoke sometime after three o'clock in the afternoon. I awoke with the sun coming through the wide bedroom window, not knowing if it was the next morning or late afternoon on the same day. In any case, I could hear the birds chirping and Marinette's children playing in the backyard. Upon looking out the window and seeing a beautiful blue sky, I began to collect myself. There was a gentle knock on the door. I said, "Come in." Danielle entered and asked me to accompany her to the Migros supermarket, one of the major chain stores in Switzerland. Our new life together had begun.

We were two weeks away from the big day. During the first week, Danielle and I traveled on the number 14 tram to Oerlikon, a sector of Zurich about two miles north of the main bahnhof (central railway station). In 1968, Oerlikon was a more provincial part of central Zurich. There were local clothing stores that carried lesser brand-name items, although there was also one ABM department store for the one-stop shopper.

Approximately five tram stops from Hirschgartnerweg 22 (Danielle's home address), we exited in front of Hotel Sternen, one of Oerlikon's finer classical hotels. Walking north from that stately hotel and bearing left, we crossed a wide plaza which doubled as a chess heaven catering to the avid local players. Often there were three games taking place at the same time and a large crowd bearing down upon all the participants. Each chess piece was about two feet tall and was made of a rather heavy white plastic, weighing three or four pounds. Hans Geering, Danielle's father, was an avid chess player who often stopped to have a look at the matches before entering the Migros supermarket.

The day after I arrived in Zurich, Danielle once again took me to Migros to do some shopping for her mother. Upon entering Migros at the street level, I was completely overtaken by the aroma of roasted chicken, pork, and beef alongside sautéed vegetables, pastries, and fresh pizza just out of the oven, all of those morsels extending across the entire counter. For the first time I was introduced to schinkengipfeli, a wonderful-tasting warm croissant filled with bits of pork and spices. It was simply out of this world. To this day, whenever I set foot in a Migros, my first stop is at the gipfeli counter.

After filling two cloth shopping bags with fresh produce, including rhubarb and prunes (that is, plums—they call dried prunes "pruneaux") for making Maman's flavorful open-faced pies encased in Migros's excellent pie crust, we walked over to the local butcher shop for some fresh ground beef, pork, and chicken before paying for all those treats and heading for home. When we arrived at Hirschi (HGW-22), we exited the number 14 tram and continued along the concrete path leading to Danielle's house. On the path, light poles came on as nightfall approached. Suddenly, we heard a loud shriek: "Yo-Ho, Guli-Guli-Goo!" Before we could turn around, an enormous burst of energy was upon us. It was Jacques, Danielle's six-foot-six younger brother. As he zipped past us I noticed a metal change purse strapped around his waist which jingled from the various-sized coins inside each chamber. He swung around the lamppost in front of us. First he gave his sister a robust bear hug, and then he wrapped his long arms around me as well. While feeling somewhat overtaken, I saw a warm and cheerful smile stretch across his face from one rosy red cheek to the other. He was so happy to see us. In his youthful vigor, Jacques gave me a feeling of renewed energy. With such warm hosts, after I had made such a long, arduous trip from the States, I finally began to feel comfortable in my surroundings.

In the days leading up to the wedding there were several important details to attend to. Of the utmost importance was a visit to the Zurich city register, in order to record our marriage. Marinette accompanied Danielle and me to the administrator's office building in town alongside the Limmat River, which I believe wasn't far from the Fraumünster Kirche (the Church of Our Lady). In an official Swiss-like manner we sat on heavy leather chairs facing a sturdy wooden desk. The magistrate, who entered our names into the official book, was tall and thin and wore steel-rimmed glasses. He was dressed in a standard light grey wool suit and white cotton shirt and wore a thin black tie, befitting his profession. I can recall that he had some difficulty pronouncing the word "citizen"; he stuttered, "Cit-cit-cit-citizen." Upon the entry of our names into that book of life, we were officially married. Having completed our official business, we three proceeded to Honold's Confiserie (Maman's favorite place to go to for an afternoon tea).

Also, during the week preceding our wedding ceremony, I visited with several close friends of Danielle's as well as more of her family. Our first stop, early in the week, was Lausanne, Switzerland, to pay a visit with Tante Yvonne and Uncle Alex, Helene's sister and brother-in-law. We boarded the nine o'clock train from Zurich to Lausanne on a warm, sunny morning. There were lots of people coming and going in all directions, as one would expect at the central station of the Zurich Eisenbahn. Alongside only a few articles of clothing fitted into a small valise, my backpack contained two sandwiches filled with fois gras, two apples, a bar of chocolate, and a bottle of water. We walked from one end of the train to the other and entered the second-class carriage. Our train slowly began to move, and after affectionately waving goodbye to Marinette, Danielle's sweet and dear sister, we were on our way to Lausanne. Allow me to pause for a moment of reflection as I retrace that lovely time in my life's journey.

Some people look back and cling to the past, while others look forward and embrace the future. I suppose there is room in every lifetime for at least a bit of both; great, enriching literature has been written from the perspective of both these ostensibly opposing views.

For the first time, as Danielle and I traveled by train from Zurich to Lausanne, the magnificent countryside landscape of farms and small villages coming into view mentally carried me from the crowded city streets of New York and Brooklyn into a dream world of Swiss charm and beauty. Watching the sloping vineyards covered by the bright sun of mid-morning, coupled with the cheerful smile of my future lifelong partner, seated there across from me, was like being on a cloud moving along to heaven. Inside the train, on the platform, and in the streets of Lausanne the talk was pure Swiss French. Putting my classroom conversational French to good use, and with Danielle's patient guidance, I was given a chance to partake of European old-world charm. I sensed that the Roman world was still alive in my surroundings. There I was in touch with antiquity, and it was a wonderfully transformative feeling.

Our first stop was at UBS Lausanne, where Tante Yvonne's husband Alex, the bank's manager, greeted us. My first impression was that he appeared to be bigger than life. He was average height, maybe five feet ten and on the portly side, but not fat. He wore a black suit, white shirt, and a conventional black tie. He had straight, shiny, thin black hair, lying flat upon a sound, shiny reddish face. Alex had already had his lunch when he greeted us at the front door of the bank. He kissed Danielle warmly and gave me a firm handshake. He took us to a mauve marble counter at the center of the room, behind which he tossed a handful of Swiss coins down the stairs and into the cellar, where the bank's vaults were presumably located. In a commanding, confident voice, he told me that this was his bank. He then put into my hand two hundred Swiss francs, equivalent, at the time, to fifty American dollars. He insisted that with it I must take Danielle to a grand luncheon cuisine at one of Lausanne's finest provincial restaurants and then later to come to his family's house for dinner.

At lunch I was treated to raclette cheese for the first time, with all the trimmings. We settled in an underground French cave-type café containing a large brick oven fireplace where the raclette was cooked and then placed on metal plates. The warm cheese and crusty bread simply and smoothly melted in my mouth. To the taste buds, that delicacy in that cloistered atmosphere of antiquity was heaven on earth. In that moment, I also realized that I was protected by a true angel—Danielle, the lady of my life.

That evening was spent at the home of Alex and Yvonne Gallay. We were greeted by Tante Yvonne, Alex, their lovely daughter Monique, her husband Michel, and Monique and Michel's four children, Blaise, Sylvain, and twins Aude and Thierry. They lived in a three-story, multi-family dwelling, settled on a spacious plot of land that contained a rustic, green garden and a comfortably shaded sitting area. Dinner, as would be expected, was a full-course experience from soup to nuts, with a tasty crêpe pour finir. And, as if all that wasn't enough, the next day was really something else—a first-time, one-of-a-kind experience.

We were up bright and early and on our way to Alex's country farm, just outside of Lausanne and at a slightly higher elevation. It was late morning when we arrived and were greeted by Monsieur Abbe, the manager of the farm. Before I realized it, we three were on the side of the barn sipping some of Alex's fine white wine while overlooking beautiful brown cows, roaming chickens, and birds, before settling down on a soft patch of grass. It was siesta time. Later on, Alex and I somehow made our way back to the large one-room chalet where we would partake of a tasty filet mignon dinner garnished with champignon de Paris in a bourguignonne sauce. Outstanding! After playing a board game called "Pigs" which Alex always won, we all retired to bed. Danielle and Tante Yvonne remained in the chalet, with room only for one bed, while Alex and I retired to the barn. For me, such a rural excursion was a first, and it was a rather interesting night to remember.

We slept on the upper floor of the barn, Alex on one bed of straw and me on another. I wore a normal two-piece pajama, while Alex was dressed in a cream-colored one-piece pajama with feet, making him look a bit like a large bunny rabbit. As I settled into my bed of straw, I could hear Alex snoring away nearby. Below me were the contented cows, mooing with cowbells clinking. Somehow, I finally fell asleep. The next morning, I awoke bathed in the glow of a vast sunny sky, which seemed to descend right into the space where I slept. After a sumptuous continental breakfast of bread, butter, jam, and wonderfully brewed café, Danielle and I were on our way back to Zurich. But first we exchanged some hugs and a hearty handshake as we left Tante Yvonne and Uncle Alex behind, for they planned to stay in their chalet for a few more days.

Back in Zurich, Danielle and I were on the go again. We suddenly realized that the big day on Sunday would be upon us quickly.

In the middle of our second week together in Switzerland, while we were going over our preparations for the wedding, we received a wonderful gift. It was a cardboard boat, painted in light blue and grey, with colorful cantonal flags draped across the top line and descending to the front and back. Along the sides of the boat were portals made from Swiss five-franc pieces. It was affectionally constructed by Marinette's closest old friends, Marianne and Fridli, along with members of Bevio, a social Swiss youth group to which Danielle and Marinette belonged.

Later, as we walked through the park leading up to the Alte Kirche Witikon (an old, beautiful church), I noticed someone standing on a hilltop, blowing into an elongated alpine horn. I realized it was a Swiss local folksong, and it was coming from the lips of Peter Geering, the younger son of Jacques and Mirna, Hans's brother and sister-in-law. For me, it was a mystical moment.

All week long Danielle kept reminding me that at the church altar, when the minister read us our vows and she squeezed my hand, I would have to respond, "Je promets." It would be the intro into a new world for me, with no turning back. I was transported, almost by sheer magic, or perhaps God's will, or divine providence; henceforth I would be ensconced in the most wonderful Swiss family, a new, welcoming second family I would retain for the rest of my life.

Danielle, my wife, partner, and guardian angel, had brought me so much unanticipated joy, with experiences I never even dreamed of. Though, funny enough, I later did remember that as a young boy of maybe nine or ten I briefly had a crush on a fictitious Swiss Miss, a woman dressed in a colorful traditional costume who sang and danced in an Italian Swiss Colony wine commercial that aired regularly on Brooklyn's local television station. Perhaps, somehow, in the unlikely surroundings of 628 Avenue V, I caught just the slightest glimpse of the charmed future that was in store for me, though it ended up being a future far better than any wine commercial that was ever made.

After the church service, we all entered the family glass-covered bus, yet another first for me. As we proceeded on our way up a mountain pass, coming around some of the narrow turns along which only one vehicle could go at one time, amidst the laughter and good cheer being had by all, there was a sudden loud but friendly horn sound: "Tee-Ta-Tow, Tee-Ta-Tow." That seemed to serve as a theme tune of sorts as we scurried along toward our midday wedding reception.

The only downside to that glorious moment was that it rained all day long. Somewhere there is a family picture of Danielle and me, along with a few family members, standing at the base of the outer stone wall of Gasthaus Hirschen, Kyburg, holding umbrellas and standing in the rain just prior to entering through the front door.

As with most joyful weddings there, fabulous Swiss food was served in a formal setting. There were perhaps forty or fifty members of the Geering family and close friends seated at several long tables, arranged in an oblong fashion allowing us to all see one another, as in one large circle. I believe it was Marinette who, with her incredible artistry, perhaps assisted by her equally creative husband Christian, constructed a miniature ten-carriage train made out of cardboard and wine bottle corks. On that wonderful creation, each car carried a specific written piece of the history of Danielle's life and the events leading up to the moment of our wedding. The train journeyed past each table so that everyone could read the text and glance at the simple but beautiful drawings by Marinette and Christian which depicted the life of Danielle. After a hearty meal, together we all formed a single line and happily danced our way through the castle. After that merriment, we returned to our places to conclude our wonderful wedding, with tasty pâtisserie, excellent Swiss café, and some schnapps. As of June 15, 1968, Danielle and I were officially united.

We spent that night at Hirschgartnerweg, in the house of Danielle's parents. On the next day I can still remember waving goodbye to Hans and Helene, Danielle's parents, and to Tante Yvonne and "Oncle" Alex, who stood together on the third-floor outdoor balcony as we walked through the household garden toward the number 14 tram. The following day we began our honeymoon in Zermatt, at the foot of the famous Swiss Matterhorn. Shortly after our weeklong honeymoon, we headed back to the States, off to a flying start in our new life together.

Looking back, in all likelihood, I think I fell in love with Danielle the very moment that I met her.

Chapter Fifty-Five

Before our trip to Zurich, Danielle's cousin Margrit had put us in contact with Mr. Waldes, for whom she worked as a private secretary. Mr. Waldes's mother had decided to go to Czechoslovakia for a summer vacation and to be with her married daughter as well. At the praiseworthy recommendation of Margrit on our behalf, Mr. Waldes had said we could live in his mother's English Tudor house in the posh neighborhood of Bayside. We were to live there just for that summer, upon returning from Switzerland, shortly after our marriage. But as luck would have it, Mr. Waldes's mother decided to remain in Czechoslovakia for a year and a half. We continued living in the house throughout that entire period, which allowed for me to finish college on a full-time schedule and attain a bachelor's degree in economics in the minimum amount of time. To make ends meet, I continued working Friday nights at Pips on the Bay and part-time during the week at the Pace College library. Danielle, meanwhile, began teaching German part-time at Hofstra University and at Pace College as well.

Mr. Waldes's mother's house had eighteen rooms spread across three floors. We occupied a suite of three rooms on the second floor: a master bedroom with a queen-size bed, an adjoining full-size bathroom, and a sitting room. From our bedroom we could descend to the first floor, directly into a full-size kitchen. From the kitchen we could also enter the two-car garage. Off from the kitchen was a raised dining room containing an extra-large, solidly built wooden table, long enough to seat no less than a dozen people. The dining room also contained a large hutch and a lowboy set of drawers that held enough flatware and fine silver cutlery to entertain at least as many people as could fit into the room.

Perpendicular to the dining room and one step down from it was a lengthy sunken living room. At the opposite ends of the living room were a reading library at one end and a television sitting room at the other. On holidays and special occasions, we invited my family and friends from New York as well as Danielle's folks whenever they made the occasional journey over from Switzerland.

I had told my nephew Frankie, my brother Gus's son, that I was looking for a car since selling my 1958 Olds, and he happened to find a 1960 Olds that suited me to a T: a white Delta 88 in excellent condition. The previous owner was a doctor who did not drive it very often. It had low mileage on the odometer and the interior was in excellent condition. Above all, the price was right, as was the timing. I thanked my nephew for putting me in contact with the good doctor and promptly purchased the car. Shortly after that transaction, Maman and Tante Frieda decided to visit us in America. It was Frieda's first time coming to the States, and we had plenty of room to comfortably accommodate them in our stately home in Bayside as well as a great vehicle in which to show them around.

While they were with us, Danielle and I decided to drive them to Montreal, Canada, to visit with a first cousin on the Klarer side of the family. In mapping out our trip, we also included a stop-off in beautiful Cooperstown, New York, home of the Baseball Hall of Fame and Museum; also, after an overnight stay, we were to head west to Niagara Falls before driving east on Highway 401 to Montreal. These were all places I had never been to before, but I looked forward to visiting them during that trip. In addition to driving those long distances for the first time, I had to put on my salesman's hat and cold-canvas for our nightly stays as we journeyed north. Needless to say, there were a few testy moments for this inexperienced traveler.

After exiting the major highway at Cooperstown, while traveling on a side street, we wound up with a flat tire on the right rear end of the Olds. My natural gifts have always manifested in my verbal skills; my mechanical skills, on the other hand, are sorely lacking. I was clueless when it came to changing a flat tire, but luckily Tante Frieda was able to guide me through the procedure. I was surprised to discover that Danielle's aunt had learned to drive a delivery vehicle during her youthful days while working for the Nievergelts in the family stationery business.

In Cooperstown we stayed overnight in a lovely New England colonial house where we rented two comfortable rooms. The morning after, we were treated to a wonderful English breakfast: eggs made to order, ham, brewed coffee and teas, and a wide variety of jams and jellies complemented by finely baked bread and biscuits. We exchanged pleasantries with our hosts, filled our gas tank at the local filling station, and continued our journey to our next stop, Niagara Falls. It was early spring, 1969. We were blessed with beautiful 70° weather throughout our trip, except for one stormy day. Happily, throughout our journey my Olds Delta 88 performed admirably, once we had repaired the flat tire.

The majesty of Niagara Falls was simply breathtaking. Viewing it from the side, we were able to feel the spray of the Falls on our faces. We stayed the night at a nearby inn and were on our way early the next morn. We picked up Highway 401 from Buffalo to Montreal, a route bordering Canada and the United States. We were in the fourth day of our trip when, at midday, we encountered a severe rainstorm. It was so strong that I could hardly see out of my car windows. We pulled off the highway and landed in Belleville, a small town that one would easily drive past under normal weather conditions.

As luck would have it, I parked the car in front of the classiest hotel in town. I led our group of four from the car, up the five or six wooden steps, across the porch, through the stately white front doors, and on to a classy carpeted floor of Turkish tapestry. The lady concierge at the desk could see that we four appeared quite shaken from having driven for quite some time under stormy rainy conditions.

She was an elderly lady, with grey hair combed neatly into a bun. Maybe 60 years old, she wore thin steel-rimmed glasses, and stood about five foot five, dressed in a light springtime suit. She greeted us warmly, stating that her name was Martha, and that she had two special rooms for us on the second floor which had just been vacated the day before. We walked up twenty steps to a center hall balcony. At the top, just to our right in the hallway, were two rooms facing each other at opposite ends, and there were two further rooms that extended beyond our own. The one that Danielle and I were to occupy had an old-fashioned bed with four high posts holding up a thin veil that was draped over us while we slept. The second room had two single beds which were quite sufficient for Helene and Tante Frieda. Each room had a full bathroom and furnishings that were most accommodating.

We were able to freshen up and then settle down to a wonderful lunch in the downstairs dining room, overlooking a beautifully landscaped green lawn that extended across several houses on the same side of the road as our hotel. The lawn extended across a wide swath of land up to railroad tracks, and beyond the tracks was a wooded forest.

For dinner we were treated to a delicious pot roast, mashed potatoes, fresh garden green beans, and freshly baked white bread. We concluded our dinner with freshly baked warm apple pie and piping hot brewed coffee, though Maman and Tante Frieda chose instead their favorites from among a variety of English teas. After dinner we spent some time in the reading room that was adjacent to the dining room. It was well-stocked with fine English classics, playing cards, and a few board games. We chose the playing cards and settled down to a game of Jass before retiring to our respective rooms.

As we were getting ready to head upstairs, Martha led us to the guestbook and pointed out to us the signatures of notable celebrities, both from the States and Europe, who had spent the night at that very same hotel. In fact, several years prior to our stay, Walt Disney and his family had spent the night there and even slept in the same bed as the one that Danielle and I shared.

The next morning, at around nine a.m., we four entered, through the dining room door, a glass-enclosed breakfast porch. We joined several other tourists who were seated at tables, partaking of breakfast. The morning sun came out in its full glory and the view overlooking the green lawn was magnificent. We watched as a traditional locomotive passed by just in front of us, blowing a cloud of white steam from the chimney of the front engine carriage. The highlight of our breakfast was a beautifully arranged platter of some thirty different fresh confitures, accompanied, of course, by the very best freshly baked breads and buns. It was a truly royal breakfast. We expressed our heartfelt gratitude as we said our goodbyes to Martha and some of her staff. From Belleville we continued onward to Montreal.

As one last stop prior to our arrival in Montreal, we stopped at old Fort Henry in Ontario, Canada, astride the St. Lawrence River. That nineteenth-century fortress gave us a glimpse of old-world charm dressed in British pomp and circumstance, as they flawlessly executed the changing of the guard ceremony.

We rested for a couple of days just west of Montreal at the home of Irwin Ahl in Mount Royal, Quebec. Irwin was somehow related to Margrit as a cousin on her mother's side of the family, the Klarers. As I recall, Irwin was retired from the business sector but still maintained a part-time connection to the business community and the local government in Montreal. Unfortunately, his wife Rita was suffering from the early stages of Alzheimer's, a debilitating affliction of the brain. They lived with their teenaged son, who played the drums in the basement of the house most of the time while we were visiting.

During our brief stay, Irwin was quite pleased to give us a tour of his wonderful city, Montreal. The view of the city from the top of Mount Royal was impressive, especially as the city lights came on at day's end. Montreal is a city of old and new architecture. I was impressed with the cobblestone streets leading to stately stone and brick colonial British- and French-style houses, with archways that horses and carriages could still pass through en route to courtyards. In later years Danielle and I revisited Montreal on our way to Quebec City, at a time in our life when we could enjoy excellent French cuisine and practice our French language skills. I discovered that Canadian French, with its slight slur, is somewhat different than Parisian French, which utilizes a more guttural sound.

At the end of our stay, it took us a little more than eight hours, in my trusty Olds, to make our way directly from Montreal to New

York City, and then back to our rent-free eighteen-room mansion in Bayside, Queens.

The second and final week of Maman and Tante Frieda's stay with us was split between visiting some of Manhattan's well-known quarters and museums, and spending some leisure time on the white sands of Jones Beach. The latter spot was a favorite of many landlocked Europeans. In later years, whenever Danielle's parents came to visit with us, regardless of the season, a trip to Jones Beach was always included in the itinerary. Maman and Tante Frieda returned to Switzerland overjoyed at their experience in the United States and Canada, and urged us to visit them again as soon as we could.

Danielle and I began to travel to Switzerland once every two years, and over the many years of our marriage it became a biannual staple; when our two sons Fabrice and Raphael were born, they too began to make the journey with us back and forth across the Atlantic. Every other year, Danielle's parents, and sometimes her brother and sister with their families, would come to the States to visit with us.

Early in our marriage Danielle and I purchased a small circular, one-level, two-bedroom wood house in the Poconos. My sister Anita and her husband Jimmy were the ones who suggested we have a look at the circular-shaped house. The price was right and we bought it. During the off-years, while we remained in the States, Maman and Papa would generally visit with us in the summer and spend several weeks at Hemlock Farms, where our little house was located, a short distance down the road from my sister's place. On our half-acre lot, we were surrounded by healthy oak trees. Papa set up a woodcutting device and loved nothing more than to cut wood and make handsome piles of logs to burn in our wood-burning stove. He would also take his daily swim in the six-lane pool at Fawn Hill, just a short distance from our house by foot.

Whenever we traveled to Switzerland, it was like being in a Walt Disney fairyland. The wonderful views start from beautiful lakes, surrounded by old-world arcades, gift shops, and café-restaurants. A short trip by boat on a tour ("Rundfahrt") offers a panorama of lush green trees and colorful gardens amidst chalet-type houses that ascend up into dense woods. On a sunny day it's simply a magnificent view. We liked to take the number fourteen tram to Triemli to arrive at the foot of the Uetliberg, a point where the edge of the forest touches the city street. A cable train took us to the top of the mountain, where we were rewarded with a breathtaking view of downtown Zurich. In our youthful days Danielle and I enjoyed hiking down from that mountaintop to the local tram. The whole picturesque landscape, even in memory, remains heavenly.

Chapter Fifty-Six

The early years of our marriage, while they were wondrous, were also quite challenging. Living rent-free for nearly a year and a half, thanks to the elderly Mrs. Waldes remaining with her daughter in Czechoslovakia, afforded me the opportunity to finish my studies at Pace College through a full-time program. At the same time, Danielle found work teaching German to students attending Hofstra University, as well as an ESL (English as a Second Language) class at Pace. I continued waiting on tables at Pips on the Bay in Brooklyn on Friday nights. During that period, Danielle and I lived on chicken wings, bircher muesli, and, on occasion, quiche lorraine.

In February 1969 we were hit with a severe winter storm, known as the "Lindsay Storm," after the New York City mayor at the time who was criticized for the inadequate assistance he offered residents in the snowy aftermath. Danielle and I had the good fortune of living through it in the comfort of Mrs. Waldes's stately home in Bayside, where the white Delta 88 was safely tucked away in the two-car garage. Within our first two years together, in courtship and in marriage, we survived two snowy winter storms. We were extremely fortunate to have safe, warm environs in which to sit them out, and to have each other's company, so we weren't tempted to unnecessarily brave nature's worst.

Apart from such stormy weather, we two youthful spirits made our way together around and about town, laying down a stable foundation for a lifetime of vision, growth, and family. In addition to the love that was there from the beginning, Danielle and I grew to trust each other, in our individual strengths and weaknesses, as we forged a path into the future.

As with so many young people of today and of yesteryear, when our formal schooling was finished we inevitably had to decide what to do with our lives. Just prior to and shortly after my marriage to Danielle, I found myself facing the simple question, What will I make of my life? What would my future look like? After I graduated from Pace College, I realized that I had to find a good and steady job. But I also wondered further, What would be my calling? Or even, in the simplest terms, What would I be good at? I knew I wouldn't be able to put off these pressing questions for much longer, but until I actually graduated they felt somewhat remote, or at least still nebulous.

To clear our minds of pending worries and to introduce Danielle to some of my childhood buddies, shortly after we moved into the house in Bayside I thought it would be a good idea to throw a party. I invited some of my old cronies from the old neighborhood, whom I hadn't seen for some time, along with a few of our newer friends from Pace College. It was in March 1969, in celebration of my twenty-eighth birthday. The list of attendees included Fat Stevee, Eddie Kwasnewski, Bobby, Frankie, cousin Benny, and a couple of other regulars from the old neighborhood in Brooklyn. From Pace College, Walter and Juliette, as well as Gunther and Rosemary, were added to the mix. There were plenty of cooked chicken wings, Swedish meatballs, and pomme chips along with some inexpensive table wine, beer, and other friendly libations.

Beatles hits, such as "Sgt. Pepper's Lonely Hearts Club Band," and other popular rock songs of the day, filled the air with lively music. Before long the sunken living room had come to life with dancing and conversation. As the night wore on, the folks from Brooklyn kept insisting that I try a little pot. I held back, even after some friendly persuasion for old times' sake. I could see the annoyance on Danielle's face as my old friends tried to lure me in, and in front of my coworkers, no less. Later on, as the evening came to an end and the folks were leaving, I could tell that the likelihood of engaging with my former comrades in the future had dwindled away.

After the party, Danielle worried that in some way I might want to return to life as it was before we met. Without any hesitation, I assuredly told Danielle that I had no desire to return to my past way of life. Even my musical tastes had been changing from rock to classical. I was not about to turn back.

On a few occasions I invited members of my family over for dinner, in some cases so they could meet Danielle for the first time. On one occasion my brother Sal, the oldest of my siblings, gave me a fatherly tap on the shoulder and told me I had made a fine choice in marrying Danielle. Coming from Sal, who was one of the most pragmatic and sensible people I knew, the compliment meant a great deal to me. In that moment, though, I thought to myself that I really didn't need anyone's affirmation to know how fortunate I was to have met Danielle.

There are certain turning points in one's life, when one must make the right decision to find the future course that one must pursue. In order to build the foundation necessary to go forward, I knew I had to finish college and attain my degree in economics as soon as possible. I managed to carry a full load of eighteen credits in the fall and the spring semesters, and to complete classes during both halves of the succeeding summer. As a result of that hard work, I graduated in January 1970. During that same period, Danielle began her master's program in comparative literature at the City University of New York (CUNY).

Mrs. Waldes returned from Czechoslovakia shortly after my graduation, but we were allowed to remain in her Bayside home for another two months. She asked us if we wanted to stay on as the butler and the maid. Needless to say, and without any hesitation, we declined the offer. While we fully appreciated getting to live in that wonderful English Tudor house for a little more than a year and a half, we knew we had to move on and make something of ourselves. With warm gratitude, we said our goodbyes to Mrs. Waldes.

Right after graduation I put together a resume and began knocking on the myriad doors of corporate America. One of my earliest stops was at a small stockbroker's office on Wall Street. The owner of the operation liked the looks of my resume, and I believe he thought my interpersonal skills were quite good. He made me an offer and I accepted. There was, however, one caveat to beginning my career as a stockbroker: Danielle and I had already booked our flight to Switzerland, so I would need to put off starting at my new job for two weeks. The owner said that was alright, and that I could start when I returned from Switzerland. When I returned, though, the position had disappeared. In my absence the company had hired someone else.

I was somewhat surprised at that outcome, but the company's decision was final. Welcome to the real world, as they say. Once again, I began knocking on doors. As of 1971 the modern use of computers, which were to lead to everyday online communications throughout corporate America, were still in a nascent stage. I had to conduct my job searches the conventional way. With a detailed, typewritten resume in hand, I put on my polished walking shoes and proceeded to enter one building after another all along Park Avenue, in midtown Manhattan, handing out my resume to as many banks and companies and institutions as I could find. Though I received a great many rejections, I kept up my search, and at last I struck paydirt. After an entrance test and two interviews, I was hired by Union Carbide, a major chemical company. I would begin my work life as a junior industrial credit analyst.

In addition to receiving a fairly good starting salary from Union Carbide Corporation, I had medical coverage for me, Danielle, and our future children. UCC would pick up whatever college costs I would incur toward furthering my education, with the one condition being that those further studies had to be business-related. With that covered, I began to take classes at Pace College at night in pursuit of a master's degree in economics. It was common knowledge that a higher education would enhance a career immeasurably, leading to upward mobility in the managerial hierarchy of corporate America. I was happy to have such an opportunity, and I felt I was in a good place in my life.

Danielle and I had begun our search for a new dwelling while we were still staying at the Waldes house. At that time, we found a two-room attic apartment in a one-family brick and stucco house just one block east of Parsons Boulevard and one block north of Union Turnpike on 79th Avenue, in Queens. Cantilall Dave and his wife and two children were the proud owners of the expanded one-family house. Mr. Dave was a highly skilled technology supervisor who had immigrated from India to the States. While learning an American style of management, he already had a great deal of mechanical and scientific knowledge to contribute to the business community.

In addition to renting the attic apartment to us, they also rented the basement apartment to a young couple from Massachusetts, Jerry and Eileen, who had temporarily relocated to New York City. Jerry Meuse, the husband, was to complete a tour of duty in the sales department of his company. Eventually, he expected to be transferred back to his home state, with a promotion to regional sales manager. At the time, Eileen was in the early stages of pregnancy. They were a handsome couple, a year or two younger than Danielle and myself. Occasionally, we would get together for dinner and a movie.

During our stay at the Daves' house, Danielle also became pregnant. It helped that Eileen and Danielle could talk to each other about their respective experiences of first-time pregnancy. Eileen had her child while we were still living in the Daves' attic apartment, and it was only a few months later that Danielle gave birth to Fabrice, our firstborn.

Chapter Fifty-Seven

Danielle was 29 years old when she gave birth to Fabrice. That glorious happening arrived in the midst of some real excitement. During the last month of Danielle's pregnancy, Jacques, her younger brother, had some time off from his studies at medical school in Zurich and decided to come to America to be with his dear sister for the final stage of her pregnancy.

On March 16, 1972, one drizzly weeknight, I was attending a graduate class at Pace College. Our baby was due at any moment. Together, Danielle and Jacques decided to fetch me at Pace, in lower Manhattan, next door to neighboring Chinatown. That morning we'd agreed to go to Chinatown to have dinner at the family restaurant of one of Danielle's former ESL students, from when she was a part-time instructor at Pace College. Jacques admirably offered to drive our car into and out of the city, but it began to rain buckets just as Danielle and her brother arrived in Manhattan. Also, just as the rain turned into a downpour, Danielle began to have mild contractions. As soon as Danielle and Jacques collected me at Pace, we all discussed what would be the best plan of action. Danielle felt that the contractions were still quite mild, and that it would be best to return to Queens to the hospital where she'd expected to deliver; and, given that the labor might turn out to take a long time, she felt that we should still stop by the Chinese restaurant before leaving the city, to pick up some food to bring home to our apartment in Queens.

We arrived back at our attic apartment at eight o'clock in the evening, having thankfully avoided any delays. We three settled down in front of the television to enjoy our Chinese treat. Jacques wanted to watch an American basketball game, as he was somewhat familiar with the sport after glimpsing a game or two in Switzerland. So, we began our dinner just at the start of a Knicks game.

As we began eating and shortly after the first tip-off to start the game, Danielle's crampy contractions steadily became stronger. We all realized it was time to stop everything and head on over to Flushing Hospital, only ten minutes away from our apartment. In anticipation of that moment, Danielle's suitcase had been prepared well in advance. I drove our Olds with Danielle and Jacques seated behind me, and it seemed as if I was floating on a cloud, instinctively taking us all to the hospital.

Dr. Lawrence and a nurse were already set up to receive us as we came through the backdoor emergency entrance. When it was clear that it would still be awhile before Danielle was ready to give birth, the good doctor advised Jacques and me to go home. When the baby was delivered, he said, we would be contacted by telephone. He further assured us that Danielle was fine and in good hands.

Back at the apartment, Jacques decided to stay up and continue watching the basketball game on TV. I was dead tired and elected to put on my PJs and go straight to bed. Understandably, with work, school, Chinatown, and rain, it had been a very long day for me.

Perhaps only two hours after I had put my tired body into bed, the telephone rang. A cheerful female voice said, "It's a healthy six-pound-eleven-ounce baby boy, and your wife is resting comfortably." Jacques was still in his dress clothes at that point and watching a late-night movie. All that TV stuff was quite new to him, since there was never a television in his house on Hirschgartnerweg. I quickly threw on my shirt, socks, trousers, and shoes, and off we went, back to the hospital.

It was 35 minutes after midnight on Saint Patrick's Day, March 17, 1972, when Danielle gave birth to Fabrice. When we arrived, he was asleep in his hospital crib and looked quite healthy. After peeking in at Fabrice, Jacques and I lit over to Danielle's room. She was resting comfortably too. Danielle seemed fatigued, yet she had the presence of mind to give us a gentle smile and say, "Isn't he beautiful!" Draped across the foot of her hospital bed was a handmade green quilt with a Saint Patrick's Day shamrock at the center. We were told that Fabrice was the first baby born on that day in Flushing Hospital.

After spending three days in the hospital, Danielle was discharged and allowed to return home with her newborn baby in her loving arms. Apparently, it was a quick, easy delivery, or at least as easy as any delivery could be for a woman to go through. In any event, we were finally home all together, safe and sound. For me, it felt so great to be alive.

Jacques stayed with us two or three more days to give us some added moral support and then returned to Switzerland to resume his studies. Danielle and I were so grateful for Jacques's calming presence at that critical moment in our lives. It is no wonder that in later years Jacques would become a wonderful doctor and caring general practitioner, in the small town of Tramelan, Switzerland. I was able to take a week's vacation from work to stay at home with Danielle and Fabrice. Maman would soon come across the Atlantic again to be with her daughter and Fabrice, her newest grandchild.

Fabrice was about ten months old when he took his first steps. Maman and Tante Frieda were visiting the United States for a second time when that event took place in our tiny apartment. It was on a cold January evening, and Danielle had just finished giving Fabrice a bath. While we were all sitting around in the living room, digesting a wonderful Swiss cheese and potato gratin prepared by Maman, I was at one end of the room and Danielle was at the other when Fabrice, stark naked, raced across the room and into my arms. After some hearty laughter by all, Fabrice went to bed and we four settled down to a friendly game of Jass.

Early into the next year, perhaps at springtime in 1973, either during a conversation with a neighbor or while on a baby carriage walk, we learned that a very nice apartment had become available in the Kew Terrace apartment complex. It was located two blocks north of Union Turnpike, between Main and 147th Street.

Apartment 2B was a spacious two-bedroom apartment with a foyer leading into a rather large kitchen, and it seemed the perfect place for our young, growing family. Between the foyer and the kitchen was a dining area that accommodated four comfortably. The dining area led one through a wide opening and straight into a spacious living room. Behind the living room was a full bathroom to the left of the small passageway, and on the right side opposite the bathroom was a large master bedroom. At the back end of the small passageway was a smaller bedroom which would soon become the room where our two sons would sleep in their Swedish red bunkbed—though, when we first moved in, Raphael had not yet been born, and Fabrice still slept near us in a crib.

Apartment 2B was located on the second floor of a three-story garden apartment building that housed four families on each floor. Next to our unit was apartment 2A, where Janet MacKay and Barbara, her young daughter, lived. Janet would be our neighbor for the next 25 years. Having three-sided window exposure afforded our apartment wonderful natural air and sunlight. It was an ideal setting for Danielle and me to settle in to family life. The rent was also quite reasonable and easy on our modest pocketbooks. For a small additional fee, we even had a large closed garage with ample overhead storage space, across the street, along a community driveway. From 1973 to 1998 we lived at 144-15 78th Road, Apt. 2B, in Kew Gardens/Flushing, Queens, NY.

In the early 1980s the Kew Terrace apartment complex converted into a cooperative and changed to the Kew Terrace Coop. Having already lived there for more than ten years, we could purchase our apartment as insiders for 50 percent less than someone buying in at the new residents' price. Later on, we were able to sell our coop-apartment for a modest gain and purchase an attached three-bedroom, two-story English Tudor house in Forest Hills, Queens. The trend toward American homeownership had become, by the end of World War II, the fulfillment of the American dream. In tapping into that marvelous opportunity, we were no exception to our generation's dreamers.

Danielle and I were, in some ways, though, an exception to the norm. As we began our family life in Kew Gardens, we realized that we wanted to maintain strong ties to our family roots; those roots included Danielle's family in Switzerland, my family in Brooklyn, Long Island, and elsewhere, and eventually our new friends from the church community we were soon to join. Even as many of our fellow New Yorkers were attempting to establish themselves in new roles and settings and breaking away from the past, we were happy to retain our connections to the people and traditions that had nourished our lives.

Danielle and I were thrilled that the elementary school at

Vleigh Place, just walking distance from our apartment, came highly recommended by some of our neighbors. As a further bit of luck and convenience, my workplace on Park Avenue, in midtown Manhattan, was just a half-hour subway ride from where we lived. Over the years we never had any desire to move from the city to Long Island, though that was a post–World War II trend for young families who were climbing up the social ladder. I was very comfortable being a New Yorker for life.

Over a span of three and a half years, I sojourned from Union Carbide to American Sugar Refining Inc. (Domino Sugar), then finally settled down at Westvaco—the new name, as of 1969, for the West Virginia Pulp and Paper Company. I spent the next 24 years in the employ of Westvaco Corporation as a senior credit analyst, in the treasury department. I had my own team of two credit analysts and a secretary from the typing pool, and we were responsible for the envelope division. Imagine selling 450 million dollars' worth of envelopes per year in 1997! We were a centralized credit department consisting of 22 people (three senior analysts, six junior analysts, plus support staff) reporting to an assistant treasurer, who, in turn, reported to the treasurer, who, in turn, reported to the financial vice president, who, in turn, reported directly to the president of a six-billion-dollar paper company. At the time, the fine paper and paper box divisions accounted for the bulk of sales at Westvaco, but additional groups included the envelope, chemical, international, and forestry divisions. It was a very dynamic and exciting place for me to be. I have fond memories of working for Westvaco.

Chapter Fifty-Eight

In the early days of my tenure at Westvaco, I was given the opportunity to work at a major paper mill in Covington, Virginia, during a significant strike. The strike wasn't so much over wages as it was about work rules. In the early 1970s many large corporations with a large workforce in both management and labor had to deal with the major changes taking place as robotics began to increasingly gain greater traction in the workplace environment. Corporations were beginning to realize the enormous potential of computers, and America was on the cusp of becoming a knowledge-based society.

Coming from corporate headquarters in New York (299 Park Avenue), I was one of the few in management with credit, finance, and accounting skills who was asked if I wanted to work at the mill during the millworker's strike. I was offered twice my salary plus twenty dollars per day as living allowance, as well as a semi-private room at a local Holiday Inn throughout my stay. Moneywise, it was a large windfall gain for me and my young family. How could I say no? I accepted and was immediately transferred to Covington, Virginia. I was assigned to work at the table of machine number eight. My tour began at eight p.m. and ended at 8 a.m., twelve straight hours per night. Physically, I never worked so much and so hard in my life.

We were served a bag lunch in the middle of the night, consisting of Southern fried chicken, a juicy apple, and a candy bar, and we ate our homemade sandwiches on the fly. I must admit that Southern food is the best. The making of coated paper started wet, when the pulp was nearly 100 percent water, and it wound its way through a series of large metal cylinders covering a distance of at least a city block. That then fed into a calendar stack of thin rollers, about three stories high, and finished its journey as white coated paper. After it came out of the calendar stack, the paper was rewound into a large roll about forty feet long that could weigh an average of about ten thousand pounds.

That giant roll of paper was then brought by a large crane-like carrier over to the slitter-winder, to be cut into smaller rolls of paper, according to job specifications. Five or six of those extremely heavy rolls would come flying off the winder and onto the table, where me and my team of six male and female personnel would receive them with open arms. Those giant rolls were conveyed and pushed along the table, to be labeled and, in some cases, individually wire-wrapped and recorded (my specific responsibility). In that speedy, high-stakes environment, I never dared miscount or fall asleep on the job. I was also responsible for making sure there were enough metal straps to wrap rolls for exporting to places like Canada. Each roll would then be lifted by a Hyster carrier and loaded into a train car resting next to our table.

By the following morning, at the end of each night shift, there would be a morning steak and potatoes breakfast, with all the trimmings, in the Covington mill cafeteria. We were a rather large group of management workers from all over the country, taking the place of the unionized millworkers who normally worked on the floor, covering no less than eight machines at the Covington mill. There were similar groups sent at that same time to the Luke,

Maryland, mill as well. After a very steady, hardworking twelve hours that left me with aching shoulders and tired feet and hands covered with metal splinters, it felt good to be breaking bread with many of my new colleagues. Back at the hotel each morning, I slept like a baby for the better part of the day. Harrison, my roommate from the marketing group in New York, had a difficult time sleeping, as the guy with a full beard from the Charleston chemical plant who rested next to him snored all night long. Harrison begged me to switch with him, but I said, "No way."

I was away from home for fifteen straight nights. I was given a five-day leave to be with my family, only to return for another twelve nights, until the strike ended. During my tenure in Covington there were a few testy moments, when the protesting strikers standing in front of burning barrels shouted some nasty words at us as we passed through the entranceway of the mill. When the strike ended, management and labor became good buds once again. After all, much of management had themselves come out of the hard-working ranks of labor at each of the mills. I, as a part of management, appreciated all of the benefits that came from the ranks of labor, to the lasting credit of the Westvaco company.

Chapter Fifty-Nine

In 1974, after I had worked for Westvaco for a little more than two years, Danielle gave birth to our second son, Raphael. Westvaco footed the bill for Raphael's delivery, and offered very good continuing coverage for our whole family. In addition to that coverage, Westvaco also paid for most of the expenses for me to attend Pace College classes at night while obtaining my master's degree in economics, for which I am eternally grateful.

Raphael was born at approximately six o'clock in the evening, on March 8, 1974. Danielle and I thought that from the beginning of her pregnancy we would attend the recently popularized Lamaze sessions designed to offer men the opportunity to assist their wives during the birth of their child inside the delivery room. We decided that, unlike for the birth of Fabrice, when Danielle was solely in the hands of her doctor and nurse, it would be more comforting for her if I could be there when Raphael was born. To further add to the gravity of the event, during the first month of her pregnancy Danielle struggled through a tipped uterus difficulty that caused her to be bedridden for nearly a month. In that period, my two sisters Anita and Barbara helped take care of Fabrice, who was barely fifteen months old. Happily, with proper rest, Danielle's uterus corrected itself. Going forward without further complications, we were well on our way toward the happy event of bringing our second offspring into the world.

On March 8th I was working at my desk at 299 Park Avenue when I received a call from Doctor Lapin's office, informing me that Danielle was being taken over to Booth Memorial Hospital in Queens. Over the phone, Danielle gave me specific orders to first go home and take care of Fabrice, and then to come to the hospital. It was three o'clock in the afternoon, and all of my colleagues, who were as excited as I was, gave me a royal send-off.

Instead of going home first to check on Fabrice as Danielle had requested, as I knew he was being well cared for by Janet MacKay, our next-door neighbor in apartment 2A, I decided, in my exuberance, to go directly to the hospital. I arrived there at about four o'clock. The nurse said that Danielle was fine, and that, of course, Danielle had not yet delivered our newborn. Danielle and the nurse told me to go home and give Fabrice his supper before heading back to the hospital. There would still be perhaps a few hours before Danielle's moment of delivery. At about six thirty, not even three hours later, I returned to Booth Memorial. With high expectations, I was ready to enter the delivery room dressed in cap, gloves, and gown in anticipation of sharing with Danielle the birth of our second child.

But it wasn't to be. No sooner had I entered the hospital than I was told to proceed to the sixth floor. Danielle had already given birth to a six-pound-eleven-ounce baby boy, and mother and child were both in good health and resting comfortably. When I entered Danielle's bedroom, she was furious with me. I had not been there to share in the delivery of Raphael, a moment that we both truly wanted to experience. It took a few days to overcome that mishap, which was completely my fault. But the joy of moving on with our family life with two beautiful sons soothed that momentary sting. Life was good.

The next few years that followed the birth of our two sons were simply wonderful. There was no better place to be than in our bed at about eight o'clock on Sunday mornings. Almost like clock-work, our two sons, when they were perhaps ages two and four, would leap out of their finely crafted red Norwegian bunkbeds to land in our bed, and nestled comfortably between Danielle and me.

Dressed in their zippered toe-to-neck rabbit-looking pajamas, the boys loved to play horseback and were ready to listen to what-ever fairytale we chose to spin. They were eager listeners and music lovers, as we often sang together wonderful English, French, Ital-ian, and German songs taken from children's songbooks. We'd often receive Swiss children's storybooks, in English translation, from either their Tante Marinette or their Uncle Jacques.

After lazing in bed for an hour or two and listening to some classical music (either Bach or Mozart & co.), we four made our way to the kitchen for some scrambled eggs, or maybe pancakes or French toast, almost always closing with Hero-brand raspberry, peach, or blueberry confiture, though personally I preferred Smucker's English marmalade.

As the clock approached eleven in the morning, we were in the habit of turning on the radio to listen to a Sunday service from either All Souls Unitarian Church or the Community Church in Manhattan. Reverend Harrington was usually the keynote speaker. At times Danielle and I also tuned in to the words of Algernon Black, an effective speaker for the Society for Ethical Culture. Danielle, coming from a Huguenot Protestant family setting in Zurich, Switzerland, and I, coming from a traditional Roman Catholic background in Brooklyn, New York, mutually embraced the sermons coming from the lips of these two very fine religious and ethical scholars. We also found a wonderful Unitarian congregation in the neighborhood of Hollis, Queens.

At the Hollis Unitarian church and congregation, Danielle, Fabrice, Raphael, and I found a home away from home. It was a space for a group of wonderful individuals and families who came together, in one unique place, from nearly every part of the United States. Some folks were also recent immigrants from other parts of the world. By some miracle we discovered a place where we could express and act out our liberal religious beliefs. It was a joyful place we loved to go to every Sunday morning.

I'd like to close this segment of my memoir at this juncture, at a point when I could safely say I was no longer alone and on my own. The years that followed our joining the Hollis Unitarian Church were filled with all kinds of happenings, some challenging and others quite rewarding and blissful. The events, stories, happenings, and friends we came upon while growing our family, and throughout a lifetime of Unitarian experiences, will fill the pages of the next segment of my memoir, which I will entitle "Memorabilia." Thank you for allowing me to recount for you my life's wonderful journey. So long for now.

Acknowledgments

A special thank you to the following good sports, who patiently listened to parts of my family history and gave me some valuable information, good wishes, and help toward completing my mission: my living siblings and their partners, Anita and Jimmy Oddo, Barbara Donnelly, Rudy Martorella and his dear friend Millette; my family and friends from Switzerland, especially Marinette and Christian, Jacques and Elizabeth, Danielle's nephews and nieces, and so many friends and neighbors in that magnificent, beautiful country; Shirley Reinfelder, Jessie Reinfelder, Steven and Philip Martorella, Frank and Erin Martorella, Louise Martorella, Fabrice and Elvira Martorello, Domenico (Nico) Martorello, Raphael and Megan Martorello, Franc Martarella, James Oddo, Jonathan and Francie Miller, and Cookie (Ann) Ellie; and a few other kind souls I greatly appreciate but who shall remain unmentioned. Thanks to Michael Tencer, my editor, for careful guidance in smoothing out the edges of my story. And finally, I thank the collective powers sent from the heavens for giving me the memory to, by some miracle, reconstruct my familial past.

Family Trees

Children of Salvatore Sr. and Carmela Martorella
>Frank
>Antoinette
>Charlie
>Joe
>Lucy
>Dominick
>Maggie
>Philomena
>Louie
>Sophie
>Salvatore Jr.

Children of Augustino Sr. and Christina Vallefuoco
>Augustino Jr.
>Lilly
>Vigence
>Caroline
>Carmine
>Nicoleta
>Anna
>Ben
>Theresa

Children of Jerry (Gennaro) and Mary Migliaro
> Anna (Antoinette)
> Josephine (Josi)
> Rachael
> Tommy
> Sophie (Tootsie)
> Marco
> Anthony (Tony)
> Gloria
> Delores
> Geraldine

Children of Frank Sr. and Lilly (Vallefuoco) Martorella
> Salvatore (Sal)
> Augustine (Gus)
> Frank Jr. (Hank)
> Rudolph (Rudy)
> Anna (Anita)
> Carmela (Barbara)
> Clayton (Cloots)

Made in the USA
Middletown, DE
27 February 2020

85442155R00186